Why Selling Sucks & Building Relationships Work?

Mak

Order this book online at www.trafford.com
or email orders@trafford.com

Most Trafford titles are also available at major online book retailers.

Printed in the United States of America.

ISBN: 978-1-4269-5558-7 (sc)

Library of Congress Control Number: 2011900666

Trafford rev. 01/24/2011

www.trafford.com

North America & international
toll-free: 1 888 232 4444 (USA & Canada)
phone: 250 383 6864 ♦ fax: 812 355 4082

Dedicated to my loving parents and children; both showed me the value of life.

Also dedicated to clients, sales and service agents, who keep showing us better ways of serving customers every day!

A Story:

Once, it so happened that a customer went to a shop looking for a product. As the product was not available at the shop, the shopkeeper asked the customer for a description of the product and requested him to wait at the shop for a few minutes. He said he would look for the product in the adjacent shops. The shopkeeper soon returned with the product, and gave it to the customer with an invoice.

Moved by the shopkeeper's dedication the customer asked the shopkeeper, "Thank you for finding me the product, but I wonder how this transaction has benefited you?"

The shopkeeper smiled and answered, "Sire, my benefit is your benefit, because you are my customer who has come to my shop, while you could have gone to so many other shops – it is not for you to thank me; I thank you for choosing my shop, and I look forward to serving you again in the future."

TABLE OF CONTENTS

FOREWORD

Call any call center or walk into any customer service area of a business enterprise, and the chances are that you'll find service standards that leave much to be desired! Similarly, when you search the net for books on "customer service," don't be surprised by the huge number of books written and available on the subject. For instance, on Amazon.com alone your search would reveal over eight thousand books, and many more on the way! The above is only indicative of how important "customer service" is to business organizations, especially for their survival and continued growth.

Severe competition due to the worldwide economic crunch, availability of a wide range of products, and ready access to product information and finance all have given customers greater choice and the power to bargain. The flip side of the same coin is that it has created considerable pressure on customers for their attention and on their decision-making. To simplify things, customers these days want to deal with service providers they can trust to sift through all of the above on their behalf and provide them with the best possible solution. They want to develop business relationships with service providers who can make their lives simpler, better, and more convenient.

Developing business relationships with customers and providing personalized service as much as possible has become the cornerstone of business success. It has necessitated the need for empowered front-line staff that are in direct contact with customers. Empowered, so they can do whatever necessary to win the customer, develop a business relationship with them, and protect their/employer's interests at the same time - the days of "efficient order takers" are definitely over!

This is the era in which every front-line staff member has to understand what the customer wants or feels, provide the service in a manner that is appreciated. Further, the service agent has to specialize in their own area of work so that they can benefit their customers in real terms. The service agents nowadays have to be experts at whatever they sell, know how to communicate effectively with their customers, and conduct business in a manner that protects the profit margins. Such service agents are an asset to the company they work for, a valuable resource for the customers, and also a blessing to the community they serve. They not only provide quality service to their customers but also manage their relationships with their colleagues, as well as the suppliers to the business; they are, in fact, the fulcrum that translates the business enterprise's goals and objectives into reality.

The irony is that although most business enterprises are aware of the importance of customer service, they habitually focus more on their products than what their customers want. The result is that their front-line staff knows much about the products they sell, but very little about customer psychology and behavior. For example, front-line staffs in airlines in general think that they are in the business of selling and issuing tickets, whereas their concern should lie in transporting passengers from one point to another safely, quickly, and in comfort. Another example would be of a hotel's staff perceiving their business as selling rooms, but more appropriately they would be providing a memorable, comfortable, and convenient stay to their guests.

Few service staff realize the fine line that threads through all businesses, and that is whatever they do, the foremost stakeholder is the customer. The customer comes first. This thread is more of a culture than it is a conscious application of customer service procedures and regulations; it has more to do with customer awareness, and above all an attitude that the business exists for the benefit of its customers.

The right attitude and aptitude are crucial in the profession of customer service. This book addresses all such issues head-on and has been written by someone who has worked at the front-line, directly supervised and also trained the front-line staff on customer service.

Mak's book is a practical guide for the front-line staff that will make them more effective in managing customers to their satisfaction and developing a business relationship with them. From that angle, it is a primer on how to persuade both internal and external customers, and also can assist professionals like doctors, engineers, and lawyers with private practices to retain and enhance their customer base. I strongly recommend this book for the front-line staff of any business that deals with customers face-to-face or over the telephone.

Ram Ganglani,

Chairman,

Right SelectioN,

ACKNOWLEDGEMENTS

My thanks to my colleagues at the Emirates Group of Companies, Dubai, who contributed to the development of the ideas and thoughts in this book, especially Zoher Campwala, Sadia Afrin, and Santhosh Joseph, and, for their valuable insights into customer service, both face-to-face and over the telephone.

A special thanks to all the delegates who attended my classes on customer service training for their perspectives and case studies in the book; they have been one of my main sources of learning.

I would also like to thank Hamid Jamil, Farida Sultana, Sarah Moosa, Abu Baker Siddique, Sarwar Jehan, Savio J Dsilva, Baba Yerra, Manzurul Islam Chowdhury, Sabiha Kabir (late), Sujatha Shetty, Charmaine Rodriguez, Abdullah Tawakul, Sundeep Honrao, Rana, Nita and my children for believing in me and prodding me on to complete the book. My son Omar showed me, not to give up no matter what. My daughters Amina and Ayesha made valuable recommendations that made the book more interesting and readable. My six years old granddaughter Zoya made me realize the value of unfettered love and acceptance. And my son-in-law showed me how to be nonjudgmental.

Finally, my profound thanks to Sarah & Alison of www.FirstEditing.com who painstakingly edited the manuscript and the staff of Trafford Publishing for making this book a reality.

INTRODUCTION

Did you know that according to a survey, 68% of customers leave a business because they feel that they are treated indifferently, and not because of any other bad experience, poor quality products, or pricing issues? Don't believe me? Well, the next time you are dissatisfied with any service you receive, check and see if it is because:

- You were not cared for or treated properly.

- You were given a defective product.

- You thought the price was too high.

- Or you were upset because of something else.

Chances are that you will be dissatisfied mostly because of a lack of attention or because you were not treated properly.

When I started coaching and training corporate staff on customer service more than a decade ago, I was surprised to find that even some of the senior delegates in the class with many years of service experience had very little understanding of customer psychology! Often, these people were experts on the products or services they dealt with, but knew very little on how to deal with their customers.

The surprising thing is that everybody seems to know all about customer service, and yet you will find few service providers who understand what their customers really want, are sensitive to their needs, or care enough to treat the customer as an individual rather than a number!

This situation is going from bad to worse as businesses are becoming automated and process-oriented. New businesses are opening up every day and new staff is inducted on a daily basis, but they are not provided with the necessary briefings, training, or resources that would help them gain the adequate knowledge/skills for properly attending to the company's customers.

Such business enterprises often assign new recruits to front-line positions without any induction or training with the assumption that the recruits will learn from experience or from their senior colleagues. Little do they realize the extent of the damage that the new recruits do before they develop any reasonable skills at managing customers! Besides, the senior colleagues pass on both their effective as well as their ineffective service skills to the new bees.

This book strives to address the above issues and focuses on the customers and how they feel by providing front-line staff and recruits with the following resources:

- How to understand their customers – customer psychology

- How to communicate effectively with customers so that they feel good – from that point of view the book is a comprehensive manual on customer communication

- Helping them learn and apply skills that build long-term business relationships with customers so that they keep coming back

- How to look at products or services from the customer's perspective: what benefits them, how to come across as reassuring, and how to make them feel at home.

The book also can assist the back office and supervisory staff to understand and support their front-line colleagues to provide the best possible service.

In fact, anyone dealing directly or indirectly with customers can benefit from it, such as field salespeople, doctors, lawyers, or any other professionals with private practices to enhance and consolidate their customer base.

This book is the outcome of training sessions with thousands of customer service staff, numerous customer surveys, and service improvement consultations with service and support departments.

Sales, marketing, and customer service overlap and complement each other to provide the best to the customer. That is why in some places, this book diverges into sales and marketing, in the context of customer service and service delivery issues. It has been written with the front-line staff in mind and in a way that is easy to read. It contains loads of case studies, real-life examples, and self-evaluation quizzes that will help you to learn and apply customer service principles and techniques effectively. There is a lot of humor in the form of cartoons, quips, and metaphors that keeps the reader interested and involved.

To simplify, the customer is at times referred to as she or he, and the words "products" and "services" are used interchangeably. This book starts with the attitude you should develop to connect with your customers, then discusses how to communicate effectively with them, followed by the skills you would need to manage them, and ends with the need for service standards, how to manage complaints, and how to work in a team. All the while, the emphasis is on customer needs and preferences, developing a business relationship with them, and above all providing quality service to benefit the customer, rather than just making a sale. The book is high on service objectives, commitments, and customer focus.

Each chapter is more or less independent in the sense that they make sense on their own; to the reader it may appear that there is a lot of repetition of issues discussed in the various chapters, but closer scrutiny would reveal that it has been done intentionally to make each chapter individually readable, and also to cover the context of discussion thoroughly.

If you are looking for a practical guide on customer service that will show you how to provide the best customer service step-by-step, or you are a CEO who is looking for a resource that can help your front-line staff to improve on customer service, then this is the book for you."

I hope you enjoy reading this book and find it useful.

Chapter 1

ATTITUDE

Once, a boy was walking down the street and he came across two masons working on a building.

Out of curiosity, he asked them, "What are you doing?"

One of the masons became annoyed and retorted with sarcasm, "I'm laying bricks...can't you see?"

The other mason replied with a cheer and a smile, "Why son, I'm building the tallest tower in town!"

Which mason do you think was enjoying his work?

The person who sends out positive thoughts activates the world around him positively and draws back to himself positive results.

Norman Vincent Peale

Case Study 1:

Carole was shopping for undergarments. She was a large woman and went to a prominent store, expecting help with comfort and fit. As she browsed the clothing sections, she made eye contact with the shop attendants, hoping one of them would offer to assist. However, most went about doing whatever they were doing, while a few afforded her a harried smile at best!

A little disappointed, Carole approached the cash register. There, she noticed a number of attendants talking to each other. They ignored Carole and continued with their discussion.

Carole interrupted them, and asked if someone could assist her with her purchase of undergarments. One of the attendants nonchalantly pointed to a far-off section and said, "Undergarments are in that section." Embarrassed and annoyed, she made her way to the undergarments section.

Carole was taken aback when an attendant appeared from nowhere and greeted her with a sweet smile, "Good morning ma'am, I'm Julie. Is there anything I can help you with today?" For the next hour or so, Julie assisted Carole in selecting undergarments as well as other apparel that Carole purchased. Carole left the store happy and satisfied. She decided to return later and see Julie for more clothes.

While driving home, Carole wondered why Julie was so helpful while other attendants at the store were negligent and aloof.

Does Carole's story seem familiar to you?

ATTITUDE MAKES ALL THE DIFFERENCE

Have you ever wondered why front-line employees in any business with similar jobs and salaries behave significantly differently with their customers? Why are a select few enthusiastic about their jobs and helpful towards their customers, whilst the rest are mostly indifferent and apathetic? Is it their attitude that sets them apart?

Let us look at customer service from another perspective. Most products and services in their own class provide the same features (e.g., international airlines offer travel in similar aircrafts, similar seating arrangements, and similar food, beverages, and onboard entertainment). Yet, is it not the attitude of the cabin crew and ground staff that makes the difference between an award winning airline and a mediocre airline?

In a nutshell, the more helpful the customer service agents are, the more satisfied their customers feel. In turn, satisfied customers attract other customers, and the process directly contributes to the business entity's bottom line and long-term success.

The greatest discovery of my generation is that human beings can alter their lives by altering their attitude of mind.

William James, psychologist

So, what is attitude?

In his book, "The Attitude Factor," Thomas R. Blakeslee describes attitudes as:

> *Crucially important to happiness because they define the way we react to the world. They can make the difference between pleasure and pain, happiness and misery, even good health and bad. Attitudes are like well-worn paths in the mind that gradually evolve as a result of thousands of little choices we make every day of our lives. They define our experience to such a degree that different people often have opposite reactions to the same thing.*

What is your attitude, especially with your customers?

- Are you happy, enthusiastic, and passionate? Or are you uninterested, indifferent, and cheerless?

- Have you trained yourself to be enthusiastic at work and to be helpful towards your customers? Or is it that you don't particularly care?

Your attitude defines how you deal with your customers.

Work is either fun or drudgery. It depends on your attitude. I like fun.

Colleen C. Barrett

YOU CAN CHOOSE YOUR ATTITUDE

Your attitude is a lens that colors everything you see through it – bright, rosy, black, or blue.

Mak

Happiness is a state of mind. If you focus on the positive things in life, you will be happy, and if you focus on the negative things in life, you will feel depressed and victimized. Positive states of mind include enthusiasm, contentment, being passionate, creative, zealous, eager, and joyous, etc. They are all ways of choosing to perceive life positively. Happiness and enthusiasm are habitual ways of thinking positively about life.

Positive thinkers stay immersed in positive and meaningful thoughts. They don't have the time for negative thoughts or paranoia. They see and expect the good side of things. Their positive thoughts give rise to positive feelings and emotions, and consequently, they are happier.

That is why money, power, and status seldom make people happy in the long term. Those things can make life physically comfortable, but cannot guarantee happiness. You could be very wealthy and yet choose to indulge in all sorts of negative thoughts that will make you unhappy. On the other hand, you could be happy with the bare necessities if you choose to focus on the positive things in your life.

Actors and actresses who undergo plastic surgery provide a great example of how we choose to be happy or unhappy. Plastic surgeons have observed that no matter how beautiful their patients are to begin with or how attractive they become after the surgery, they are never fully satisfied with the way they look! Many prominent actors and actresses from both Hollywood and Bollywood resort to plastic surgery many times over to appear younger and more attractive.

According to plastic surgeons, most of these screen idols are never fully satisfied with the results of surgery. They just keep coming back to make more changes to their faces and bodies! Why do they do so?

It is because in their zeal to become physically perfect, these actors and actresses tend to notice only the negative aspects of their physical appearance. When it comes to their bodies, they have trained themselves to be overcritical. They have forgotten how to appreciate their natural beauty and the miracle that is the human body.

For people who choose to be happy, even insignificant things like a flower, a passing courtesy, or a child's innocent babbling could be enough to make them happy. Happiness can and usually does come from the little things in life. Happy people are generally more enthusiastic and have a clearer sense of direction; they know what they want or don't want in life. They are more passionate about what they do. *They are in control of their lives because they* **exercise their choice** *to manage their thoughts, emotions, and feelings.*

Unhappy people, on the other hand, let life events or other people control them. It is almost as if they give their remote control to others who make them feel good or bad!

For example, some people believe that they are worthy only when others around them say so. They constantly seek and need validation from others to feel worthy as human beings.

In a nutshell, external elements like money, power, and status can give us more options in life. As super coach, self-help writer, and advisor Anthony Robbins aptly states, with money, you can arrive in style...but can it guarantee contentment and happiness? Contentment and happiness are intrinsic to you; only you can choose to be happy.

*You, and **only you**, can **choose** to be happy.*

WHAT HAS ATTITUDE GOT TO DO WITH CUSTOMER SERVICE?

Everything!

Your attitude influences your overall disposition and behavior. If you're happy and content, you're more positive towards your customers, others around you, and life in general.

Conversely, if you're unhappy, you tend to be aloof and negative towards anyone and everyone that you encounter.

Recall how you behave with others when you were extremely happy – are you not all smiles, helpful, overly accommodating, and forgiving?

In contrast, what happens when you feel below the weather? Are you not short-tempered, snappy, and irritable?

However, that is not where it ends - your emotions and feelings influence the mood of the customers you serve, as emotions and feelings are contagious.

The chart on the next page shows how your attitude influences your customers.

If you are not using your smile, you're like someone with a million dollars in the bank and no checkbook.

Les Giblin

EMOTIONS AND FEELINGS ARE CONTAGIOUS

Your *attitude* towards your customers triggers

Customers develop an *attitude* towards you that reflects *your attitude* towards them in the first place.

Your *emotions and feelings* towards your customers and that

Customers' *thoughts* about you trigger their *emotions & feelings*

Stimulates *your thoughts* about them

They *reciprocate* by mirroring your *thoughts* (which they read from your attitude and behavior)

And your thoughts modulate *your behavior* towards your customers

Your customers *perceive* your *attitude and behavior* towards them

It is obvious that when you feel positively towards your customers, they feel positively about you and even themselves. Similarly, when you harbor negative feelings towards your customers, they respond negatively towards you.

If you are not enthusiastic or passionate about your products, your customers subconsciously read your feelings and beliefs towards your products and don't feel positively about them either.

In a way, you cannot influence your customers with emotions that you don't have or feel. Attempting to influence customers that way would be an uphill task, because faking emotions that you don't have is difficult – you will not be able to sustain the act for long, and eventually customers will see through your facade.

Enthusiasm and passion, like most other emotions, are highly contagious.

ENTHUSIASM ATTRACTS CUSTOMERS LIKE HONEY ATTRACTS BEES!

We influence others with the way we feel. When we are lively, others in contact with us feel cheerful, and similarly, when we are dejected, we depress the people around us.

When we are enthusiastic with customers, they sense our enthusiasm and develop confidence in dealing with us. Customers then see more value in the products or services we provide and are easily convinced to buy from us. To clarify the concept, imagine discussing a problem with a friend who is an optimist. Do they make you feel hopeful and relieved? Alternatively, have you ever noticed how we avoid paranoid people that zap our energy and leave us feeling somewhat sorry and miserable?

You, as a customer, may have noticed that an enthusiastic salesperson attracts your attention and appears more credible. As a result, you tend to buy more from them.

Customers keep coming back to enthusiastic service providers.

FIND OUT YOUR ATTITUDE TOWARDS LIFE

(Self-Assessment - 1)

Sr. No:	QUESTIONS	SCORE	REMARKS
		Give yourself marks on a sliding scale of "0" to "10" ("0" is the lowest and '10' is the highest).	**Do this only after you have scored yourself.** Note any positive attitudes that you should continue to nurture or any negative attitudes that you need to improve. For example, you may want to improve your attitude if you tend to be indecisive or judgmental. Also, note down ideas on how you can improve.
1	Do you know <u>exactly</u> where you want to be in three to five years' time? (Have you taken any <u>specific</u> action/s towards this? Then, and only then, it is a want. Otherwise, it is only a wish.)		
2	Do you take full responsibility for your current situation (successes and failures) in life?		
3	Are you a caring person? (Think back over the last six months and score yourself based on something that you did for someone else without expecting something in return. Be ruthless in assessing yourself.)		

4	Once you have thought things through, are you decisive?		
5	Do you listen to others' opinions and keep your own council?		
6	Do you believe that the world is full of opportunities?		
7	Do you believe that all people have the right to their own thoughts, judgments, opinions, and feelings?		
8	Do you boldly go where no woman/man has gone before?		
9	Are you tolerant and patient of others, no matter what or who they are?		
10	Could you accept if a relatively inexperienced colleague gets promoted before you? Alternatively, if you're self-employed, do you take it in stride when one of your competitors lands a juicy contract?		
11	Do you think most of your colleagues/friends would rush to assist you if you were in trouble?		
12	Do you believe "honesty is the best policy?"		
13	Do you believe that to be successful, you should "beat your own drum" so others know your capabilities?		

14	Do you believe that to be successful in today's world you should count favors done and received?		
15	Do you believe that only people with proven capability should be at the helm of a company?		
16	Do you believe that you should only empathize with people who deserve it?		
17	Do you think it is foolish to take risks no matter what is at stake?		
18	Do you think that the world is full of people with impaired judgment? Do you believe that these people should be told what to do or think because otherwise everyone could suffer because of their folly?		
19	Do you believe that it is a "dog-eat-dog" world?		
20	Do you believe that there is only one way of doing things and that is the right way?		
21	Do you believe one should always be cautious and wait for the smoke to clear before taking action?		
22	It is foolish to help people attacked by thugs on the street? After all, your involvement or calls for help could attract the thugs' attention to you, and they could attack you as well!		

23	Do you think that you could have done better in life if you had had a better upbringing and education?		
24	Do you believe that providence has etched your destiny in stone and you cannot do anything to change it?		

SCORE YOURSELF:

Step 1:   Add your scores for question numbers 1 to 12 (x)

Step 2:   Add your scores for question numbers 13 to 24 (y)

Step 3:   Deduct x – y to get your score (for any negative score, consider yourself in the '<0 to 24' bracket)

37 & above   Excellent – you have a mature, non-judgmental, and positive attitude that is rare and exceptional. People perceive you as a caring, respectable, and reliable person. Most people in your life probably tend to treat you in the same caring manner in which you treat them.

25 to 36   Not bad, although there is room for improvement; identify the high scores in the Step 1 questions and maintain them or work towards enhancing those scores further. Similarly, identify the high scores in the Step 2 questions and note the restrictive attitudes on which you need to work and improve.

<0 to 24   This score should be a matter of concern! Review the questions in Step 1 and identify any score below 7. Similarly, identify the questions in Step 2 with scores above 5. Contemplate your response to each such question identified, and ponder if there could be a better perspective or response.

CAN YOU BE ENTHUSIASTIC ALL THE TIME?

No, obviously not!

We all feel anxious or physically run-down sometimes either for a good reason or due to something inexplicable. To conquer such mood swings, especially when attending to customers, many service gurus recommend "switching off" such negative states of mind and putting on an act of enthusiasm. I agree that at times, the strategy works. However, it is not always possible to put on an act in all situations. For example, if your loved one is in intensive care, or if an intimate relationship ends, you may find it challenging to act as if nothing is wrong!

In many cases, remaining in denial could severely complicate the situation and prevent you from taking steps towards resolving the issue.

Consider a hypothetical situation in which your infant has a high fever and you have to leave her in the care of an elder sibling or a neighbor. Even if your infant was under the supervision of a doctor, you would probably be worried sick, and it would undoubtedly affect your enthusiasm and productivity at work. Perhaps the best thing that you could do would be to have faith and focus on your work.

It is important to note that as human beings, we are emotional. Contrary to popular opinion, we cannot switch off intense personal issues when we go to work. If that were true, it could make us utterly insensitive and uncaring towards our customers as well.

What we can do is acknowledge the situation and not ignore it. It is more practical and effective to accept things as they really are and work towards managing the negative emotions resulting from such situations.

That way, we have a better chance of managing any runaway emotions and containing them effectively. By looking reality in the face and being aware and in acceptance of our predicament, we can be more in control of our emotions, and thereby attend to our customers more effectively. However, sometimes there are deeper personal issues that gnaw at our very sanity. When facing such issues, it takes a mammoth effort to stay calm and composed at work. Troubled intimate relationships or chronic physical conditions like cancer or other serious diseases can make it difficult to keep smiling, especially at work.

Let me illustrate this point with an example. I frequently pick up groceries from a supermarket that is just a five-minute drive from my house. One of the ladies manning the cash register at this store is usually cheerful and courteous. In the past, I didn't mind waiting in her queue, even if the other queues were relatively lighter, just to be inspired by her bubbling enthusiasm.

However, one day, she seemed extremely disturbed. She surprised me by literally throwing the grocery items to one side after scanning them, and in a rebuking tone, suggested that I didn't buy so many things just before closing time! Her outburst was so unexpected that I did not know what to say or feel. Instinctively, I knew that something was wrong and that she was not her normal self. I chose to ignore her rude behavior, as there were other customers waiting their turn and I didn't feel like making a scene.

A few days later, on my next visit to the supermarket, I casually broached the incident with the manager. He told me that he was aware of the situation because of complaints from other customers as well. According to him, she was one of their good staff members, and was going through a bitter and painful divorce. He was moving her to the back office until she recovered from the personal tragedy.

Learn to manage your personal problems, for you cannot switch them off!

HOW TO KEEP WORRY OR ANXIETY AT BAY WHILE AT WORK

First be *aware* of the difficult situation you are in. *Accept* and *acknowledge* it, *do everything in your power* to alleviate the situation, and last of all, *focus on your work* and *expect the best*. Each of the above steps assists you at looking reality in the eye and remaining calm – the process empowers you to respond appropriately rather than react emotionally. <u>Do whatever you can to solve or alleviate the problem, and understand that you have done your best.</u>

For example, if your wife or husband is sick and you have arranged for someone responsible to look after her/him, worrying about your spouse will hardly alleviate the situation.

Instead, focus completely on what you are doing – your conscious mind cannot focus on two different issues at the same time. Therefore, when you get busy with your work and focus on it, the mind stops processing thoughts related to anxiety, depression, or worry, and becomes preoccupied with the task at hand, your work.
You may have noticed that sometimes, even though you were worried about something, it didn't bother you as long as you were busy at work. However, the moment you left work, the anxiety returned instantly.

Expect the best and have faith – remember, the body follows the mind and vice versa. They follow, feed, and amplify each other. When the mind is in a negative state, the body follows suit and becomes stressed. The stressed body then provides negative feedback to the mind, and a vicious cycle ensues.

The trick is to break the cycle by focusing your mind on various parts of the body, one at a time. For example, focus on your right foot, left foot, right shin and calf, left shin and calf, and move upwards to cover the rest of the body.

While you focus on a part of your body, notice how that part of the body feels. Your mind becomes fixated on how you're feeling; it cannot think negative thoughts or send depressing signals to the body.

When the mind becomes fixated on how the body feels and is unable to send negative signals to the body, the body gets a chance to recover. In turn, the body doesn't produce any negative vibes to reflect back to the mind. Thus, in effect, you disrupt the negative energy lines by which your mind and body feed each other.

Whenever you are in extreme worry or anxiety, try this in private with your eyes closed for a minute or two. It will help you to focus on your work and remain calm.

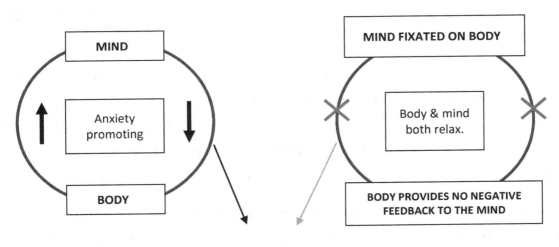

Negative feedback

Fig 1

In times of great stress or adversity, it's always best to keep busy, to plow your anger and your energy into something positive.

Lee Iacocca

IF YOU LIKE WHAT YOU DO, IT IS NOT WORK, BUT PURE JOY!

Imagine your supervisor asks you to go outside and stand in the sweltering heat of the desert for only ten minutes. Once outside in the heat, I bet you will question the supervisor's sanity in less than five minutes. However, if your supervisor were to ask you to go outside and play your favorite game, say football, basketball, or cricket, chances are you would enjoy staying out in the sun for the next hour or two without complaining. The next day, you would probably request to go out and play again.

Why is it that in the first scenario, you were questioning your supervisor's sanity in five minutes, and in the second scenario, you were happy to stay out in the heat for more than an hour?

There are two main reasons: The first scenario didn't serve any purpose and you didn't have any reason to tolerate the heat. However, in the second scenario, you were happy to stay out in the harsh weather because you were enjoying the game. Enjoying the game was good enough reason to tolerate the heat. As a matter of fact, because your focus was on the game, you didn't notice the heat in the first place!

Considering the fact that we spend more than half our waking life at work, if we don't enjoy our work, aren't we subjecting ourselves to lifelong pain? Is that fair to us, our customers, our employers, or even our colleagues?

On the other hand, if you were more enthusiastic about what you do:

- You would be happier and more satisfied with your life
- You would be more active and creative
- You would be more committed to your customers
- Your enthusiasm would bring out the best in you

- You would progress rapidly in your career.

Enthusiasm fires you up and makes you passionate about what you do; it can transform your life into a lifelong vacation.

HOW POSITIVE ATTITUDE MAKES THE DIFFERENCE BETWEEN SUCCESS & FAILURE

Positive and helpful attitudes promote customer satisfaction and build long-term customer relationships. Satisfied customers keep coming back for more, again and again. They also tell other customers about your superb service. Word-of-mouth advertising doesn't cost a dime, and it is the most effective form of advertisement.

Positive attitudes and enthusiasm are contagious. Our positive emotions influence our customers, and their emotions become positive. Customers in positive moods buy more than customers in negative states of mind. Personalized care and attention are the byproducts of a positive attitude; they make the customer feel important and pampered. They become lifelong partners in our business, and the value of lifetime customers is enormous for any business.

A calm and composed attitude boosts customers' confidence; they feel relaxed and enjoy the soothing ambiance of being in your care. For them, the enjoyment and relaxation leads to a positive experience.

Positive attitudes are contagious – they infect your customers, who respond positively.

WANT TO KNOW THE DIFFERENCE BETWEEN POSITIVE AND NEGATIVE PEOPLE?

Positive people are proactive. They take preemptive action to get what they want. On the other hand, negative or reactive people wait for things to happen! The former take control of what happens to them in their lives, while the latter allow themselves to be at the mercy of the situation they are in or the actions of others around them.

Below are three states of mind in which positive people stay immersed.

1. **Positive people are passionate about anything they do; they have goals and objectives.**

   Goals have two main components:

   a. ***Goals should be specific:***

Happy people have specific goals. For example, if it is one of their goals to own and drive an expensive car, they can see it in their mind's eye. They know the exact model, year, color, and other minute details of the car. It is almost as if they already own the car and are driving around in it. Why? This is because the goal then appears real and tangible to them. Once their mind identifies with the goal, it goes to work planning a path to achieve it.

The problem is that most of us don't know what we want! You may find it difficult to believe. However, just to test yourself, imagine that an angel comes down from the heavens and offers you one wish. What would you ask for?

Most people make statements such as:

"Please, my last wish is to have three more wishes!"

"I would like to be a millionaire."

"I would like to be happy."

"I would like my children to grow up to be good human beings." Notice that all of the above statements are very subjective and ambiguous.

How many millions do you want, by when, and in what currency or form – cash or kind? What would make you happy? How do you define a "good human being?"

In contrast, when you have a specific goal to save U.S. $1,000,000 by the end of 2011, your mind can fully comprehend what you want and can work towards achieving it.

Until and unless you can be absolutely clear and specific about what you want, how can your mind work towards getting it?

b. *Goals should be time bound:*

Have you noticed that in all the above statements (except the specific goal of saving $1,000,000 by the end of 2011) there is no mention of deadlines or "by when?" We don't live forever, and therefore every second counts.

When we set deadlines, our mind gives the goal the right priority and focuses on its achievement urgently. Otherwise, the goal keeps getting relegated in favor of other unimportant things and remains a dream forever!

What you do today determines your tomorrow.

2. Positive people strategize, take action, and expect the best:

Positive people strategize and develop plans to get what they want. Once they have the plans in place, they can't wait to dive headlong into action. They focus on the results, and their belief in their visions is so unwavering that they expect only the best. That is what keeps them motivated to strive against all odds.

They believe that their goals are worthwhile and are passionate about them. Their self-worth depends on how much they dedicate themselves towards the achievement of their goals. Their goals become their visions, which they consider larger then themselves. They cannot wait to make their vision a reality, and take all necessary action to achieve their vision, no matter what.

It doesn't matter to them if they will be successful in their endeavors or not; what matters to them is that they dedicate themselves to what they believe in. Their desire is so intense that they can't keep themselves from taking action to achieve what they want.

If they fail, they try again, and if they fail again, they try something new, and the process goes on and on until they have what they set out to achieve. This is different than daydreaming, where people build castles in the air that have no foundation beneath them – their dreams float in and out with the wind!

> *When you live for something bigger than yourself, life becomes meaningful and rewarding.*

3. Positive people enjoy doing what they do:

Happy people enjoy what they do. They are passionate and thrilled by what they can create and give it their best shot. It is a never-ending cycle that keeps feeding itself; the more involved they get with something that they like and enjoy, the more motivated they become.

> *For positive people, success is secondary - doing what they do is intoxicating to them.*

Below are some positive side effects of having goals, strategizing, taking action, and *enjoying doing what you do*:

- Higher self-esteem
- Greater job satisfaction
- Greater inquisitiveness
- Greater creativity and innovation

> **Success is a journey, not a destination. The doing is often more important than the outcome.**
>
> Arthur Ashe

- Greater determination and perseverance
- More patience and tolerance
- Excellence in the work that you do and professional growth.

The people who get on in this world are the people who get up and look for the circumstances they want and if they can't find them, make them.

G. Bernard Shaw

SOME THINGS PEOPLE WITH POSITIVE ATTITUDES DO

Ironically, people who value themselves care for others. People who lack confidence feel victimized and blame others.

In a way, we are all like mirrors. Generally, whatever we project onto others is what others reflect back to us. If we greet others, they respond by returning our greeting, and if we are rude to them, they reciprocate with rudeness to us. Positive people want good things for both themselves and those around them - a win-win for all. Below is a list of five practices of positive people that make them highly effective:

1. ***Give first:*** Have you ever heard anyone say, "Take and give?" No, you haven't, because that is absurd. One cannot expect to receive before giving. That is why the adage is, "Give and take."

   Giving first is a kind of commitment and pledge that is given without any condition. People with positive attitudes practice giving first.

   Employees who deal directly with customers need to instill and practice this attitude so the customers feel cared about.

2. **_Understand before expecting to be understood:_** Effective service
   agents focus more on their customers and their needs than on their own needs to
   make sales. Because their focus is on what their customers want, they try to
   understand their customers by listening to them.

   Ineffective service agents, on the other hand, are more concerned with their own
   needs to sell. They expect that their customers would understand and respond to
   their sales pitches. Because the agents don't take interest in their customers and
   what they need, their customers find their sales pitches boring; they either don't
   buy, or they never return!

3. **_Focus on solutions and not problems:_** Effective service agents understand that
   their _customers want solutions to their problems_. They understand that their
   customers should not be bothered with company policy, manpower problems,
   system breakdowns, or failures on the part of the seller. They know that, for
   their customers, the equation is very simple: the customers are paying their
   hard-earned money and giving them their business, and in return, the customers
   expect them to deliver without any excuses or hitches.

4. **_Value relationships above all:_** Developing and fostering relationships is the
   number one priority of positive people. They work hard at building strong
   relationships so both parties can benefit from the synergy of mutual support and
   growth. Wise service agents build strong business relationships with their
   customers, who keep coming back with their patronage. Both the business and
   the customers benefit from the arrangement; the business gets more revenue and
   the customers get better, personalized, and more reliable service at no extra cost.

5. ***Operate from the position of integrity and honesty:*** In any relationship, the most important element is trust. Even the best relationship is doomed to fail without trust. Customers expect that the service agents at their favorite stores will look after them and protect their interests. They want to be able to blindly trust the service agent they deal with, and that is why effective service agents operate from the position of integrity and honesty.

I once read somewhere that you're allowed to tell a lie, as long as you don't get caught. The problem is that to cover one lie, you need to tell many lies, and eventually, the truth slips out. Note that it takes time, hard work, and commitment to build trust, but it takes only one instance of dishonesty and deceit to break that trust.

Therefore, if you don't know the answer to your customer's question, don't bluff him. Most customers are smarter than you think and they can see right through you. If they are treated like that, they won't bother to come back. However, if you tell the customer that you don't know and that you will find out and let them know, the customer may not be pleased with your answer, but you will retain his trust and patronage!

We don't sell; we build trust and relationships with our customers.

CAN YOU CHANGE YOUR ATTITUDE?

Yes, contrary to popular belief, it is possible to change your attitude. What we need to understand is that it is *extremely difficult* to change one's attitude and requires immense effort, dedication, and work.

Attitudes don't form overnight; they take a long time to take root. For example, if you are pessimistic or paranoid, it is because you made hundreds and thousands of little negative choices over a long period.

Taken all together, they make you negative. It is identical to how the coral in the sea accumulate, one on top of another, to form massive coral reefs.

If you have a negative attitude, you literally have taught and trained yourself to process events in your life negatively to cope with things that were outside of your control, and to avoid taking responsibility for the things that were in your control. Now, years later, the process has become automatic, and you tend to see the negative in all things, as it has become a part of your character.

Similarly, positive people have developed positive attitudes by making positive choices over a long period of time, which ultimately cemented into positive approaches towards life. A positive person tends to notice the glass as half full, while a negative person tends to notice the same glass as half empty! These positive or negative attitudes transform into beliefs that we have about different aspects of life.

Refer to the diagram on the next page, and notice that our beliefs reside in the deepest recesses of our minds that are unconscious. Our beliefs modulate our feelings and attitudes that give rise to our thoughts; our thoughts drive our behaviors, and our behaviors are visible to all around us.

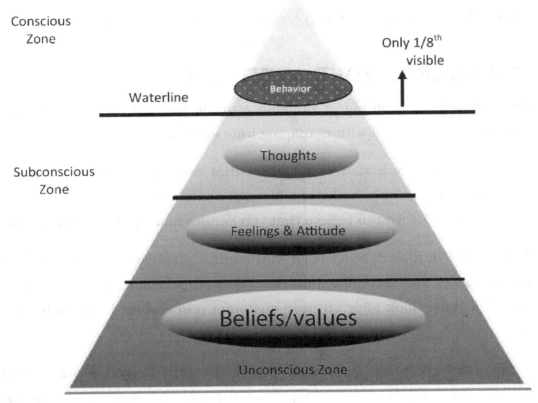

Iceberg – 7/8th below waterline

This is why attitudes are almost impossible to change by forcefully managing them. The way you can manage your limiting attitude is to identify the related belief that modulates it, and change that belief first. That seems simple, but the problem is that, as previously mentioned, beliefs reside in the deepest recesses of our mind, and we are seldom conscious of them!

Therefore, we need to be aware of our beliefs and learn to question them first. It may be that the belief in question was applicable and beneficial at an earlier time, but now that the circumstances in our lives have changed, it is no longer appropriate.

Therefore, we need to identify redundant beliefs, weed them out of our systems, and replace them with appropriate sets of new beliefs.

Learn to question your limiting beliefs before you try to manage them.

HOW TO CHANGE YOUR ATTITUDE

- First, identify the limiting or problem attitude that you want to change. For example, "I'm not good with managing irate customers!"

- Trace the belief (outdated or negative) that feeds the limiting attitude. For example, you may have had a terrible experience with an irate customer a few years ago that led you to believe that you cannot manage irate customers.

- Replace the outdated belief (that you cannot manage irate customers) with another belief that is more appropriate, ethical, practical, and worthwhile. For example, "I can look after an irate customer and resolve their issues to their satisfaction."

- Avoid or be on guard for people who make fun of you or your efforts to change. Also, stay away from people or situations that make you negative; the idea is not to reinforce unwanted behaviors or attitudes.

- Relentlessly think, speak, and hear the newly-installed belief until it takes root or becomes spontaneous; let it recede naturally into your unconscious mind to support the new and desired attitude.

For example, if you are one of those people who get tongue-tied in front of the boss, it could be that your parents discouraged you from expressing yourself openly in their presence. You were supposed to speak only when spoken to.

Over the years, the belief that you should stay quiet in front of your parents or others holding a similar position of power and reverence was unconsciously ingrained. It could be that your subconscious mind draws a parallel between your strict parents and your boss, and inhibits you from speaking freely in front of her. That way, you don't go against your belief, and this keeps you from expressing yourself in front of people in positions of authority.

To get rid of your limiting beliefs, first identify them and then develop a workable strategy to delete such beliefs one by one. Replace them with viable beliefs that support your desired attitude. In this case, you would need to reason away the limiting belief with the following facts:

- Your boss is not one of your parents
- Your boss wants to be communicated with; otherwise, work would suffer
- It would be out of place not to communicate with the boss.

Now, install a new belief that you should communicate freely with your boss on work-related issues. Support your newly-installed belief with the above mentioned facts. Apply the new belief by taking the opportunity to speak to your boss as often as possible until the process becomes unencumbered and natural.

If you don't like something, change it; if you can't change it, change the way you think about it.

Mary Engelbreit

WHAT SHOULD YOU WATCH OUT FOR?

What do you say to yourself when you talk to yourself? If you find yourself engrossed in negative thoughts, casually correct yourself by choosing positive thoughts instead. Don't blame yourself, as blaming will initiate negative emotions, and negative emotions will reinforce the habit of negative thinking.

How do you take what others say to you, especially when, knowingly or unknowingly, they put you down? Register what others say to you or about you, but don't internalize these statements. The fact is that even if you have done something wrong, it doesn't mean you are an incapable person or deserve to be condemned. You can learn to correct whatever you did wrong.

Be non-judgmental: When you become judgmental, you become emotional and lose your capacity to remain objective. Moreover, why judge others when judging others will induce others to judge you in return?

Guard and keep your motivation high: Remember "Success = Motivation x (knowledge + skills)." The beauty of the equation is that even if you have all the knowledge and skills in the world, if you're not motivated, you will never apply your knowledge or skills to produce anything good because you lack motivation.

Substitute knowledge and skills with a value, say 100 each, and make motivation zero. What do you get? Zero! Now, try reducing knowledge and skills to 50 each, and make motivation 50 as well. Now what do you get? [50 x (50 + 50) = 5,000!] Therefore, watch out for any person or situation that diminishes your motivation (positive attitude) and avoid them like you would avoid the plague.

There is no failure, only results: What this means is that there are no failures or successes, there is only feedback. If you take appropriate action, you will experience success, and if you take inappropriate action, you will experience failure. Therefore, avoid branding yourself a failure, because if you believe you are a failure, you will tend to give up before you even attempt anything!

When something doesn't work, try something new: For anything that you do, there will be positive feedback (success), or negative feedback (failure). Negative feedback only means that you need to do something differently to get what you want.

If you don't succeed, try something else till you find a way that works. The trick is to keep trying and bettering your batting average for positive feedback (successes). In simple language, failures are signals for you to change the way you do things and prompt you to take a different course of action.

Watch out for anything that dampens your thoughts, motivation, and belief in yourself.

Summary

1. The person who sends out positive thoughts activates the world around him positively and draws back to himself positive results.

2. Your attitude defines how you deal with your customers.

3. You, and only you, can choose to be happy.

4. Enthusiasm and passion, like most other emotions, are highly contagious.

5. Customers keep coming back to enthusiastic service providers.

6. Learn to manage your personal problems, for you cannot switch them off!

7. Enthusiasm fires you up and makes you passionate about what you do; it can transform your life into a lifelong vacation.

8. Positive attitudes are contagious – they infect your customers, who respond positively.

9. Until and unless you can be absolutely clear and specific about what you want, how can your mind work towards getting it?

10. What you do today determines your tomorrow.

11. When you live for something bigger than yourself, life becomes meaningful and rewarding.

12. For positive people, success is secondary - doing what they do is intoxicating to them.

13. We don't sell; we build trust and relationships with our customers.

14. Learn to question your limiting beliefs before you try to manage them.

15. If you don't like something, change it; if you can't change it, change the way you think about it.

16. Watch out for anything that dampens your thoughts, motivation, and belief in yourself.

When you do things from your soul,

you feel a river moving in you, a joy.

When actions come from another section,

the feeling disappears.

Maulana Rummi

Chapter 2

RAPPORT

Stop selling – start building relationships!

Mak

Case Study 2:

John took his seat in business class and buckled up as the aircraft's engines whined to a sharp pitch in preparation for takeoff. The cabin crew was busy serving the welcome drinks, distributing newspapers, taking passengers' coats, and helping them stow away their carry-ons in the overhead compartments.

Like many other passengers who don't travel by air often, John found it disconcerting sitting in such proximity to total strangers. Although he knew better, John could swear that everyone was looking at him! To cope with the discomfort, John pulled out a worn out in-flight magazine from the pouch in front of him and pretended to be lost in it.

John became apprehensive as another passenger took the seat next to him; he didn't know what to expect. How he could remain seated with a complete stranger for the next six hours? What should he say and how should he behave? They exchanged a dry greeting, which to John was more like a ritual whereby both agreed to refrain from bothering each other unnecessarily.

Soon, the aircraft was airborne, and for some inexplicable reason, John felt a sense of relief. Everyone in the aircraft became busy with their own things: taking off their shoes, reclining their seats, and fiddling with the in-flight entertainment system.

John was surprised to notice that the stranger sitting next to him was wearing a Rolex wristwatch that was exactly like his. Not being able to withhold his excitement, he pointed it out to the stranger. The stranger, one Mr. Smith, was equally surprised at the coincidence and the subject became an icebreaker for both of them to start up a conversation.

Thereafter, it didn't take long for the two of them to open up to each other. They got busy talking about topics like the worldwide economic recession, the depletion of the ozone layer, the melting of the ice caps, the promise of stem cells in curing cancer, extraterrestrials, and whatnot.

Their excitement turned into frenzy when they discovered that both of them were avid fans of cricket and relished eating oysters and frog legs.

John had a quiet moment after dinner when Smith dozed off. He wondered how he could have felt anxious about Smith sitting next to him a few moments ago, and yet within a short while, he felt as if he had known Smith for a long time.

What do you think happened that brought John and Smith close to each other?

WHAT IS RAPPORT?

Although our lifestyles have changed drastically over the last three to five hundred years, our physiology hasn't. Our brains still scan our surroundings for anything unknown or unpredictable that can be dangerous. It automatically puts us on guard against anything unknown, such as strangers.

When we interact with strangers and find that we are from the same country, our brains find it reassuring and a little less threatening, and if another **_commonality_** emerges, the situation becomes more relaxed for both parties.

If there is enough commonality between two people, they develop rapport.

Rapport is a connection between two individuals that indicates a comfortable level of acceptance, understanding, and predictability. For instance, if John and Smith had discovered that they both were going to Oxford Street in London, the rapport between them would have gone up another notch. If they discovered that they were both married to American women, they would have become even closer.

A series of commonalities between them would ultimately precipitate a strong bond of friendship.

In order to sell a product or a service, a company must establish a relationship with the consumer. It must build trust and RAPPORT. It must understand the customer's needs, and it must provide a product that delivers the promised benefits.

Jay Levinson

Similarly, a great deal of rapport also develops through _commonalities in body language, interests, and attitudes._ Much of the scanning process for detecting commonality happens subconsciously and influences our feelings more intensely than we realize.

For this reason, you may have noticed that sometimes, you meet people for the first time, and for no apparent reason, you have an instant like or dislike of them. It is possible that in the deeper recesses of our minds, the person resembles someone we were fond of, like our late grandfather – a commonality that builds rapport. Alternatively, perhaps the person reminds you of a colleague from a previous job who was very obnoxious – something that inhibits rapport.

Commonality, safety, and amiability promote rapport.

To get anybody to buy from you requires three things: rapport, logic, and emotion. Rapport means that the buyer trusts you. Logic means that buying makes sense. Emotion means that buying feels good. Use all three tools.

Mark Sanborn

RAPPORT FROM THE CUSTOMER'S POINT OF VIEW

One way or another, most of us have learned to hide our true feelings and become experts at manipulating words to hide what we really feel! For example, you greet your boss, with whom you don't particularly agree, and yet the words you use are congenial. You could be saying, "Good morning boss," whilst your feelings could be screaming, "See you in hell!"

You could be effectively hiding your real feelings by manipulating words, but a keen observer will be able to make out from your body language and tone that the words you are uttering are not coming from your heart. For example, you could be verbally greeting the customers warmly, but from your body language and tone, they would know that you're just being courteous and don't mean a word you say.

Further, few people can synchronize their body language, tone, and words to convey the same message or feelings. How often do you (as a customer) come across service agents who say the right words to you but don't mean any of it? Simple things like a sincere smile, greetings from the heart, or an inviting gaze or tone go a long way in making customers feel comfortable and at home. When you're sincere, your customers can almost hear you whispering into their ears: "Welcome, what I can do for you today?"

Any difference in what your customer sees and what they feel is going to make them uncomfortable and question your intentions.

RAPPORT FROM THE SERVICE AGENT'S PERSPECTIVE

Effective service agents scan the customer's speech, body language, and tone to ascertain the emotional and mental state of the customer. They do this to moderate their own behavior and become accommodative of their customers, so that the customers feel welcome and comfortable. Remember, building rapport or connecting with the customer involves *focusing on customers as well as being aware of your own responses to them.* Rapport makes your communication with your customers more effective because:

- Customers feel they are on familiar turf and any apprehensions they have fade

- They become more trusting and at home, and they start seeing things positively

- Their judgment takes a back seat and a sense of excitement and discovery takes over

- They forgive little irregularities on the part of the service agent

- Customers feel safe and expect help without condition

- Customers open up and share their feelings and what they want with you

- The customer develops a sense of belonging after the first few transactions.

Be aware not only of what you say and how you say it, but also of how you feel while attending to your customers.

STEPS TO DEVELOP & MAINTAIN RAPPORT

Effective service agents habitually apply the rules of developing rapport with their customers. However, a great majority of service agents lack the sincere feelings and commitment while dealing with their customers. Both feelings and commitment complement each other; when one goes up, the other automatically goes up, and when one goes down, the other follows suit.

Feelings and commitment are byproducts of attitude, which we discussed in the previous chapter. We can make our jobs as customer service agents more rewarding and interesting if we start taking a sincere interest in our customers and build stronger business relationships with them.

Taking on the responsibility of assisting and satisfying our customers makes our work worthwhile; it gives us a great sense of purpose.

Let us now take a brief look on how we can develop and maintain rapport with customers:

1.   **Acknowledge:** Acknowledging customers can be as simple as a smile or a nod. It is a crucial step nonetheless, because this triggers the beginning of a relationship between the service provider and the customer. Executed properly, the customer is reassured that they are welcome and have come to the right place. Acknowledgement sets the tone of your attitude towards the customer, and they feel more comfortable and secure in dealing with you. In particular, when customers are waiting their turn, a smile or gesture from the service provider assures the waiting customer that they will be attended to shortly. When you assure your customers that you will attend to them promptly, they don't fidget, and they wait their turn in a relaxed state of mind.

Acknowledgements can be classified into three main categories:

i.   **A neutral response:** This is when service agents totally ignore their customers as they walk into their premises. They look through their customers as if they don't exist. The customer reads the attitude as conveying the message, "Whether you buy or don't buy, I still get my salary."

ii. **Annoyance:** This is when the service agents acknowledge the customer, but with *passive reluctance*. The acknowledgement is cold and dry, devoid of any feelings. The customer reads the acknowledgement as conveying the message, "Don't you have anything better to do than walk into this place?" or "Let us get this over with quickly, as I have better things to do!"

iii. **Welcome:** However, when you welcome customers from your heart, the customer hears, ***"Welcome! How can I be of service to you today?"***

An acknowledgement should be your signal to the customer saying, "We are glad to see you and be of service to you."

2.   Greet: Greetings are explicit expressions that address customers to welcome them, show respect, and offer assistance. Greetings are usually formal, such as, "Good morning Ms. Sanders, how may I assist you?" or can be informal with regular customers (e.g., "Hi, Ms. Sanders, I haven't seen you for a while. Is there anything I can do for you today?").

Acknowledgements and greetings go hand in hand. There could be situations in which you are busy with one customer and acknowledge other customers waiting their turn.

Service agents should be mindful of the norms and culture of their place of business and use appropriate greetings. In cosmopolitan environments, standard greetings are appropriate and acceptable (e.g., "Good morning" or "Good afternoon").

However, greetings based on religion, culture, community, or country can be made more personal when you can be sure of your customer's origin. For example, service agents can use greetings like "Namashkar" for Hindu customers, "As-Salamu Alaykum" for Muslim customers, and "Ohayou-gozaimasu" or "Konnichiwa" for Japanese customers. Stick to what is appropriate; *what really matters is that you greet your customers from the heart so that they feel welcomed.*

Greetings from the heart make your customers feel good and at home.

3. **Use your customer's name:** Our names are the sweetest words to us. When you address your customers by name, they feel good and you grab their attention. Try going into a crowded place, like the bazaar or a party, and shout out a name, for example, "John." You will be surprised to find that all Johns will stop doing whatever they were doing and look at you, while the rest of the people will hardly notice that you called out a name (Do this at your own risk; I did this once in a fish market and some Johns there were not very appreciative of what I did!).

Addressing people by name requests their attention to the exclusion of all others, thus personalizing your address. It is like tuning in to a particular radio station.
In particular, when you want to emphasize something to your customers or want to appease them for something that went wrong, addressing them by name creates a greater sense of rapport and connection.

Addressing customers by name personalizes your interaction with them and makes your communication more effective.

4.   Smile: The smile is a universal way of connecting and accepting that knows no boundaries. Even infants recognize a smile as a sign of goodwill, and they too often express their pleasure by smiling back at their mothers.

Smiling is something that comes naturally and impacts everyone; the person smiled at feels elated, and the person smiling feels connected. People who smile help to spread a bit of happiness around them, and those smiled at, smile back – a spontaneous response. It is not ironic that what you give out is what the world around you reflects back at you. When you smile at your customers, they smile back at you, and the ensuing good feelings help to develop rapport.

Moreover, as stated earlier, your body follows your mind, and your mind follows your body. When you smile, you feel good, and it triggers positive thoughts. Positive thoughts give rise to positive feelings. Positive feelings make you more enthusiastic, active, and energetic. The customer perceives your positive vibes and responds positively towards you. It may surprise you to know that it takes fewer facial muscles to smile than to frown. Frowning takes more effort than smiling, and it takes only one second to smile, so why not smile?

When you smile at your customers, they smile back at you, and the ensuing good feelings help to develop rapport.

5.   Shake hands when appropriate: Shaking hands is a more personalized form of acknowledgement that complements the greetings in both personal and formal situations. Since we shake hands at the beginning or end of a meeting, let it be warm and firm; it leaves the other party feeling good.

Fortify your first and last impressions with your customers by smiling and wishing them greetings from the inner core of your heart. Address them by name if you know them, and where applicable, welcome and see them off with a firm handshake.

A word of caution, though . . . Have you had the experience of shaking hands with someone who, in their zeal to impress you, squeezed your hand so vigorously that all of the bones in your hand were almost crushed? Alternatively, have you experienced the opposite, where someone offers his or her hand but it felt limp, like a dead fish? What message do these overpowering or lifeless handshakes give you?

Additionally, there is another group of people who make things worse by not letting their grip go even after the preliminary courtesies have been exchanged! Some overly eager males often perpetrate this crime when they meet attractive ladies! In some conservative cultures, shaking hands between males and females is not acceptable, so be discreet.

Shaking hands creates the first and last impression; be zestful and sincere.

6.   **Breaking the ice:** When people meet for the first time, especially at an unknown place, they are usually on guard, as they don't know what to expect. Similarly, customers who come to your premises for the first time are not familiar with your organization and may feel apprehensive or anxious.

Their apprehension and anxiety makes it difficult for you to reach them until you assist them in developing an adequate level of confidence and trust in you.
You can gain the confidence of new as well as existing customers by:

a. **Genuine appreciation or compliments:** We all like appreciation and compliments. When someone compliments us, we feel good towards that person and begin to connect with them. However, one should be careful that the compliments are genuine and not insincere or flattery; customers see through flattery. It is manipulative and demeaning.

The most effective way to achieve right relations with any living thing is to look for the best in it, and then help that best into the fullest expression.

Allen J. Boone

b. Empathy: Simply put, empathy is your ability to feel and share the pain of others. When you empathize with others, they feel cared for, supported, and understood. Then, people see you as an ally.

This is where most service providers fail. Most are good at giving technical information, enumerating service procedures, and providing other details. However, when it comes to responding to customers' emotional needs, they fail miserably! Simple expressions such as, "I know how you must be feeling," or even, "I cannot possibly fathom what you must be going through!" can go a long way in helping you connect with your customers.

Appreciation and empathy are the royal roads to building rapport.

c. Listen attentively: Take interest in what your customers have to say. One of the most effective ways to listen to what others are saying is to take genuine interest in them. Taking interest in others is a matter of choice that becomes a habit over time.

Attentive listeners invariably develop strong relationships that benefit both parties in a conversation. Listening attentively is one of the hallmarks of people who are good service providers, and such people are usually more effective in their personal and professional relationships as well.

If you want to be heard, be attentive to what others have to say.

d. Establish credibility: Customers find it reassuring to deal with professionals. Such service providers are usually service matter experts and have a deep understanding of customer psychology. Therefore, it is sometimes prudent to establish your credibility as someone who can assist them in a professional manner. However, don't build credibility by being loud and boastful of your abilities.

e. Build your credibility subtly and in a casual manner, making relevant statements such as, "From my fifteen years of experience in this field, I recommend that you consider product 'X' with an all-inclusive warranty."

Customers like to deal with service agents who are confident and empowered subject matter experts.

BE CAREISH

a. Let the customer feel that they are in **Control.**

b. Be **Appreciative** of them.

c. **Respond** by focusing on the customer: their needs, concerns, and feelings.

d. **Empathize** by responding to their mental or emotional states.

e. Take **Interest** in your customers by listening to them attentively.

f. Take care not to hurt customers' **Sentiments**: their ideas, values, and beliefs.

g. Be **Humble** and accommodating.

If you want to cheer up, cheer somebody else up.

Richard Denny

WAYS TO BUILD RAPPORT

- **Courtesy:**

1. Greet your customers
2. Listen to them intently
3. Ask their permission to ask questions where appropriate
4. Thank them for any information given
5. Do not keep the customer on hold over the telephone for a long time
6. Use positive language
7. Thank the customers and invite them to come back again.

- **Feelings & emotions:**

1. Be friendly and helpful

2. Empathize – this means sharing the customers' feelings, emotions, and pain while understanding what they must be going through. Don't sympathize, as it refers to superficial feelings for a customer's plight (i.e., not feeling sorry for them, but pitying them)

3. Be responsive to their emotional concerns

4. Reconfirm your understanding of what the customer wants, as well as reviewing the main points that were discussed at the end of the conversation to ensure full understanding and management of the customer's expectations

5. Call back with any necessary information, updates, or any changes to the agreement with the customer.

- **Service & providing solutions:**

a. Be confident
b. Take initiative

c. Focus on the benefit to the customer rather than the product/service

d. Recommend appropriate solutions

e. Where applicable and practical, follow-up after providing the service to find out if the customer is satisfied with our services

f. Resolve customer complaints quickly and to their satisfaction.

TEST YOUR RAPPORT-BUILDING ABILITY

Fill in the "Your Response" column first and then fill in the remaining two columns accordingly.

(Self-Assessment – 2)

Sr. No:	Question	Your Response 1 (low) to 5 (high)	Your strengths & areas to improve	How do you plan to work on areas that need improvement?
1	Do you take genuine interest in others?			
2	Do you know what you appreciate in others?			
3	Even if you do not agree with others, can you stay non-judgmental towards them?			
4	With a view to understanding others, do you try to look at things from their perspective?			
5	When you have differences of opinion with others, would you rather change the subject than win the argument?			
6	Can you share your feelings (positive or negative) with others relatively easily?			
7	Can you let go of little differences and focus on the positive aspects of your relationships?			

8	Do you feel a sense of satisfaction when you can be of assistance to others?		
9	Do you make it a point to appreciate, empathize with, or encourage others?		
10	Do you take time to acknowledge your gratitude when others are of assistance to you?		
11	Are you sensitive to others and their feelings?		

Your score:

42 to 55   Excellent! Your score indicates how easily you connect and communicate effectively with others. By the same token, others probably find it relatively easy to connect and communicate with you.

27 to 41   Not bad; however, there is ample room for improvement. Identify all items with scores less than 3, mark them in the column entitled "Your strengths & areas to improve," and work on them. Write down how you plan to improve your communication skills in the identified areas.

11 to 26   Your score is a matter of concern. Identify the weak areas as indicated above (any score equal to 2 or below) and work on them one at a time until you have significantly improved in each. Explain what you're trying to achieve to people close to you, and ask them for their honest and candid feedback. Ask them for their suggestions and keep trying to improve until you succeed. One word of caution, though . . .

Seek assistance from people who are encouraging, rather than critical of you.

When people are like each other, they tend to like each other.

Anthony Robbins

Summary

1. Stop selling – start building relationships.

2. Commonality, safety, and amiability promote rapport.

3. Any difference in what your customer sees and what they feel is going to make them uncomfortable and question your intentions.

4. Be aware of not only what you say and how you say it, but also of how you feel while attending to your customers.

5. Taking on the responsibility of assisting and satisfying our customers makes our work worthwhile; it gives us a great sense of purpose.

6. An acknowledgement should be your signal to the customer saying, "We are glad to see you and be of service to you."

7. Greetings from the heart make your customers feel good and at home.

8. Addressing customers by name personalizes your interaction with them and makes your communication more effective.

9. When you smile at your customers, they smile back at you, and the ensuing good feelings help to develop rapport

10. Shaking hands creates the first and last impression; be zestful and sincere.

11. Appreciation and empathy are the royal roads to building rapport.

12. If you want to be heard, be attentive to what others have to say.

13. Customers like to deal with service agents who are confident and empowered subject matter experts.

14. If you want to cheer up, cheer somebody else up.

15. When people are like each other, they tend to like each other.

Chapter 3

BE CAREFUL OF WHAT & HOW YOU CCOMMUNICATE!

They may forget what you said, but they will never forget how you made them feel.

Carl W. Buechner

Case Study 3:

Russell usually purchases his monthly groceries from two stores that are located near his house. One is called "Kwality Supermarkets." It is the larger of the two, and caters to a group of higher-income customers in the area. They have a large range of consumer products and the quality is better than most other stores in town.

The other store is a much smaller setup called "Shopper's Paradise." The quality is not as good as that of Kwality Supermarkets, but they are more affordable. In fact, if one were to compare the quality, packaging, and quantity offered by both the setups, the deals offered by Kwality Supermarkets are superior and more attractive.

Russell finds the upscale ambience of Kwality Supermarkets refreshing, but he finds the staff somewhat indifferent. Even though he frequents the store, no one there knows him by name. Once, Russell wanted to return a defective mixer that he had bought from them, and they promptly replaced the item. Russell felt that the staff at Kwality Supermarkets handled the situation quite well, but lacked the personal touch that is so natural to the staff at Shopper's Paradise.

Russell purchases a sizable amount of his groceries from Shopper's Paradise as well. The attendants at Shopper's Paradise know Russell and all of his family members by name. They even know Russell's granddaughter, Charmaine, who is six years old. Russell loves to have Charmaine with him while shopping for groceries, as it gives him extra time with her. The Shopper's Paradise attendants seem to sense this, and every time Charmaine is at their store, they make it a point to pamper her with toys, ice cream, and chocolates. Although Russell insists on paying for such items, he appreciates their gestures.

At times when Russell is very busy, he calls Shopper's Paradise and gives them a list of items he needs. The staffs at Shopper's Paradise keep the order ready and Russell picks it up later at his convenience.

They have an understanding that if Russell doesn't like an item, he can return it during his next visit to the store as long as it is unpacked. The cost of the returned item is adjusted in Russell's next purchase from the store.

If you were the manager of Kwality Supermarkets, what would you do to get Russell and similar customers to buy all their groceries from your store?

Anything and everything you do or don't do with your customers can be described as communication with your customers.

FRONT-LINE STAFF MAKES THE DIFFERENCE

Friendly staff, layout, décor, displays, cleanliness, quality, price, and convenience all contribute to how effectively you communicate with your customers. When customers are with you in person, they take particular notice of the climate of your premises, what you say, what you do, and how friendly you are towards them before they decide to buy from you regularly.

Most businesses in the same class offer more or less similar services. As mentioned earlier, it is the people who provide the service that make the difference between a mediocre service provider and an excellent service provider. Why? This is because it is the people (front-line staff) who respond to the customers' needs, emotions, values, and sentiments. They are the only ones that interact directly with the customers and can build a meaningful business relationship with them.

Fortunately or unfortunately, depending on how you look at it, most of the front-line staff is usually young and relatively inexperienced, but eager to learn. Many don't have adequate knowledge, training, or skills to provide superior customer service. However, they have the spunk, energy, and innocence that give them an advantage over many experienced staff who have lost their motivation to put their best foot forward.

Nevertheless, the front-line staff makes all the difference between mediocre and excellent customer service. It is not only what they say to their customer that is important, but also how they say it.

By far, success and failure at customer service is made by the front-line staff and how they interact with their customers.

As far as customers are concerned, you are the company. This is not a burden, but the core of your job. You hold in your hands the power to keep customers coming back – perhaps even to make or break the company.

Anonymous

KNOW YOUR CUSTOMERS SO YOU CAN RESPOND TO THEIR NEEDS

Take interest in your customers: You should know as much as possible about your customers: what motivates them, their expectations, concerns, preferences, and desires, etc. Their buying habits, income levels, marital status, family size, business, profession, nationality, religion, culture, and tradition all help you to know your customers better and equip you to deal with them accordingly. When we make friends, don't we find out more about them? We may not do so consciously, but don't we take interest in them?

The more interest we take in our friends, the better we understand them. When we take interest in them we learn more about them, and when we know more about them, we can interact with them in a manner that appeals to them. They in turn find us interesting, and a close bond develops. The same process applies to our customers and our relationship with them.

The point is that the more you know about your customer, the better position you will be in to respond to them and satisfy them. For example, if you could read your customer's mind and found out that he is a cricket fan and that the Australian team is his favorite, it would be very easy for you to impress him just by supporting the Australians.

Although the above would be manipulative, the example is just to show how customer information puts you on a better path to influence them. As stated earlier in the chapter on Rapport, the customer's subconscious mind will recognize the similarity between his views and yours, and he will likely feel more comfortable with you.

You can make more friends in two months by becoming really interested in other people than you can in two years by trying to get other people interested in you.

Dale Carnegie

Speak the customer's language: You should know your customer's level of understanding about the services you provide. That way, you will be able to communicate with them in a manner that is easy for them to understand.

For example, most elderly people have difficulties understanding modern electronic gadgetry. If you're not electronically savvy like me, you would probably have a hard time deciding which of the dazzling models to choose.

Imagine a shop where an attendant helps you understand what an electronic gadget, like a mobile phone, can do for you (in English!) and recommends the one that suits your requirements. Wouldn't you keep going back to that service agent every time you needed an electronic device?

History: Even information on the customer's history of dealing with your organization, their loyalty, and what they think about you can help you to manage and satisfy them in ways that keep them coming back. You may be asking, "How is it physically possible to know the profile of each and every customer that walks in through the door?" I agree with you; you can only keep track of a few customers, and even for that, you would probably need the help of a computer program. Moreover, knowing each and every customer may not serve your purpose either, because most customers that walk in through the door are not regular customers.

80/20 rule: We need to know as much as possible about only those customers that give us their business regularly. According to the 80/20 Rule, 80% of the revenue in any business is generated by approximately 20% of the clients. This is also known as Pareto's Law.

Pareto was the sixteenth-century philosopher who propounded the theory. If you check for the validity of the rule in your line of work or business, you would find the above to be more or less true. If 20% of your customers give you the bulk of your business, then does it not make sense to focus on them? This makes the task of managing hundreds of customers much more manageable. Therefore, the question we should ask ourselves is, "Do we know who our regular customers (20%) are who give us the 80% of our business?" If not, we should obtain the information so that we can retain their patronage and further increase our business with them.

One word of caution: *You cannot afford to ignore the other 80% of your customers. We still have to provide them with our quality service, a must given to one and all.* You never know which customer from amongst the 80% will become your regular customer in the future, and besides, an unfulfilled customer can spell disaster for your business by badmouthing you!

We should provide a highly personalized and efficient service to our major or regular customers who give us the bulk of our business and also give quality service to all of our walk-in customers.

Personalized service is service that you tailor to a major customer's particular needs, such as what Russell received from Shopper's Paradise, as mentioned in the case study in the beginning of this chapter.

> *Know your major customers and build strong business relationships with them.*

Food for thought:

Think about the following questions. Jot down your first reactions, and then contemplate their merit.

a. Do you know the major customers (20%) who give you 80% of your business? Do you think knowing them is important, and if so, why?

----

b. Do you know why the above customers give you their business? Write down at least three reasons that explain why they keep coming back to you rather than going to your competitors.

----

c. What can you do in your personal capacity at the customer contact point that can make your services more attractive to your major customers?

----

d. Do you think it is important to find out if your major customers are happy with the way you treat them? In addition, how can you find out if your major customers are happy with you and your services?

The customer is the king.
Handle him with care and he will make you rich.
Ignore him and he will banish you from business!

Mak

WHAT'S IN IT FOR ME? (WIIFM)

Whether you accept it or not, we are all predominantly interested in ourselves. There is nothing wrong in that; after all, it is only when we are truly interested in ourselves that we can be genuinely interested in others. Whenever someone talks to us, we search for meaning or value in their speech. We question whether what they say to us is meaningful or of interest to us. If their communication appreciates us, or provides information that we need, or has something of value for us, we find their communication interesting, and we listen to them.

Similarly, when we talk to our customers, they consciously or subconsciously ask, "What's in it for me? Why should I listen to this service provider?"

Remember, earlier on, I had mentioned that we are all like mirrors: **whatever we project onto others is what they reflect back to us.** Well, that is exactly what happens in our transactions with our customers.

If we take interest in them and the things they want, they too take interest in us and the things we say to them. Then, they collaborate with us to make the transaction mutually beneficial.

In short, when you communicate with others, they subconsciously inquire, "What is in it for me?" If what they hear is interesting, they will listen to you. Otherwise, they may hear what you say, but not take interest in the communication. They may even look at you, and nod in agreement to show that they are with you, but in their minds they are somewhere else!

Let me elaborate by asking you a question. Imagine you're at a party and mingling with a lot of people, some who are known to you and others who are not. To whom would you like to spend time talking? A person who is more interested in telling you about their affluent life style, expensive trips abroad, and coveted status, or someone who wants to know more about you?

Learn to look at things from the other person's perspective.

SPAN OF ATTENTION:

Unconfirmed sources claim that even if people give you their full attention, their continuous and maximum span of attention lasts approximately 9 to 11 seconds. If it is true, and people were listening to you intently, they would probably think about something else every 9 to 11 seconds. Can you imagine what their span of attention would be if they were not interested in you or what you said to them?

When we take interest in our customers and their needs, they listen to what we say to them. They feel important, in control, and recognized as individuals rather than just as customers. Customers reciprocate by finding us interesting and responding to our communication. That is why you will find that effective service providers take interest in their customers.

For example, if you notice that the customer loves his dog, you could remark to the customer that he has a nice dog and ask questions about the dog. The customer subconsciously believes that since both of you like the dog, you must be allies. Furthermore, complementing the dog is indirectly complementing the owner of the dog.

Customers are like mirrors; they reflect back what we project on them.

The way we communicate with others and with ourselves ultimately determines the quality of our lives.

Anthony Robbins

LEARN TO OBSERVE

One of my first jobs was with British Airways in Dhaka, thirty-five years ago. I was in the town office issuing tickets and making reservations. During the peak season, I was sometimes assigned to the check-in desk at Dhaka International Airport. The supervisor there was a jovial person. He used to give us words of wisdom, some of which I will never forget. One piece of his advice was to practice observing the customers from 100 yards away and be able to predict what that customer needed. According to him, the day we could do that accurately, we could consider ourselves experts at reading customers.

Let us look at some more examples to elucidate this point. If you see a passenger dressed formally, traveling alone, and only carrying a briefcase, would it be safe to assume that the customer was on a short business trip? If so, what would be the expectations of such a passenger? Obviously, a quick and hassle free check-in would be in order. However, if you have a family traveling on vacation, you can take it for granted that they would like to sit together with at least one window seat for the younger ones.

A word of caution: Avoid assuming what your customers want or feel, for your assumptions could be totally out of line and annoy them. Trying to read your customers and assuming what your customers want are two different things. The first helps you to prepare yourself mentally to better manage your customer. The latter is highly subjective and could result in ignoring the needs of your customers or even being disrespectful to them.

HOW CAN YOU LEARN TO OBSERVE?

If you would like to learn how to observe, try doing so when you are stuck in a traffic jam. Have you ever been in a traffic jam? Most of us have been at one time or another. Some of us probably experience it on a daily basis, no matter where we live or what we do! However, the next time you're in a traffic jam, pay attention to the body language of the people in the vehicles around you. Try not to appear too nosy or obnoxious, and discreetly notice what they do. It may surprise you to discover that just by observing the body language of people; you can quite accurately make out the general climate in the vehicle.

I once noticed a casually dressed young man tapping the steering wheel with his fingers, as if listening to rock music. From the way he was rocking in his seat, I concluded that he was in a good mood and was looking forward to wherever he was going, perhaps a get-together with friends or a date.

You can avail yourself of other good opportunities to observe and learn at restaurants, bars, and public places. Just be quiet and observe without prying into the privacy of other people. If that is embarrassing for you, you could try watching movies with the sound muted! You could also watch the eventful scenes in slow motion. It is fun when you compare your readings with what you discover when you replay the movie at normal speed or with the sound.

Let me take this opportunity to tell you a short story that shows how important it is to be observant. A servant who used to work at a farmer's house from morning until night was paid only $150 per month by his employer. In contrast, a teacher who used to come to the farmer's house every third day to tutor the farmer's daughter for an hour or so was paid $2,000 per month.

To add salt to the wound, the servant noticed that whenever the teacher came, everyone seemed to bend over backwards to make the teacher comfortable. The farmer personally greeted the teacher, and his wife pampered him by offering tea, coffee, biscuits, and whatever the house could offer a revered guest. The servant felt that this was unfair. Here he was, cleaning the entire household, cooking, washing, and running errands for one and all throughout the day, and he received a paltry salary compared to what the teacher got for a few hours of work. He decided to take the matter up with his master.

The farmer seemed to appreciate the servant's grievances, and asked the servant to inform him the next time the teacher came by. Thereafter, when the teacher came, the farmer asked the servant and the teacher to go to a remote and abandoned room in the farthest wing of the mansion and report back on what they saw there.

The servant reported back saying that there was nothing in the room except a cat. The farmer asked the servant what color the cat was and whether it was a male or female. The servant couldn't answer the questions and didn't see the relevance of noticing such things.

However, the teacher noticed that the cat had large white and black irregular spots and was about to have kittens. It was looking for a suitable shelter to deliver the kittens. He suggested providing the cat with food, milk, and a cardboard box with linen so that the cat would feel safe and secure in giving birth to her kittens. The exercise clarified for the servant, once and for all, why the teacher was receiving a much higher remuneration!

Observe your customers closely so you know what they need.

STEPS TO ATTENDING A CUSTOMER FACE-TO-FACE

- **Greet the customer** :

 A pleasantry like "Good morning," that shows the customer that you, the service provider, are glad to see her, want to attend to her, and are eager to take care of her needs.

- **Offer assistance with a smile:**

Offer to assist with something like, "How may I help you today?" or "What can I do for you?" This sets the stage for a conversation between you and your customer. The customer feels comfortable and this prompts the customer to open up with her needs. It also alleviates any hesitation on the part of the customer to start a fruitful discussion.

- **Listen attentively:**

This doesn't only entail listening to the customer. It also involves maintaining eye contact, observing the body language, noticing the customer's tone of voice, and understanding what she is saying and <u>what she is not saying.</u>

While you listen, don't forget to show the customer that you are listening and understand what she is saying. Nod your head or say something like, "Yes," "Uh-huh," or "Right," etc. Try not to interrupt your customers unless you feel you don't understand what they are saying or want to support them in what they want to say using short and concise prompts.

If in doubt, repeat your understanding, or paraphrase so that both you and your customers don't miss out on anything. Customers often don't verbalize their expectations and take it for granted that you understand. Therefore, it is also important to listen for what they are omitting. For example, while purchasing furniture, the customer may expect immediate delivery. He may be totally oblivious to your logistical limitations!

- **Ask questions and listen:**

This helps you to find out what your customers need. Focus on what your customers want to achieve through your services. As you ask questions, observe your customers' body language and listen to their tone of voice to determine what they are feeling.

Asking relevant questions, listening intently, and observing their body language will give you an accurate idea of what they expect. A word of caution: Do not abruptly start firing off questions, as the customer may feel intimidated or offended. This often happens when customers don't understand why you're asking so many questions.

Accomplished service providers don't leave room for any such misunderstandings. Instead, they seek the customer's permission to ask questions and explain how the questions would help them provide the customer with better service. Something like, "Can I ask you some questions? It would help me to understand your needs clearly, and that way, I will be able to serve you better."

- **Offer alternatives and recommend:**

Try to offer alternatives rather than one option. Offering alternatives makes the customers feel that they are in control and have the privilege of exercising their choice. Do you remember the famous quote by Henry Ford? "An American can have a Ford in any color, so long as it's black." Explain the relevant pros and cons for that customer. Recommend or suggest the option that you think would be better for the customer. Present your recommendations in such a way that they don't sound condescending or compelling. Recommending an option tells the customer that you're a subject matter expert, that you're interested in benefiting them, and that you're ready to practice what you preach. In short, it promotes customer confidence in you and your services.

- **Agree on an option:**

Come to an agreement on which option the customer wants so that there is no ambiguity on what course of action to take.

- **Tell them what you're going to do:**

Most service providers don't apply this important step. As a result, they fail to manage the customer's expectations. Perhaps the easiest way of explaining this would be through an example. Imagine you took your car to a renowned garage because of an unusual noise coming from the rear wheels. The mechanic checks your car and asks you to leave the car at the garage and pick it up at the same time the next day.

Would you leave the car there? Would you be satisfied with the mechanic's response? No, of course not! You would probably want to know what is wrong with the car, what the mechanic is going to do to fix the problem, how much it will cost, and what guarantees are in place to ensure that the problem will not recur.

Similarly, when you don't tell the customer what you are going to do, they don't know what to expect and they have a feeling of uncertainty that is disconcerting. However, when you tell your customers what you're going to do, they get an idea of what to expect and it is a confirmation to them that you have understood their needs.

- **Take action:**

Once you tell the customer what you're going to do, proceed to execute the order as agreed.

- **Thank the customer for their business and invite them to come back again.**

- **Update if necessary:**

If the nature of service dictates, keep the customer informed on progress. In the case of any deviation from what had been originally agreed, inform them upfront and before they call you. It tells the customer that you care and gives them the option to seek alternative solutions should they so desire.

Many service providers don't take the initiative of informing customers of any changes, and the customer finds out only when they inquire about their work! This makes the customer suspicious of the service standards. Then, the customer feels uncomfortable, even when the change that is applied produces a product or service that is better then what was in the originally agreement.

Don't deprive your customers of the opportunity to take alternative action by not informing them of any changes in time. Besides, when the customers call to check on their work, they expect completion of their work or significant progress, and not hitches. When you call the customer with unexpected changes before they call you, they are more accommodating and appreciative of your caring attitude.

- **Follow-up:**

Don't forget the customer once the service has been provided. Where practical, it is always nice to call up the customer to check and see if they are happy with the services provided. Follow-up calls show the customer how committed you are to them and helps to build a relationship with them by keeping in touch.

Manage customers' expectations by keeping them in the picture all the time.

LEARN TO COMMUNICATE EFFECTIVELY

Before you communicate with your customers, you must know exactly what you want to communicate. You should be specific about what you want to address and communicate it in a simple and effective manner.

Complicated communications and too much detail confuse customers and they tend to move away from such ranting.

Customers prefer simplified, concise communications to which they can relate.

The customer should be able to see how what you're communicating is going to benefit them.

Ask yourself the purpose of your communication. What is it that you want your customers to know or do? Next, ruminate on how you can get the customers' attention and make your proposal appealing to them. Clarifying the purpose and intent of your communication often yields ideas on how to communicate with the customer effectively.

We have to understand that customers nowadays are inundated with information. Innumerable competitors are vying for the customer's attention, and to cope with the incessant calls for their attention, customers have learned to switch off from anything they perceive as hard to relate to, complicated, or uninteresting.

If you surf the net, you know what I mean; try making sense of a webpage that has too much detail on it. It can be hard work and requires considerable concentration and patience to decipher what the site is offering. Other websites present their core message in a simple, easy, and accessible format. The owners of such websites are clear on what they want their customers to know or do. They present the information in a manner that goes straight to the point.

INNOVATE & DIFFERENTIATE

You can attract your customers' attention and keep it by differentiating yourself. You should stand out from your competitors in order to catch and keep your customers' attention. Customers also want to deal with reliable and honest service providers. This need is greatly heightened these days, as there are many service agents who sell products that are questionable, or that do not exactly match the specifications they advertise.

I once had the privilege of witnessing a sales demonstration at a shopping center that spoke for itself. This demonstration was so convincing and powerful that most of the customers watching the demonstration bought the product immediately. It was the Eid holidays, and we were shopping at one of the largest shopping malls in Dubai. We happened to be in a section that displayed traveling accessories like trolleys, bags, and suitcases of all shapes and sizes. The place was swarming with shoppers looking for a bargain, and it was difficult to walk straight without running into someone else.

A salesman appeared out of nowhere and clapped his hands so loudly that all the shoppers in the vicinity stopped in their tracks, not knowing what to expect. The salesman than coolly proceeded to open a rather large suitcase and took smaller suitcases out of it. He took three smaller suitcases out of the larger one, and the smallest was a cute vanity case with wheels. Without saying a word, he slammed all the cases shut and started hopping on the largest suitcase, which was lying flat on the ground!

The salesman was at least 65 to 70 kilos, and soon, he was jumping madly from one suitcase to another, all the while, looking at us with a broad grin on his face. Thereafter, he put the suitcases back inside of each other, bowed to the crowd a number of times, and left. I don't have to tell you the loud accolades the salesman got from the watching crowd!

We didn't particularly need a set of suitcases, but my wife said we would be traveling in six months' time and maybe we should buy a set because the product was sturdy, attractive, and the price was a bargain. I couldn't have agreed more, and like many other shoppers, we too purchased a set of suitcases! We are sure all of the shoppers who purchased the set of suitcases were very happy with their purchase; it was a well-tested bargain, and therefore the customers perceived value in it.

Demonstrate to differentiate, such demonstration speaks louder than words.

Jesus does not give recipes that show the way to God as other teachers of religion do. He is himself the way.

Karl Barth

PRODUCT DETAILS VS. BENEFITS

In the race to dominate the market, manufacturers are innovating and launching new products every day. It has become difficult to keep up with the new and ever-changing technology. Nowadays, service agents have to know the technical details of such new products and be able to explain to their customers how the products can make their lives easier.

Unfortunately, only a handful of service agents keep themselves updated on the ever-changing technology. The business owners are busy managing their businesses on a day-to-day basis. They seldom invest in training and developing their service agents; however, those that do reap long-term rewards.

As a result, when you want to buy products using new technology, the service agents hardly can tell you what the product can do for you except give you the technical details from the product brochure. This is especially true for electronic items or gadgets with complicated technology. The manuals that come with the product are difficult to understand and the information therein is mostly scant and haphazardly presented.

Recently, my youngest daughter and I went to a well-known electronic store to buy a mobile phone. The attendant showed us a few models and showered us with a lot of information in jargon, such as: MP3, AAC, mega pixel, GPRS, zoom, Palm Operating System, TFT screen, talk time, standby time, 64 MB flash memory, WAP, and whatnot. When I asked him what all that meant, he wasn't quite sure how all of that related to us! Fortunately, another attendant who was watching us from a distance must have read the frustration on our faces and volunteered to assist us by explaining what each of those features meant and how we could benefit from them.

Then it made a lot of sense, and we were happy to purchase the mobile phone of our choice.

Tell your customers what the product can do for them rather than how great the product is.

The first salesman told the customer everything about the car – it was enlightening. The second salesman told the customer that with this car, the customer would be the first one to arrive – he sold the car!

Mak

BE RESPONSIVE & SENSITIVE TO YOUR CUSTOMERS' FEELINGS

An airline cargo call center located in Dubai received a call from a customer who wanted to send two dogs to his mother in the U.K., as he was going on a holiday to Australia. From the customer's words and tone, it was obvious he was not very happy about sending the dogs unaccompanied. The dogs had never flown without him, and he was concerned about their safety.

The call center staff responded by telling the customer, in one short sentence, not to worry, and promptly detailed the forms that needed to be filled and other formalities to be completed. The customer kept asking questions like, "Who is going to feed the dog?" and "What if the dogs fall sick?" The call center staff kept repeating that he needn't worry, as all of the procedures were in place to look after the dogs.

Do you think it would have been better if the call center staff had focused on the emotional needs of this customer and reassured him first, before giving him the booking procedures and other details? To alleviate his concerns, the staff could have explained to the customer how the dogs are cared for onboard and on the ground.

The staff could have followed up by explaining that they have been transporting dogs almost daily for the last so many years to all parts of the world, safely and without any untoward incidents.

Take another instance. I was once visiting a friend of mine, George, who was hospitalized for severe pain in the lower abdomen. Tests revealed that he had appendicitis and required immediate surgery. The surgeon briefed George on the procedure in considerable graphical detail. He told George how he would cut open his abdomen, there would some bleeding and of course no pain, as George would be unconscious under anesthesia, and so forth.

What do you think happened to George? You guessed right. George was terrified and panicked. In spite of the pain that he was in, he contemplated fleeing the hospital! It was only after reassurance from family members that George agreed to the surgery.

I wonder if it would have been better if the surgeon had told my friend that the procedure was simple and would be over in a jiffy. Even better would have been if the surgeon had told George that he could go home in a week's time and that he would feel much better after the procedure, focusing on the positive results. Some testimonials as to how others had recovered rapidly from this routine procedure could have boosted George's morale and would have been comforting.

Reassure your customer often; reassurance makes the customer hopeful and confident about your products and services.

DON'T JUDGE YOUR CUSTOMERS

Sometimes, service agents fail to be sensitive to their customers by discriminating against them on the basis of their ethnicity, religion, or creed. Although most service agents are discreet about their feelings when attending a customer, they would do better by not harboring such feelings. No matter how discreet you are; customers often perceive your negative feelings towards them. Your body language and tone of voice gives you away without you being aware of it. Customers treated with contempt feel disrespected, hurt, and unwanted, and they are highly unlikely to return with repeat business.

Has a service agent ever sneered at you? Have you ever felt that service agents were talking behind your back? Perhaps a reluctant service agent may have kept you waiting? If so, you know how frustrating it can be! In the service industry, judging customers is tantamount to a felony.

Don't judge your customers.

USE HUMOR WITH CAUTION

Some people believe that one should use a lot of humor when dealing with customers, and I can see where they are coming from. Good humor and jokes, properly delivered, can be helpful in developing good cheer. It can make the environment more hospitable and welcome for customers.

However, you have to be careful not to say things to the customers that you may regret later! It is one thing to be cheerful and another to tell jokes that are not appreciated. No one objects to good cheer and decent humor, but in the wrong place and time, they can do more damage than good.

Delegates in my class often ask when humor is applicable and how much is okay. My response is that it all depends on the situation and context; however, I have the following recommendations:

1. Add humor to your communication only when you know the customer well and are absolutely sure that it will be well received.

2. Keep your humor well connected to the topic at hand and find ways to compliment either the customer or the service you are providing.

   For example, "Did you know that our 'Research and Development' has recommended that this product be downgraded because of its durability? It seems most customers buy it once and it lasts them a life time; sometimes too good can be bad for business!"

3. Do not try to win customers by telling jokes that are vulgar, racist, personal, or culturally insensitive. You could put the customer off, and even if that does not happen, they may think of you as frivolous.

Respond to customers' humor cheerfully. Smile and take advantage of the customer's disposition by quickly drawing his/her attention back to the service at hand. Your balanced and controlled response will keep the communication with your customers going and save you a lot of time.

Humor can be helpful, and customers always appreciate good cheer.

Our customers will come here for the first time and then keep coming back. It's a really fun environment; we joke with each other and have a good time.

Terri Frasnelli

SERVE FROM THE CORE OF YOUR HEART

Do you know the difference between great actors and unaccomplished actors? Great actors get into what is called "state," whereas most actors put on an act. **Getting into state means you become the person you are portraying.** That way, you don't have to consciously think about what to say, do, or feel. It all happens spontaneously, as if you were that person in real life.

It is said that Ben Kinsley, who acted in the epic film "Gandhi," lived a life akin to the Mahatma's while he prepared for the role of Gandhi. Although this could be nothing more than rumor, one can imagine that if it were true, Ben must have practiced living like Gandhi by eating, sleeping, and spinning the charkha (spinning wheel) like Gandhi before he was ready to play Gandhi's role.

In short, Ben must have started to think and feel like Gandhi, so that whatever he did resembled the actions of Gandhi. Is it any wonder that many say that Ben's portrayal of Gandhi was so real, or that it was almost as if Gandhi had returned from the dead to act out his own biography?

You can try this for yourself and see how much difference getting into state can make. Imagine that you are the managing director of a large corporation and you are giving a speech to the board of directors on how badly the group has performed for the fiscal year and how much loss they have incurred. First, try to act like a managing director and make the speech in front of close friends so they can give you their feedback. Alternatively, capture the whole thing on video to watch later.

Do the exercise again, but this time, sit alone in a quiet place and imagine that you **are the managing director** of the corporation and get into the "state." When you feel like you have become the managing director, make the speech. Ask your friends or compare the two videos, and undoubtedly you will find a better and more convincing performance in the second speech.

Having worked for over thirty-five years in customer service and related environments, I am observant of the service standards in any service situation. I was once on a flight to Baku (Azerbaijan), and the flight was very light. A young and beautiful airhostess served us, and I was quite impressed by the immaculate way she looked after the passengers in business class.

On finishing my assignment in Baku, I returned by the same flight to Dubai a few days later. This time, another airhostess, who was also young and equally attractive, gave us fantastic service that was also memorable. Both the airhostess did things by the book and everything was perfect.

However, the airhostess on the way back from Moscow seemed better, and I wondered why. Some contemplation revealed that the young lady who served us on the way back from Baku was not only following the service procedures, but also, and more importantly, doing it from her heart. **She was enjoying serving us.** Her smile, eye contact, and tone of voice were all spontaneous and reassuring.

Providing service requires dedication. You have to enjoy being a professional who speaks from the heart.

One act of beneficence, one act of real usefulness, is worth all the abstract sentiment in the world.

Ann Radcliffe

KEEP A TAB ON YOUR EMOTIONS

Be aware of your body language and your tone, and use appropriate words. It is relatively easy to hide your feelings by manipulating words, but it is difficult to hide the feelings that are exposed through your body language and tone of voice.

For example, you can easily greet the customer by saying "Good morning," even though you may not mean it. However, the customers will likely pick up the annoyance or negativity on your part through your body language and tone of voice.

Service agents often have genuine reasons to be upset. It could be because of a problem of a personal nature, a disagreement with the peers or higher-ups at work, or even a customer who was aggressive or manipulative. When service agents in a negative state attend to customers, the customers pick up the negative vibes and feel uncomfortable. They don't understand the reason for this apathy or indifference on the part of the service agent, and they react to it. They either leave in a hurry or become overly sensitive and irked; one thing leads to another, and sometimes, the situation becomes volatile.

What we have to understand is that customers expect the best from us and they have a right to expect that; they pay for our services with their hard-earned money!

Let us not forget that the customer has a choice; she can walk away and deal with our competitors instead!

I can almost hear some of you say, "So what? Let the customer walk away. My life is not a bed of roses either!" You may be right, and yet we cannot correct one wrong with another, can we?

So what is the solution? It is quite simple and can be extremely rewarding. Step back from the incident that upsets you, take an objective view of the situation, and realize that life is made of ups and downs. You need to learn to take things in stride and not let such putdowns disrupt your work or life in general. If required, it is better to sleep on disturbing issues and then respond in a cool and calculated manner then to react to them. Respond only when you are emotionally composed and balanced. For now, it is a customer's time, and you're committed to giving her your best. Besides, who doesn't have problems in life?

When you stand behind the service desk, you have to connect your self-esteem with being helpful and nice to your customers, no matter what. With that kind of an attitude, the more challenging a situation becomes, the more resourceful you become in managing the situation.

Your personal and moral obligation to your customers is much larger than the job you do.

PRIME YOUR CUSTOMERS BEFORE YOU SELL TO THEM

Once, I met a watch salesman whom I hadn't seen before in an elevator. Without a word of courtesy or introduction, he exposed the insides of his jacket. Rows of wristwatches of all sizes and shapes lined his jacket. "Want to buy a watch?" he said. His crude approach took me by surprise, and I spontaneously blurted out a loud "No!" I promptly walked away as the elevator arrived at my floor, feeling somewhat embarrassed.

The first thing that you should do as service agents is to develop a rapport with your customers and get them into a frame of mind where they are more receptive to you. Let me explain this through an analogy. Imagine it is 1 p.m. You want to go for lunch and you want a colleague of yours to join you.

However, your colleague has been working on an important project and is totally engrossed in it. Therefore, he passes on your offer and says he will join you the next time.

Have you noticed what happened here? Your colleague was not ready to accompany you for lunch, as he was totally engrossed in the project. Instead of asking him to accompany you for lunch directly, what if you had asked him what time it was?

You asked the question deliberately even though there was a large clock on the wall and you were wearing a wristwatch. In answering your question, your colleague's subconscious mind probably told him that it was time for lunch. However, suppose your ploy didn't work, and he just told you the time and went back to peering into the monitor.

What if you asked him, "Do you smell the roast chicken?" Do you think, being conditioned to associate the aroma of food with lunchtime, he would smell the roast chicken in his imagination? Would you say that the chances now are higher that he would take you up on your offer and accompany you for lunch?

Suppose that your colleague still remained unmoved. What if you made him aware of the need to take a break by asking, "John, how long have you been sitting in front of the computer? Aren't your shoulders cramped? Come, let us take a break and go for a bite!" Now, do you think John would move? It is more than likely; <u>this is because you have prepared him and made him feel what you wanted him to feel.</u>

Make your customers ready; make them feel the need to buy before you sell to them.

Mankind is governed more by their feelings than by reason.

Samuel Adams

KEEP WAITING CUSTOMERS ENGAGED

Keep your customers engaged, informed, and involved: When the customer walks into your premises, he expects immediate service. No customer likes to be kept waiting. There are three main reasons why customers don't like to wait in a queue even if they have the time:

- They feel ignored, unrecognized, and treated as a number.

- They feel deprived of their choice and freedom to do anything else.

- They don't know how long they will have to wait, and the focus on the waiting makes the time drag. The time taken by the service agents to service the customers at the counter seems unreasonably long.

This happens because the waiting customer cannot see what is going on at the counter and cannot assign any reason to the time being taken to service the customers ahead of them. Without a reason, the time taken to service each customer appears inordinately long. That is why you will find that customers waiting in a q-matic facilitated area (a mechanized customer queue flow management system) are much more relaxed and composed. The q-matic gives them an idea of when to expect their turn; the progression of numbers tells them that things are in progress and that it will soon be their turn. Then, they find it easier to divert their attention to a magazine or a newspaper.

You see, the human brain is always thinking, and when put into any uncertainty, it goes into a negative mode by default. The main purpose of our brain is to keep us comfortable and free from danger at all times. If a customer feels uncertain or constrained standing in a queue, his brain goes into an alert

"And they lived happily ever after..."

mode that reads even the minutest delay as offensive. In that mode, the brain tends to notice more negatives than positives. The negatives are focused on and amplified to ensure that no danger or unpleasantness goes unnoticed. That is why if you have to wait your turn, and you don't know how long it will take, you become jittery.

Let me give you an example. I was once waiting my turn in a queue to pay the electricity and water bill at the payment counter of the Water & Power Department.

When my turn came, the cashier left his seat without a word and went to the back office. He seemed to engage in a long telephone conversation, and thereafter, started looking for something in the drawers. Inward, I was infuriated at the cashier for keeping me waiting, and some of the customers behind me in the queue were becoming loud and vocal about the delay.

Hearing the commotion, the cashier returned and explained to us that the computer system was down unexpectedly and that he was trying to arrange acceptance of payments manually so we didn't have to wait. No sooner had he said the words, everyone in the queue calmed down. Some even appreciated the cashier's initiative in trying to accept payments manually.

Therefore, it is imperative that you do the following for a customer waiting to be served:

Whenever possible, show the waiting customer that you are aware that they are waiting their turn and that you will be with them as soon as possible. It tells the customers that they are cared for and that something is being done to serve them. From time to time, keep reassuring them; even a well-directed smile can be very reassuring to the waiting customer.

Where appropriate, and if the situation allows, initiate a side conversation with the waiting customers; discuss the weather, news, sports, or anything you know that interests the customer. However, don't discuss politics or any other subject that is controversial in nature.

When possible, offer tea/coffee and/or an ample supply of the latest magazines of general interest, not outdated and dog-eared publications that are only fit for the waste bin. Keep your customers engaged in something interesting and they will gladly wait their turn. *Remember, an engaged customer has very little inclination or time to judge you or your services critically.*

If you happen to be working in an area where you have long queues the whole day long, then make sure that the customers walk in and take their position in the queue, and that those waiting from before are served first. There is nothing more irritating than customers jumping the queue while service agents condone or ignore such rash and irresponsible behavior.

Sometimes, a customer in the second or third position in the queue may just need one moment of your attention, and it is unfair to keep such customers waiting, especially when such customers have some urgency and request your assistance. Examples of this may be a mother with a sick or crying infant, or someone who has double-parked their car due to lack of parking space. In such situations, make sure you obtain the consent of the customers ahead of the customer with the urgency and explain the situation; assure them that it will only take a minute.

Better yet, if possible, redirect the customer with the urgency to a colleague in the back office who can attend to this customer immediately.

Keep the customers engaged while they wait to be served.

No matter how busy you are, you must take time to make the other person feel important.

Mary Kay Ash

STRATEGIES FOR EFFECTIVE COMMUNICATION

Remember in the beginning of this chapter how we touched on that anything and everything that we do to win the patronage of our customers amounts to effective communication? Keeping that in mind, it is obvious that you need to assess all your business strategies, activities, and operations from the customer's point of view. Below are some strategies for ensuring that you communicate effectively with your clients at all times.

1. Put yourself into your customers' shoes and evaluate your services or products from their point of view–everything from the time they meet you to the time the service is completed. Question and make anything that doesn't put the customers' interests first dispensable.

2. Check all your communication with your customers. Does your communication style focus on the service or the way in which the service can benefit the customer? The former only informs, while the latter motivates the customer.

3. Make your services as accessible as possible. Keep the servicing procedures simple, hassle free, and flexible to accommodate the customers' needs.

4. Be in constant contact with your customers and keep them informed. Remember, *out of sight* is equivalent to *out of mind*.

5. Adopt the PET strategy – **P**ersonalize, **E**voke interest, and provide **T**estimonials – a strategy that will keep your customers coming back for more.

6. Create many channels for the customers to complain, and respond as if the complaint is a life-and-death situation.

7. Run frequent surveys and service evaluations, and involve your customers in the whole process, especially in guiding you in the right direction. After all, they know what, when, and how they want it, and at what price.

8. Coordinate above and below the line advertisement; they should all say the same thing.

9. Empower yourself as front-line staff; after all, it is the front-line staff that can make the business more responsive to its customers. Customers are attracted to responsive service providers like bees to honey.

10. Innovate, be creative, and differentiate your business to stand out from other service providers, and invest in new technology or more efficient ways of serving your customers.

11. Be objective in everything and anything that you do. Build long-term objectives on the shoulders of short-term objectives, all pointing towards customer satisfaction and retention.

Customers always come first.

QUIZ - 1

(Check the most appropriate option)

1. **When you deal with customers, you should:**

   a. Behave in a professional manner so the customers think highly of you and your organization.

   b. Focus on building a close business relationship with customers so they like to deal with you and keep coming back for more.

   c. Ensure that you explain everything about your products or services to your customers so they will buy.

2. **The long-term success and growth of your organization depends more on:**

   a. The marketing strategy developed by the head office; after all, they are the experts.

   b. The quality of the products and services you provide.

   c. How you deal with your customers.

3. **You should know your customers so that:**

   a. You can serve them without them taking the trouble of telling you what they want.

   b. You know their credit worthiness before you deal with them.

   c. You can deal with them in a manner that makes them feel good and pleases them.

4. **The concept of "What's in it for me" (WIIFM?) means:**

   a. At a subconscious level, we all (including customers) ask ourselves this question to make decisions that benefit us.

   b. Most customers are selfish in a way, and ask themselves why they should deal with you.

c. That you should know exactly what you want from your customers and ask for it directly, rather than wasting their time.

5. We should closely observe our customers so:

a. We can respond to them the moment they ask for any assistance.

b. We can know better how they feel and respond to them accordingly.

c. We can make sure they don't engage in any shoplifting activity.

6. Before you ask your customers questions, you should:

a. Become deadly serious in your facial expression and tone so customers are convinced that you mean business.

b. Smile profusely to distract them while you easily extract all the information that you need from them.

c. Where appropriate, seek their permission to ask questions and explain how asking questions will help you to understand them and help them better.

7. After the customers agree on buying a product or service, you should:

a. Tell them what you are going to do so they can visualize how the service will be provided and how their expectations will be met.

b. Quickly close the sale before they change their minds.

c. Enumerate the features of the product in question once again to ensure that the customers really know what they are in for; otherwise, there is always the chance that they will return the product and ask for a refund.

8. You should differentiate yourself from your competitors because:

a. It makes you stand out from the crowd and you get noticed by your customers.

b. That is the marketing fad that most Fortune 500 companies are following these days.

c. In addition to getting noticed by your customers, they perceive greater value in your products or services.

9. **You should be sensitive to your customers' feelings because:**

a. It will make it easier for your customers to part with their hard-earned money.

b. When you hurt the feelings of your customers, they are likely to take their business somewhere else, badmouth you, and drive potential customers away.

c. It is morally wrong to hurt people, especially your customers.

10. **You should use humor with your customers:**

a. Only when you know the customer relatively well, are sure that the humor relates to the subject matter being discussed, and only in a way that compliments the transaction with the customer.

b. So you can entertain them by telling them your favorite jokes while they wait their turn to be served.

c. So that you can laugh loudly and acknowledge or appreciate jokes that they tell you.

11. **It is important that you serve your customers from your heart:**

a. Because you want your customers to know that you have feelings too, and that if they are disloyal, they had better not expect any favors from you.

b. Because when you serve from your heart, the best in you shines through no matter what, and customers naturally recognize this.

c. Because you want them to feel guilty when they want to take their business somewhere else.

Scoring:

The most appropriate answer is indicated below. For every correct answer, give yourself five points.

Sr. No:	Option a	Option b	Option c	Remarks	
1	-	√	-		**0 – 15 points:**
2	-	-	√		Poor score; you need to improve on your understanding of customer psychology.
3	-	-	√		
4	√	-	-		
5	-	√	-		**16 – 35 points:**
6	-	-	√		Average score; there is a lot of room for improvement.
7	√	-	-		
8	-	-	√		
9	-	√	-		**36 – 55 points:**
10	√	-	-		An excellent score; keep up the good work!
11	-	√	-		
Your total score:					

Summary

1. *Anything and everything you do or don't do with your customers can be described as communication with your customers.*

2. *By far, success or failure in customer service is made by the front-line service providers and the way in which they interact with their customers.*

3. *Know your major customers and build strong business relationships with them.*

4. *Learn to look at things from the other person's perspective.*

5. *Customers are like mirrors; they reflect back what we project on them.*

6. Observe your customers closely so you know what they need.

7. Manage customers' expectations by keeping them in the picture all the time.

8. Demonstrate to differentiate, such demonstration speaks louder than words.

9. Tell your customers what the product can do for them rather than how great the product is.

10. Reassure your customer often; reassurance makes the customer hopeful and confident about your product and services.

11. Don't judge your customers.

12. Humor can be helpful, and customers always appreciate good cheer.

13. Providing service requires dedication. You have to enjoy being a professional who speaks from the heart.

14. Your personal and moral obligation to your customers is much larger than the job you do.

15. Make your customers ready; make them feel the need to buy before you sell to them.

16. Keep the customers engaged while they wait to be served.

17. Customers always come first.

Chapter 4

NEEDS, WANTS, & EXPECTATIONS

Needs are basic, wants are one level above them, and when you provide excellent service, the customer says "wow," and that is the kind of service customers expect.

Mak

Case Study 4:

Mohammad was working in his office, and from the corner of his eye, he saw an encyclopedia salesman trying to convince his secretary to let him into his office. The encyclopedia salesman reminded Mohammad of his early days on the road as a salesman selling porcelain decorations. Mohammad was interested in surprising his seven-year-old son with a children's encyclopedia set as a birthday gift, so he asked his secretary to let the salesman come into his office.

The salesman promptly entered Mohammad's office, lugging two heavy suitcases, and after the usual courtesies, took his seat. Without another word, the salesman started laying out the encyclopedia samples on the table and embarked on a monotonous lecture on their content.

Mohammad noticed that the salesman was showing him the latest edition of the "Encyclopedia Britannica," which already decorated the shelves in his study. He wanted to tell the salesman that he was interested in a children's encyclopedia set for his son, and waited patiently for the salesman to stop talking. However, to Mohammad's surprise, the salesman just kept on rambling without any regard for what Mohammad wanted.

The salesman went on with his monotonous speech like a railway locomotive out of control, speeding away without a destination! Frustrated, Mohammad had to pound hard on the table to get the salesman's attention, and told him that he already had the "Encyclopedia Britannica." The salesman looked surprised and stopped his lecture. For the first time, he looked intently at Mohammad and said, "Why didn't you say so?" Thereafter, the salesman packed the entire sample of books back into his suitcases, thanked Mohammad for his time, and walked out of the office!

Mohammad was surprised that the encyclopedia salesman didn't make any effort to find out what he wanted. Considering the manner in which the encyclopedia salesman was selling, Mohammad wondered if he was selling at all.

If you don't know what your customers want, you cannot possibly even attempt to satisfy them.

TODAY'S CUSTOMERS

Would you agree that today's customers are much more aware, educated, and demanding? Would you agree that most of them have a higher disposable income than customers of yesteryear, or that they are smarter because they are better informed? State of the art telecommunication systems, live worldwide media coverage, and the ever-expanding Internet are all making the world smaller by eliminating boundaries.

Present-day life has taken on a fast pace that is unprecedented. There is no time to waste or take it easy. Speed is the name of the game. As they are better aware of what they want, are armed with the latest product information, and have access to easy finance, *customers want instantaneous solutions to satisfy their needs.* The customer is the king and literally dictate what is to be produced, how much, and at what price. That is why customer intelligence and trends are setting the future direction of large conglomerates and businesses the world over.

"God only knows what the damn fellow wants!"

Intergalactic Salesman

Customers decide what they want to buy, how, and what to pay for it.

UNDERSTAND YOUR CUSTOMERS

If you want to satisfy your customers, you need to understand what they want. Otherwise, you will not be able to give your customers what they want in the manner they want it.

Everyone on this planet has wants and needs (in this context, wants and needs are essentially synonymous). The only way you can satisfy your customers is to first know what they want. Customers have needs (i.e., products or services they want to buy). The sellers or service providers also have needs (i.e., their clients' patronage from which they can make profits). The customer brings the cash to the transaction and the seller brings the products or services, and they both satisfy each other's needs.

*In a way, customers' needs are **problems** they have. You, as service providers, provide the **solutions** to their problems.*

Other sellers in the market, the competitors, also want to have your customers' business. To make sure that your customers do not go to your competitors, you have to provide solutions that are **AWE**-fully good:

1.   **A**ffordable.

2.   **W**orkable and effective in solving your customers' problems.

3.   **E**asy to access and apply.

To an extent, most service providers try to provide the solutions that have the above attributes, but extraordinary service agents provide the above and more. Their solutions are more pleasing, personalized, and effective.

They give a **memorable experience** to their customers, and the customers perceive greater value in the services received.

> *You need to understand your customer to satisfy their needs, respond to their expectations, and build a relationship with them that is mutually beneficial.*

Seek first to understand, then to be understood.

Anonymous

HOW TO FIND OUT WHAT YOUR CUSTOMERS NEED

Ask Questions:

The only effective way to find out what your customers want is to ask them what they want.

Most customers, when asked, will gladly tell you what they want. Further questions are diagnostic tools that help the service employee to pinpoint the needs of their customers. Asking pertinent questions is the key to effective customer service communication.

"Was it before or after the sentencing that you felt the remorse?"

State Appeal Lawyer

It is similar to when a physician checks a patient for pulse rate, blood pressure, fever, and runs a host of other tests to diagnose a disease. Questions help you to find out what your customer wants, and therefore are integral to effective customer service management. Asking pertinent questions is also an

> Knowing customers and what they want is 80% of the job; the rest is relatively easy.
>
> Mak

effective method of persuading customers, as will be discussed in the next chapter.

Observe & Listen: In addition to asking questions, another way to understand your customers is to observe and listen to them closely. Observing the body language of your customers will help you to understand their level of comfort, preferences, and concerns. Although you should be careful not to judge your customers based on observation alone, with a little bit of practice, you should be able to determine if they are buying into what you are offering.

Different customers have different needs, expectations, and priorities. Questioning and keen observation of their body language will help you to zero in on their individual needs and feelings.

Be "Custuitive:" "Custuitive" is a word that I have coined; meaning developing the intuition to understand customers with different personality profiles and needs.

Custuitive = Customer + Inquisitive.

To be custuitive, you will need to be inquisitive and keenly observe your customers with the intention of learning to decipher their states of mind and feelings. This requires that you learn to read and understand their body language – what their words, their tones of voice and their body language reveal.

For example, when customers cross their arms, it usually indicates that they are defensive, in disagreement, or uncomfortable about what is being discussed. Similarly, when customers look up it means that they are imagining, assessing something from memory, or considering something.

The science and art of Neuro-Linguistic Programming (NLP) can assist you greatly in deciphering what customers feel and want. Or for that matter any book on reading and understanding body language will give you adequate idea on the subject.

In the beginning, you may find it difficult to talk to customers and observe them at the same time to notice what they are feeling, but with practice it becomes natural to your interaction with customers. Practice being custuitive, and soon you'll find that you have become more adept and effective in your dealings with customers.

Ask your customers what they want, and they will gladly tell you.

Case Study 5:   *Customer Expectation*

John and his mom were setting the table for lunch when his mom asked him, "John, what is the date today?" John casually replied that it was the 2nd of January, and inquired as to her reason for asking. John's mom replied, "Oh, it's nothing important." John noticed that his mom tried to hide the tears in her eyes by quickly heading for the kitchen.

They had lunch in relative silence, and after lunch, John left for a walk. John returned in a while with a bouquet of flowers, a box of chocolates, and a lovely dress for his mother; it was his mother's birthday! When John's mother saw the birthday card and the flowers, she started crying again! *What do you think happened here? Why did John's mother cry twice?*

It is prudent to under-promise and over-deliver; let your actions speak louder than words.

THE DIFFERENCE BETWEEN CUSTOMER NEEDS, WANTS, AND EXPECTATIONS

To develop the right attitude and be able to provide excellent customer service, we need to understand the difference between customer needs, customer wants, and customer expectations. Perhaps the easiest way to explain the difference between the three is through an example. Suppose that you are hungry and you go to a restaurant to have a meal. The food is what you need, the Chinese food that you prefer is what you want, and the ambiance at the restaurant, the friendly staff, cleanliness, hygiene, choice of dishes, value for the money, etc., all fall under the gamut of your expectations.

Customer expectations are the preconceived ideas that customers have about products (or services) they consider buying or using. These preconceived ideas or perceptions are unique for each customer and can originate from previous experience, the opinion of friends and relatives, or media reports on the product.

The point to note here is that the customer expectations have little to do with the intrinsic value of a product. Customer expectations depends more on what the customers think or feel about a product. Customers are dissatisfied when the product does not match their expectations, and are satisfied when a product matches their expectations. *However, when the product exceeds their expectations, it is a **memorable experience**, and they keep returning for more.*

Customer expectations are tricky to manage, as they are like double-edged swords. The higher the customers' expectations, the more demanding they are. It becomes so much more difficult to satisfy them, and should something go wrong, the customers are disappointed to that much of a greater extent.

Notice that the same applies to personal relationships as well. We expect more from people who are close to us, and that is why it hurts more when people close to us don't live up to our expectations.

Similarly, when customers expect more from us, they too hurt more when we don't live up to their expectations. If your services are better than that of your competitors, but not as high as what your customers expect of you, the customers may appreciate the competitor's inferior service over yours, especially if the competitor provides a service that is relatively better than what the customers expect of them.

Most businesses strive to provide services from their own point of view, as to what they think their customers want and expect, whereas progressive businesses find out what their customers want and expect, and then develop and deliver their services around their customers' wants and expectations!

Don't try to tell the customer what he wants. If you want to be smart, be smart in the shower. Then get out, go to work and serve the customer!

Gene Buckley

As stated above, customer expectations are directly proportional to their levels of satisfaction; higher expectations that are fulfilled lead to higher levels of satisfaction. Left unfulfilled, higher expectations lead to higher levels of dissatisfaction.

Customer satisfaction depends on how much a product or service fulfills the customer's expectations, and seldom on the intrinsic value of the product.

SEVEN ATTRIBUTES OF A TYPICAL CUSTOMER

1. Customers are more emotional than logical:

Some of us like to think that we as human beings are logical. However, when you consider how we become attached to people, belongings, status, and even ways of doing things, it becomes clear that we are more emotional than logical. If you were only logical, relationships would have no meaning! One moment, you would be nice to someone because you needed something from them, and the very next moment, you would be totally cold towards the same person, because logically, you don't need anything from them anymore!

The truth of the matter is that we as human beings are influenced by needs as well as expectations – expectations are one of the byproducts of emotions in human psyche. **Otherwise, we would be happy with the food, and not care so much about service levels.**

Emotions are formed by the way in which we perceive things or by the memories thereof. The interpretation of any incident leads to feelings, and feelings repeated many times over precipitate emotional patterns that can be different for different people. That is why different people have different perceptions about the same thing.

Consider a customer who, while shopping at a store, requests assistance. No one responds to his call. The customer concludes that the store attendants don't care, and takes the lack of attention personally. He goes home upset about the way he was treated. Tossing and turning in his bed, he replays the incident many times over, and each time he replays it, he assumes even worse reasons for being ignored. Now, if the same thing happens to him a number of times, the customer consequently develops an aversion towards that store.

The opposite could have been the case if the shop attendants had responded to his call for assistance or even if they were busy, acknowledged him and explained that as soon as they were done with other customers before him, they would attend to him. When customers are acknowledged, they feel welcomed, and when they are ignored, they feel rejected. Fear of being rejected, ignored, or treated disrespectfully generates powerful negative emotions that can damage any relationship.

Customers are more emotional than logical; respond to their emotions first.

2. Customers do things to either avoid pain or get pleasure:

Anything and everything that we do is to get pleasure or avoid pain; we either move towards pleasure or move away from pain. In fact, everything that we do has elements of both pain and pleasure. If the pleasure is perceived as greater than the pain, we seek the activity, and if the pain is perceived as greater than the pleasure, we avoid the activity.

For example, if the customer wants to buy a watch, he considers the pleasure of having the watch, but there is the pain of parting with his hard-earned money to pay for the watch. If he perceives the pleasure to be greater than the pain of parting with his money, he would purchase the watch. If he perceives the pain of parting with the money to be greater than the pleasure of having the watch, he would defer the purchase, or decide not to buy the watch at all.

However, pain is a more powerful motivator than pleasure.

Imagine there is rumor claiming that due to logistical problems, there is going to be a shortage of food and water in your area. What would you do? Wouldn't you rush to stock up on food and water just in case the rumors were true?

You would have moved with urgency to stock up on food and water to avoid the pain of hunger and thirst.

On the other hand, if there was a general reduction in the prices of commodities and food items, would you rush to stock up with the same urgency as when you perceived an impending shortage of food and water? Obviously not - your survival was not at stake when the prices dropped. Pain is more motivating than pleasure because the thought of pain creates fear in our mind, and fear is a powerful motivating emotion.

Advertisers take advantage of this fear by broadcasting, "This offer ends tonight," "Offer valid while supplies last," etc. The customer feels (fears) that if she doesn't purchase the product by the deadline given, she will be deprived of the opportunity to purchase the item at a cheaper price (pleasure).

Customers are motivated more by pain than pleasure.

Point to ponder: Do you think it would be a good strategy to increase the customers' pleasure associated with your products or services while increasing the pain associated with the competitor's products or services? If so, how can you do that in the selling of a product of your choice?

_____

_____

_____

_____

(Hint: Ask questions that invoke the appropriate pain and pleasure responses in your customers' minds)

3. Customers buy because of emotional as well as logical reasons:

Customers buy for both emotional and logical reasons. Depending on customers' preferences and the nature of the purchase, the levels of emotions and logic vary. For items of necessity, logic usually prevails, and for fashion, status, or health-related purchases, emotions takes precedent. For example, if you want to buy a mobile phone only to keep in touch with friends, you would logically purchase a standard model that serves the purpose. However, if you buy a mobile phone as a novelty as well, you would probably go for the top of the line model that looks impressive and has many options. When emotions and logic pull a customer in two different directions and there is a tie between the two, the customer may not be able to make a decision to buy. However, customers usually buy more for emotional reasons than logical reasons.

Nonetheless, can you imagine what happens when both the emotions and logic are on the same side, complementing each other? The customer's need to buy intensifies and she perceives the purchase as a bargain. For example, if a lady buys a diamond necklace that will elevate her status and adorn her beauty on formal occasions, she is buying for emotional reasons. However, if she considers the high investment value of diamonds as well, she is buying for logical reasons as well.

Since emotions are greater motivators, start by appealing to your customers' emotions first and then support this with logic, such as, "The dress complements your beauty, and it is affordable/durable, too."

Usually for consumer items, logic prevails, and for health or status-related products, emotions prevail.

4. Your customers don't care how much you know until they know how much you care:

Customers like to deal with people who care. Caring service providers take interest in their customers' needs, preferences, and concerns. Caring for customers helps to build a close and lasting relationship with them. The customer feels empathized with and reassured. From customer's point of view, empathy is pivotal in any relationship that is healthy and sustains differences and conflicts.

> *Customers like to deal with caring service providers.*

5. Customers value trust and commitment:

Trust and commitment are integral to any healthy relationship. Trust and commitment complement each other. If, for any reason one of them is missing, the relationship goes sour. Customers trust you when you are honest with them. Violate their trust once, and they will find it difficult to trust you again; it takes ages of commitment to build trust and only seconds of neglect to destroy it.

When trust is broken, most customers move away quietly rather than protest. You won't know how many have slipped through your fingers until it is too late. Inferior products, substandard service, and cumbersome procedures all erode customer trust over a period of time. Moreover, trust can be broken in an instant when the customer's sentiments are hurt.

> *Customers value trust and commitment.*

6. Customers want to buy and don't want to be sold to!

When we buy, we derive pleasure from the very act of buying. No wonder so many people shop to distract themselves or to relieve their stress. We, as customers, like to credit ourselves for making a purchase that we think of as a bargain. It involves an element of pride, and it feels good to make such a good buy. Have you ever seen how excited and enthusiastic people get when they show off the items they bought to their near and dear ones after a shopping spree? *Therefore, don't hard-sell, rather soft-sell.*

In soft-selling, you let the customers decide what they want to buy. You assist them with all the relevant information and make recommendations so the customers can exercise their choices and buy what they want to buy. Hard-selling is <u>telling</u> the customer what to buy or what not to buy, treating him disrespectfully. The customer feels stifled when he is <u>told</u> what to buy or not to buy.

You can get away with hard-selling once or twice, but you are likely to lose the customer forever! Customers want to feel that they are in control, and hard-selling deprives customers of that feeling. It is better to suggest or recommend a product and substantiate your recommendations with evidence. Support your recommendations with testimonials from other customers who have used the product to make your sales pitch more persuasive. Customers want to make an **educated choice** and greatly value the recommendations of a trusted service provider.

Customers like to decide what they want to buy, and your job is to help them make an educated choice.

7. Customers value long-term relationships that are based on mutual benefit:

Customers like to deal with professional service providers that are reliable and dependable. They also like personalized attention and treatment. It makes their lives hassle free, secure, and it saves them time. When you attend to them promptly, they feel important, and the attention gives them a sense of self-worth. They feel pampered and cared for, and keep coming back for more, again and again. Soon, a mutually beneficial business relationship develops between the service provider and the customers.

Some of the biggest challenges in relationships come from the fact that most people enter a relationship in order to get something; they're trying to find someone who's going to make them feel good. In reality, the only way a relationship will last is if you see your relationship as a place that you go to give, and not a place that you go to take.

Anthony Robbins

Customers value long-term relationships.

CUSTOMERS WANT *SATISFIERS*

S =   **S**implicity and convenience when dealing with you

A =   **A**ssurance and dependability

T =   **T**echnology for better and quicker ways of satisfying their needs

I =   **I**ndividual attention and treatment

S =   **S**olutions to their problems

F =   **F**lexibility to accommodate their special needs

I =   **I**mmediate and prompt action towards resolution of their problems

E =   **E**mpathy

R =   **R**esponsiveness

S =   **S**ervice that is hassle free.

WHAT CUSTOMERS DON'T WANT

Negative Language

Often, service providers have to turn down a customer for a variety of genuine reasons. For example, if a customer wants to travel on a particular flight the next day, and you find out that not only is the requested flight fully booked, but all other flights for the day are also overbooked, you would have to turn the customer down. You would probably inform the customer by telling him something like, "Sorry, we can't provide you with a seat on the flight you requested for tomorrow as it is fully booked, and even the other flights for the day are also overbooked!"

The moment the customer hears the words "sorry," "can't," "fully booked," or "overbooked," he feels denied at a subconscious level. Therefore, it is good to reframe the situation and present it to the customer in a manner that doesn't result in the feeling of denial.

Avoid using the following words:

1. Don't
2. No
3. Can't ⎫ These words have negative connotations.
4. Shouldn't
5. Will not

The trick is to tell the customer _what you can do for them first_, and then tell them the reason for not being able to comply with their wishes. In the above example, you could have said, "Mr. John, we can offer you seats the day after tomorrow, as all flights tomorrow are overbooked." Notice that no negative word has been used in the sentence.

Let us look at some more examples. Suppose you are working at a rental car outlet and your customer wants a vehicle that is not available. Instead of telling him that you don't have the car, offer what you have first, and then give the reason why you cannot comply with his wishes. For example, "Sir, we have a Toyota Corolla or a Honda Civic that you may want to try; the Nissan Sunny you requested is out at the moment."

Similarly, if in a hotel, the guest requests to move to a suite from a room and the suites are not available, normally one would tell the customer something like, "Sorry, Ms. Janice. All our suites are fully occupied at the moment." Instead, why not offer what you can do for the guest before you tell them why you cannot? For example, "Ms. Janice, we will be glad to move you to a suite tomorrow afternoon, as right now all of the suites are occupied." This sounds better, doesn't it?

When you rephrase your response and place what you can do for your customer first, it sounds more compliant, and you don't have to use negative words that can put the customer off at a subconscious level. Below are some negative words and phrases that one should avoid when dealing with external customers:

1. **"Sorry"** – This word should be used in proper context (i.e., only when you empathize with your customers or when service levels have been compromised). For example, you might say, "Sorry, we don't accept checks." Instead, say something like, "We accept cash or credit cards, as our system has no provision for accepting checks."

2. **"But" and "However"** – These words connote the mental construct of "us and them." It is more acceptable to the customer if these words are replaced with "and;" it sounds better and is not adversarial. For example, instead of saying, "Yes, but this product is more sturdy and durable than the one you mentioned," you could say, "Yes, you are right, and this

product is more sturdy and durable." You're not contradicting the customer, and at the same time making your point.

3. **"Under the circumstances"** – This makes it sound as if your opinion and your customer's opinion may not be the same.

4. **"Keeping things in perspective"** – Whose perspective? Yours or your customer's?

5. **"Shall I tell you the truth?"** – Is that not what the customer expects from you?

6. **"I will try my best"** – Are you not supposed to try your best?

Avoid using negative language with your customers; use positive language.

"I would like to assist you, but it is against company policy to attend to patients after 5 p.m."

POLICY:

The customer does not care about your company's policy; they are more concerned with having their problems solved. In situations where your company policy does not allow certain services, it is more palatable if you express yourself in a way that does not sound like you are denying the customer, and at the same time delivers the message in an effective manner.

Imagine a situation in which the customer wants to pay for services rendered in a currency you don't accept. You could nicely inform the customer of the currencies you accept first, followed by the fact that you cannot accept the currency offered, as you don't have any arrangements for handling that currency. That way, you are offering your customer alternatives and not outright refusing him.

Furthermore, when you say you cannot do something because of company policy, you may invoke the customer's negative emotions towards the company you work for, and that is not good for business. It is better to state the real reason why you cannot comply with the customer's request than to point at the company policy.

For example, instead of saying, "I am afraid we cannot accept your goods for shipment because of company policy," say, "We would love to assist you with your shipment, and we don't accept inflammable items on the aircraft for safety reasons."

The customer couldn't care less about your company policy if your company policy doesn't care for the customer.

Mak

Follow up immediately with some alternative suggestions, if possible, such as shipping by sea. Ask the customer if there will be anything else. Thank him for considering your services, and invite him back again with an assurance that you will do better next time. *This approach may help in keeping your relationship with your customer intact.*

In situations where you have to say 'no' to your customers, sugarcoat your response so they do not feel badly about it.

Note: However, there could be situations in which you wouldn't hold your punches and you would simply say 'no' outright because you want to be assertive. This rarely happens, but it is usually when some customers try to take advantage of your generosity; for example, they want you to do something for them that is against the law.

Even then, you would say no politely and state the reason for your refusal to comply.

JUDGE

One day, not long ago, I found myself looking at some gorgeous wristwatches at a newly-opened shop. My wife was going on vacation to Toronto, and I wanted to send gifts for some of my friends and relatives living there. The wristwatches were so beautiful and dazzling that I had difficulty in making up my mind which ones to buy. I may have requested that the salesman show me the watches a number of times and asked for the prices many times over, trying to make up my mind.

After a while and to my surprise, the salesman became irritated with my inquiries and sarcastically blurted out, "Are you going to buy a watch or are you just looking?" I was embarrassed and taken aback at such a question. After having gathered my wits, I retorted that he was right, left the shop in a hurry, and bought three wristwatches from the shop next door!

On another occasion, I went to a car showroom to purchase a car. When I asked for the price of the model that I was interested in, the showroom manager nonchalantly responded by saying that the car was very expensive. I had to ask him more than once before he told me the price. He made it obvious to me that he did not believe that I had the money to purchase the car!

Has something like that ever happened to you? If it did, I am quite sure you did not like being judged like that. You probably left that shop and purchased the same item from another shop where the attendants were more polite and sensitive.

Don't judge your customers by their behavior or clothes; rather, focus on their needs.

YOUR PROBLEMS: Customers want solutions to their problems, and they are not interested in your problems. Personal problems or problems relating to your employer should never be discussed with your customers; they are not interested in such things, and they have their own problems to manage. Your problems do not amuse your customers. Telling your customer your problems makes you and your employer look petty and unreliable. Even if the customer sympathizes with you, he or she may never return to your establishment for business!

Remember, the customers want to deal with the best there is, and are attracted to professional service providers who take their business seriously.

> *Remember, customers are not interested in your problems; they are concerned with solving their own problems.*

The service provider lamented, "My boss shouts at me, my wife wants to leave me, my children don't listen to me, my dog bit me, and now, even my car doesn't start!" The customer empathized, but never came back!

Mak

DON'T TAKE THEM FOR A RIDE!

Do not take your customer for a ride. As discussed earlier in this chapter, customers these days are more aware and smarter than you imagine.

When you make excuses for sloppy service, your customers can see through them and lose respect for you. It is tantamount to insulting their intelligence, and as indicated above, no one likes to deal with someone they don't respect or trust.

> *Don't take your customers for a ride; it is tantamount to insulting their intelligence.*

QUIZ – 2 (Select the most appropriate option)

1. **When you talk to your customers, on what do you focus?**

   ☐ Making sure they understand what a fantastic product/service you have.

   ☐ Your body language, smile, eye contact, etc., to ensure that the customers feel that they are dealing with a professional service provider.

   ☐ What your customers have to say and what they want.

2. **When you want to emphasize a point to your customer, you should:**

   ☐ Tell them in no uncertain terms that they had better take your advice.

   ☐ Show them documentation and evidence to prove your point.

   ☐ Recommend or suggest solutions from which they could benefit and substantiate your recommendations with appropriate testimonials.

3. **Do you think that customers always know what they want?**

   ☐ Yes, customers always know what they want.

   ☐ No, they never know what they want.

   ☐ Usually, customers know what they want; however, there could be situations in which they are not very clear about what they want.

4. **How can you find out what your customers want?**

   ☐ Based on your experience; make a good guess by reading the looks of your customers.

   ☐ Politely wait for your customers to explain what they want.

   ☐ Ask your customers how you could assist them.

5. **A customer draws attention to himself by telling you how much he knows about your business. In a situation like this, you should:**

☐   Politely but firmly change the subject of discussion or ignore him.

☐   Look for gaps in his knowledge and try to educate him accordingly.

☐   Show surprise and compliment his vast knowledge about your business, and then politely bring his attention back to the business at hand.

6. **A customer asks too many questions about a product. Do you take it that the customer is:**

☐   Just window shopping?

☐   Comparing your product with that of your competitors?

☐   Interested in your product, but has some concerns that need clarification?

7. **A customer starts haggling over the price of a product. You should:**

☐   Tell him very firmly that the price is not negotiable.

☐   Give in to make the sale, as long as the price is not reduced substantially.

☐   Respect the customer's position and enumerate the benefits that the product has for the customer.

8. **A customer jumps the queue and says her car is double-parked. She seeks a service that will take a few seconds to provide. You should:**

☐   Firmly ask the customer to take her place in the queue.

☐   Believe her and attend to her out of turn.

☐   Explain the situation to the customers in front of her in the queue and seek their permission to assist the lady out of queue.

9. **A customer chats with you, totally oblivious to other customers waiting in the queue. You should:**

☐ Tell the customer you do not have the time for such chitchat and say goodbye to him.

☐ Invite the next customer to come to the counter, insinuating that the customer should take leave.

☐ Express interest in the customer's chitchat and offer to catch up later, explain other customers are waiting their turn.

10. **A customer turns up just as you're closing shop. You should:**

☐ Politely tell her it is closing time.

☐ Inform her of your business hours and ask her to come back the next day.

☐ Attend to the customer nevertheless and inform the customer of your business hours to avoid them turning up again after business hours.

Scoring:

Give yourself 1 point for each first box checked, 2 points for each second box checked, and 3 points for each third box checked. Add up all of your numbers to determine your grand total.

26 – 30   Excellent understanding of customer care and feelings; keep it up!

16 – 25   Good although there is ample room for improvement. One good way of improving would be to observe those who excel at managing their customers.

10 – 15   You are lagging behind and it would be advisable for you to educate yourself on customer psychology; read a book on customer service or attend a relevant course.

Summary

1. If you don't know what your customers want, you cannot possibly even attempt to satisfy them.

2. Customers decide what they want to buy, how, and what to pay for it.

3. You need to understand your customers to satisfy their needs, respond to their expectations, and build a relationship with them that is mutually beneficial.

4. Ask your customers what they want, and they will gladly tell you.

5. It is prudent to under-promise and over-deliver; let your actions speak louder than words.

6. Customer satisfaction depends on how much a product or service fulfills the customer's expectations and seldom on the intrinsic value of the product.

7. Customers are more emotional than logical; respond to their emotions first.

8. Customers are motivated more by pain than pleasure.

9. Usually for consumer items, logic prevails, and for health or status-related products, emotions prevail.

10. Customers like to deal with caring service providers.

11. Customers value trust and commitment.

12. Customers like to decide what they want to buy, and your job is to help them make an educated buying decision.

13. *Customers value long-term relationships.*

14. *Avoid using negative language with your customers; use positive language.*

15. *In situations where you have to say no to your customers, sugarcoat your response so they do not feel badly about it.*

16. *Don't judge your customers by their behavior or clothes; rather, focus on their needs.*

17. *Remember, customers are not interested in your problems; they are concerned with solving their own problems.*

18. *Don't take your customers for a ride; it is tantamount to insulting their intelligence.*

Chapter 5

"For God's sake Gerry, what will happen to your chances of getting appointed dean of pharmacology if you give up on this project now?"

THE POWER OF ASKING QUESTIONS

The questions are diamonds you hold in the light. Study a lifetime and you see different colors from the same jewel. The same questions, asked again, bring you just the answers you need just the minute you need them.

Richard Bach

Case Study 6:

Joseph was waiting his turn to see the doctor for a minor ailment at a local clinic. He couldn't help overhear the conversation between a doctor and a pharmaceutical salesman next door to the waiting area where he was seated.

Joseph was the sales manager of a large retail establishment that employed a large number of sales personnel working both indoors and outdoors, and he always took keen interest in the sales pitches made by sales personnel.

Often, he would discuss the pros and cons of such interactions with his sales personnel to enlighten them on how to be more persuasive and efficient at selling. Joseph was not surprised to note that the pharmaceutical salesman was hardly ever talking about his products; rather, he was asking a lot of questions, and at the end walked away with a hefty order for a variety of medicines.

Questions like:

- Are you happy prescribing medicine "X?"
- Have your patients complained of any side effects after using "X?"
- Do you think the price of "X" medicine is affordable for many of your low-income patients?
- Would you replace "X" medicine if you could prescribe another medication that had little or no side effects, was more affordable, and came highly recommended by medical specialists at the top hospitals around the world?
- How do you think this new medication will impact your patients' perception about you as a doctor and your clinic?

Joseph smiled to himself and decided to emphasize the power of asking relevant questions to his team the next time they met at their weekly sales meeting.

He also intercepted the pharmaceutical salesman on his way out and invited him to pass by his office to discuss better job prospects with his company!

Why do you think the pharmaceutical salesman was able to persuade the doctor to make a large order, and why do you think Joseph offered the salesman a job with his company?

If you are not moving closer to what you want in sales (or in life), you probably aren't doing enough asking.

Jack Canfield

ADVANTAGES OF ASKING QUESTIONS

Given below are some of the reasons why asking relevant questions is an effective tool for persuading customers to buy.

Attention: When you talk to your customers, there is always the chance that the customers hear you but don't register what you're telling them. This often happens because their minds wander off to other things that are either more important or interesting to them. However, when you ask them questions, they cannot wander off. To process an answer to your question they have to be present and listen to you, otherwise they won't be able to respond to you.

Asking questions holds your customer's attention to what you discuss with him.

Involve customers: Asking questions is a good way of involving the customers, as it makes your interaction with them more interesting. The customers get a chance to express their opinion, thoughts, and feelings about what they want or about your proposal. Within the customer's response you can find helpful clues or customer likes and dislikes that can assist you in selling more effectively. The discussion becomes a two-way exchange of information and ideas that keeps customers with you. The customers feel they have more control because they get the opportunity to express their ideas and feelings and readily collaborate with you in the process of buying from you.

Asking questions is an effective way of involving your customers so they collaborate with you in the sales transaction.

Higher impact: When you ask questions, it triggers your customers' imaginations, and when they imagine a thing, event, or situation, they perceive it through all or many of their physical senses: seeing, hearing, smelling, touching, and tasting. For example, when you tell your customers, they only hear what you say. However, when you ask, "Mr. Crawford, how would you feel if you were on an un-crowded and clean beach…?" it triggers the customer's imagination. Therefore, it is more effective to ask questions so customers can imagine things and perceive the effect of what you tell them through most of their physical senses.

Another example: You tell your customer that you have some new suits that may interest him. As compared to telling, you could ask the customer if he would like to try some new suits that would turn heads whenever he wears them. Chances are that the questioning approach will be more effective in prompting him to have a look at your suits.

Don't tell customers, but ask relevant questions to be more persuasive

Higher buy-in: Another reason why persuading customers by asking them relevant questions is more effective is because when customers answer your questions, it is their own idea or feeling, and consequently they don't reject their own reasoning. For example, you could tell the customer that the product is easy to operate and maintain. This is processed more like information to him.

However, if you were to ask a question such as, "Would you like a product that is much easier to operate and maintain than similar products in the class?" and if the customer concedes to your question, then the idea that the product is easy to operate and maintain is more his idea than yours, and consequently the customer's buy-in is higher.

When customers concede to something because you asked them a question, their buy-in is higher than when you tell them the same thing.

TYPES OF QUESTIONS

There are many different kinds of questions that can be effectively used to persuade and win over customers, and given below are the four major ones that can greatly facilitate sales:

Open Questions: Open questions are questions that you cannot answer with a "yes" or "no," and usually start with "who, what, when, where, why," and "how." One easy way to remember them is to think of a husband (the first letter of **h**ow) with five wives (the first letter in **w**hat, **w**hen, **w**here, **w**ho, and **w**hy).

Open questions entice and encourage the customer to express themselves, and within their discourse you get hints about their preferences, priorities, thoughts, likes, and dislike, etc.

For example, you ask your customer an open question such as, "Why is it that you like product 'y' so much?" The customer may respond, "I like product 'y' because it is durable and easy to use." Now, from that answer you can safely conclude that the customer is high on durability and ease of use. You then can highlight those very attributes of your product to the customer to enhance his appeal in your product.

Customers give you clues as to their needs and preferences when they respond to your open questions.

Closed Questions: Close questions are questions that the customers can respond by either saying "yes" or "no." For example, if you ask your customer, "Do you like this product?" The customer's response can be either "yes" or "no," but nothing more or less. Note that close questions are weak questions in the sense that they tell you what the customers like or dislike, but they don't tell you why. With responses like that you can hardly do anything to improve your services to them.

For example, you ask a customer if she likes your services, and she responds with a yes or no. Now, because you don't know what or why she likes or dislikes your services, you cannot isolate things in your services that please or offend her; you cannot do more of what she likes or avoid doing things that she dislikes. Close questions are questions that are usually asked to verify your understanding or while seeking clarification. For example, you ask the customer, "You don't want the delivery to be made before noon, and it should be in three large cartons?" The customer responds, "Yes, and the containers should also be waterproof for protection against rain." Now you know what you had missed out on, i.e., the waterproofing part.

Close questions help you to verify your understanding of a customer's needs, understanding, and expectations.

"What if" Questions: What if questions are questions that test the position of the customer about something. For example, you ask the customer, "What if we offer you free servicing for the first year; would you buy it then? If you accept, I will have to get management's approval." You haven't made any commitment, but are just testing how the customer feels about your proposal. If the customer accepts to buy because of the offer, you could then apply for approval and finalize the deal.

"What if" questions are test questions that allow you to verify the customer's position on something without making a commitment.

Leading Questions: Leading questions have the answer to the question in the question itself, and thereby lead customers to think in the way you want them to think. For example, you ask the customer, "Wouldn't packing it so tightly damage the suitcase?" In a roundabout way you have told the customer that if she packs the suitcase so tightly, it may damage her suitcase. These questions are useful when you don't want to contradict your customer, but at the same time want to suggest something else. For example, "I know you like this beautiful compact car, but would your family of seven fit into this car comfortably, especially during the long drives that you often indulge in?"

Use leading questions when you want your customers to think in a certain way, or to make your point without contradicting them.

Summary

1. Asking questions holds your customer's attention to what you discuss with him.

2. Asking questions is an effective way of involving your customers so they collaborate with you in the sales transaction.

3. Don't tell customers, but ask relevant questions to be more persuasive.

4. When customers concede to something because you asked them a question, their buy-in is higher than when you tell them the same thing.

5. Customers give you clues as to their needs and preferences when they respond to your open questions.

6. Close questions help you to verify your understanding of a customer's needs, understanding, and expectations.

7. "What if" questions are test questions that allow you to verify the customer's position on something without making a commitment.

8. Use leading questions when you want your customers to think in a certain way, or to make your point without contradicting them.

Chapter 6

"Darling, don't worry; just tell him to go to hell!"

THEN SHUT UP & LISTEN

Just be a good listener and others will hear you loud and clear!

Mak

Case Study 7:

Sam was one of the best sales executives on the team, representing an international group of garment manufacturers. The managing director of the company gave Sam a lead to a large account in the Ministry of Interior. Sam conducted his investigations before setting up an appointment with the financial director in the ministry so that he could convince him to buy the uniforms for the over 55,000 police and security personnel in the country from his group.

Mr. George Abdullah, the financial director, was a stout person who was succinct and terse with suppliers. On the day of the appointment, when Sam was ushered into Mr. Abdullah's office, he felt a little nervous. He had no idea how to approach Mr. Abdullah, as all he knew from his research about Mr. Abdulla was that he was a tough buyer who demanded straight answers and commitment on the spot.

Mr. Abdullah was busy examining a file, and at the same time, talking to someone over the telephone. He gestured to Sam to take a seat and continued talking. After finishing the telephone conversation, Mr. Abdullah continued examining the file and asked Sam to tell him why he should give him the uniform order, and told him to be

> To listen well is as powerful a means of influence as to talk well, and is as essential to all true conversation.
>
> Chinese proverbs

brief about it. Sam had barely finished thanking Mr. Abdullah for his time when the telephone rang again and Mr. Abdullah became busy with another call.

This pattern continued over and over again and Sam hardly got a chance to talk to Mr. Abdullah, as either the telephone would go off, or a clerk would interrupt for his signature, or some colleagues would pass by just to say hello.

Frustrated, Sam resigned himself to the situation and became quiet, hoping that at some point, Mr. Abdullah would give him five to ten minutes of uninterrupted attention so he could talk about the uniform order.

During one such interruption, Sam's attention veered to the extraordinary décor of the office. Artifacts and handicrafts from all over the world decorated the walls of the office, and the pattern gave the room a unique and intriguing look.

Sam's wife had ventured into opening a handicraft shop a few years ago, so Sam knew a thing or two about handicrafts. Sam could tell that the handicrafts in the room represented an exquisite collection that someone had invested a lot of money and time to acquire.

Sam walked around the humongous office, examining the crafts. He was taken aback when he noticed that Mr. Abdullah was standing next to him and smiling, as if not to distract Sam from the crafts.

Thereafter, Mr. Abdullah asked his secretary to bar all incoming calls and guests, as he was busy with Sam, and for the next hour and a half, he gave Sam a tour of his collection. Mr. Abdullah briefed Sam on where each handicraft came from, how long it took to make them, etc. By noon, the tour was over, and they had completed two rounds of tea, coffee, and biscuits. Thereafter, Mr. Abdullah invited Sam to lunch at a gourmet restaurant located at a five star hotel.

At the restaurant, Mr. Abdullah did most of the talking, and enlightened Sam as to his trips around the world and the manner in which he had procured his collection of handicrafts over a period of over ten years. Sam patiently listened and asked questions every now and then to keep the conversation going.

When the time came to part, Mr. Abdullah surprised Sam by asking him to pass by the office the next day and see the procurement and logistics manager to finalize the deal. He said that Sam was a smart lad, and that he was confident that Sam's company would deliver.

Sam never got the chance to make the proposal, and yet, he won the order! What do you think happened here?

Listening, not imitation, may be the sincerest form of flattery.

Dr. Joyce Brothers

THE DIFFERENCE BETWEEN HEARING & LISTENING

Life has evolved and become complex over the last millennia; however, our physiology has remained unchanged – it still has its original capacity to handle complexity. For example, a few centuries ago, we did not have electricity, radio or television, motor vehicles, airplanes, antibiotics, or the Internet. The more we progressed, the more demanding life became. From dawn to dusk, people now have to go around like dogs, trying to cope with the numerous demands of modern living, especially those who live in large cities.

In present day living, everyone is seeking our attention, and on top of that, we have to contend with noise from various sources. For example, colleagues talking in the office, family members having conversations, friends, radio, television, and noises on the road are all seeking our attention, not to mention the various types of attention-seeking through written material! To cope with such an incessant demand, our minds have learned to filter out anything that we don't consider important or that doesn't impact us directly. *The brain has simply learned to focus on what is important to us and filter out the rest.*

For instance, have you ever been in a situation where you sat peering into the television but hardly noticed what was going on because you were engrossed in other thoughts? If at that moment someone walked in and inquired what was showing on the television, you would probably go blank and feel somewhat embarrassed.

Therefore, hearing means letting sound or noise in through one ear and letting it out through the other ear! Listening, on the other hand, is quite different – it is hearing with the intention of trying to understand what the other person is saying and where he is coming from. Listening requires complete and undivided attention to the other person. For example, you may need to pay full attention if your boss is giving you a performance review, or if a close friend is giving you feedback on a presentation for which you're preparing.

If you're a person who listens carefully, you will understand what your boss is really trying to tell you or what your friend thought about your presentation, and take necessary steps to improve on your performance or make your presentation better, respectively.

So when you are listening to somebody, completely, attentively, then you are listening not only to the words, but also to the feeling of what is being conveyed, to the whole of it, not part of it.

Jiddu Krishnamurti

Therefore, listening carefully is an essential element in understanding your customers because:

- It helps you find out what your customers really want.

- Sometimes, customers themselves don't know what they want, although they have a vague idea of what they need. For example, they know that they require a storage facility at the office, but haven't made up their minds as to whether it should be a filing cabinet, a plain cupboard with shelves, or an overhead locker, etc.

- Often, customers don't tell you what they want; they assume that that you know, or just plain forget to tell you.

In all of the above situations, you need to *ask probing questions and then listen intently to the customer's response*. That is, you should notice not only what the customers say, but also how they say it, their body language, and even what they don't say. For example, when you ask your customer if he likes what you have shown him, his tone of voice, facial expression, mood, and questions will indicate his position. Some may even try to avoid responding to your question to feign lack of interest for a better bargaining position; all of these clues can help you to understand them better.

Asking questions and then listening intently can help you to deal with your customers more effectively.

Successful people, regardless of their profession, have one thing in common, which is that they ask a lot of questions, not only to others, but of themselves as well.

Asking questions would be useless if one didn't listen to the responses. *Therefore, questioning and listening are the opposite faces of the same coin; one without the other has no meaning.*

Asking questions and listening are the opposite sides of the same coin.

The most important thing in communication is to hear what isn't being said.

Peter F. Druck

WHY LISTEN?

Listed below are the main reasons why listening to your customers is essential for building strong business relationships with them:

- ☐ It allows you to gather information.
- ☐ It helps you to find out what the customer wants.
- ☐ It helps you understand your customer.
- ☐ It shows the customer respect.
- ☐ It helps you manage customers' expectations.
- ☐ It helps you fulfill customers' wants.
- ☐ It is a way of acknowledging customers.
- ☐ It can help to pacify customers.

> Listening is such a simple act. It requires us to be present, and that takes practice, but we don't have to do anything else. We don't have to advise, or coach, or sound wise. We just have to be willing to sit there and listen.
>
> Margaret J. Wheatley

Listening is the key to building relationships.

A good listener tries to understand what the other person is saying. In the end, he may disagree sharply, but because he disagrees, he wants to know exactly what it is he is disagreeing with.

Kenneth A. Wells

BARRIERS TO LISTENING

The following are some of the common barriers to listening to your customers:

- ☐ Not taking interest in your customers
- ☐ Judging your customers (e.g., assuming they are just window shoppers)
- ☐ Assuming that the customer does not have the financial capability to purchase
- ☐ Branding them as inferior (e.g., from a cultural, religious, or political point of view)

- [ ] Being too absorbed in administrative work or anything else while attending to customers
- [ ] Not feeling well, either physically or mentally
- [ ] Renovation work at the premises that is loud and noisy
- [ ] Distractions or break in workflow due to an equipment or system breakdown (e.g., computer breakdown, electrical failure)
- [ ] Superiors asking you to do something urgently, and in the process the waiting customers are ignored
- [ ] Sometimes, though not often, loud and noisy demands of an irate or abusive customer.

We have two ears and one mouth so that we can listen twice as much as we speak.

Epictetus

HOW TO LISTEN TO CUSTOMERS SO THEY FEEL GOOD, LIKE YOU, & LISTEN TO YOU

Listed below are some tips that can help you to communicate more effectively with your customers so that they like you, buy from you, and above all, keep returning to you.

1. Give the customers your full attention and stop doing anything else.

2. Take interest in your customers: find out more about them and their interests, make them feel important, treat them with respect, and attend to their needs promptly. Don't judge them based on their appearance, religion, race, creed, or nationality.

3. Ask relevant questions to seek clarification so the customers feel that you are taking interest in them and trying to understand their needs.

4. Take notes as and when necessary, so you don't make your customers repeat what they have already told you.

5. Listening helps you to ask relevant questions; ask the correct questions and you will get right answers. By asking and listening, you can progressively narrow down your diagnosis of what the customer really wants.

6. Listen to read between the lines; find out the real reason behind any communication. Don't take only the literal meaning of what your customers say, also try to discern any undisclosed interests, concerns, or mindsets.

7. Don't interrupt or digress from what the customer is discussing until and unless it is irrelevant. Even then, you need to do so with finesse and grace so that your customer doesn't feel bad about it.

8. Show the customers that you are listening to them by maintaining eye contact, using open gestures, nodding, and saying things like "umm," "okay," "yes," "right," etc. At times, make an exclamation to keep the conversation going, such as "really?" "no!" "it can't be true!" or "don't tell me!" However, don't overdo it or sound artificial.

9. Offer them suitable alternatives, collaborate with them to identify and define their problems, and suggest the best possible solutions.

10. When the customer selects a product or option, reassure them that they have made a good choice. Let them know that you are there for them both before and after the sale, and make sure you are sensitive to their emotional needs.

11. Encourage and assist your customers in purchasing and make them feel good about it. Ensure that the customer perceives the value in the product so that they consider it a bargain.

12. Appreciate the customer for their patronage. Thank them and invite them to come again.

> Listen with your ears, listen with your eyes, listen with your mind, and above all, listen with your heart.

> To listen is an effort, and just to hear is no merit. A duck hears also.

Igor Stravinsky

Summary

1. Listening, not imitation, may be the sincerest form of flattery.

2. Asking questions and listening are the opposite sides of the same coin.

3. Listening is the key to building relationships.

4. We have two ears and one mouth so that we can listen twice as much as we speak.

5. Listen with your ears, listen with your eyes, listen with your mind, and above all, listen with your heart.

Chapter 7

REASONS, CONSEQUENCES, & TESTIMONIALS

Reasons and consequences, the self-perpetuating motivators

Mak

Case Study 8:

My colleague and I were once involved in a unique project at one of the largest and fastest growing airports in the Middle East. The problem was that some passengers, after checking in, wandered off into one of the most attractive duty-free shopping facilities in the region. They would get so engrossed with their last-minute shopping that they would completely forget to report to the boarding gates in time for the flight's departure.

Late reporting involved considerable hassles for the airlines, as they had to search for the passengers and then rush them through the formalities at the boarding gates, often causing costly flight delays. Sometimes, when the airlines could not locate such passengers in time, they had to let the flight go after removing their baggage from the aircraft as a safety measure. Our investigation revealed that the check-in staff was clearly spelling out the closing time and the gate numbers while giving out the boarding passes. What was surprising was that the check-in staff also told the passengers to pay attention to the boarding announcements that were made over the intercom at regular intervals all over the airport. However, some passengers, who otherwise seemed to be responsible people, failed to report to the boarding gates in time; they had to be located and herded like cattle aboard the aircraft at the last minute!

What do you think was the problem?

You may have guessed it. People usually have a million things on their minds, especially while traveling. Buying gifts and indulging in last-minute shopping never seems to end. People absorbed in shopping usually lose track of time or plain forget to report to the boarding gates on time!

We discovered that until and unless we got their attention by giving them a good **reason** for reporting to the gates on time, and explained the **consequences** of failing to do so, they wouldn't take the matter seriously and kept failing to report to the gates on time. Thereafter, we advised the check-in staff to tell the passengers the following, as well:

1. "Please report to boarding gate number 14 by 1210 hours latest, as it will close by then." (*Reason*)

2. "Not reporting to the gate in time could result in you missing the flight, and your luggage may be taken off the aircraft for safety reasons." (*Consequence*)

3. Another consequence could include the difficulty of getting seats on subsequent flights, as most flights were full. Further, they would have to go through the hassle of lugging their baggage back and forth to and from the airport until they got on a flight. Finally, the whole family might not be able to travel together due to lack of space on the flights!

4. Worst of all, the airport security police could question them as to why they did not make it to the boarding gates on time.

The response was astounding and every bit worth the extra time and effort spent in briefing the customers at the check-in counters. Most passengers started reporting for their flights well before the gates closed, and everyone was relieved. Although there were still some passengers that failed to turn up at the gates on time, the situation became manageable.

Reasons and consequences make your communication meaningful.

To proceed from one truth to another, and connect distant propositions by regular consequences, is the great prerogative of man.

Johnson

WHY GIVE REASONS & CONSEQUENCES?

When you give reasons, it becomes easier for your customer to understand you. It clarifies to them what they should or should not do. The message you convey is complete and clear; there is no ambiguity or assumptions made on the part of the customer.

Consequences, on the other hand, motivate the customer to do your bidding. When you neglect this, there is a chance that the customer may still do something other than what you recommend or expect them to do. For example, if a tour guide informs a group of tourists that it is not safe to go to a certain area of the town after sundown, the tourist may wonder why. If they don't get a convincing reason, they may ignore the guide's warning and let it go in through one ear and out the other!

However, if you give them a reason, e.g., inform them that it is not safe because of the muggings that have taken place in those areas after sundown; the customers can make sense of what you tell them. The message you convey becomes more convincing. Further, if you add that in some cases, miscreants kidnapped tourists for a ransom (an even worse consequence), your message becomes very compelling indeed.

> *When you give reasons, your customer understands; when you add consequences, you motivate them to take action.*

HOW TO REASON & SPELL THE CONSEQUENCES?

Listed below are some suggestions that will make your communication more effective by presenting the reasons and consequences in a manner that is easy for your customers to comprehend.

1. Relate them to the customer's situation or context so that he has a better understanding. Emphasize the positives or negatives as appropriate.

2. Explain to the customers how taking or not taking action as per your recommendations will affect them; be specific and absolutely clear about it. Encourage the customers to do what you want them to do for the reasons and consequences mentioned. For example, don't say, "Something undesirable may happen," say, "You will miss your flight!"

3. Give them step-by-step instructions on how to achieve what they want to achieve; the most mediocre service providers fail to do this properly.

> *Put yourself into your customer's shoes before enumerating the reasons and consequences to ensure complete understanding on the part of the customer.*

EMPHASIZE THE CONSEQUENCES

☐ Consequences complement the reasons and make the message more compelling by completing the picture. The synergy of reasons and consequences provides a holistic picture that spells out the short and long-term implications.

- Similarly, consequences accentuate the reasons and show the customers what will be gained if the instructions are followed, and what can be lost if they are ignored.

- Making the consequences more graphic makes your call to action more powerful and persuasive.

- Overall, when your message is well defined, the customer's understanding of the pros and cons of your communication becomes clearer. They can think for themselves and decide on their most suitable action to take.

Emphasizing consequences motivates customers to take action; they convince themselves.

PROVIDE INFORMATION IN A WAY THAT LEAVES NO ROOM FOR MISUNDERSTANDINGS

It may be worthwhile to mention here that whenever we receive incomplete information, our brain fills in the missing bits of information by assuming things, which are often erroneous. The process results in misunderstandings or miscommunication. For example, if you were to ask a number of people to fill in the blank in the sentence, "I ---- you," different people would respond by filling in the blank with words that fit their own understanding and mood at that moment in time. Some may fill in the blank with "love," while others may even respond by saying "hate!"

Similarly, customers fill in the missing information themselves to make sense of what you tell them, and this leads to serious misunderstandings and chaos. For example, a travel agent may inform a customer that her flight departs at 9 o'clock, meaning 9 a.m. However, the customer may assume the departure time to be 9 p.m.!

Please note that most customers fill in the missing information with negative assumptions. For example, if you greet me and I do not respond, you are likely to assume that I have an attitude problem. Whereas in reality, I may not have heard you!

As explained earlier, the human brain's primary function is to protect us from danger. In the event of a lack of information, the human brain usually fills in the missing information with things that have negative implications. It does that to be on the safe side, as it doesn't want to take anything for granted.

Customers with incomplete information usually fill in the missing information on their own, and that often leads to misunderstandings and confusion.

In addition to the above, customers are more comfortable with information presented to them in a logical, organized, and structured manner. They find it easier to absorb when it is relevant to them and presented concisely. Therefore, when you communicate a number of things to your customers, make sure you mention them in proper sequence, stress items with high priority, and summarize everything in the end.

Customers find it easier to absorb information that is presented to them in a logical, organized, and structured manner.

THE POWER OF TESTIMONIALS

A testimonial is a positive statement made by other customers in favor of your products or services that you quote to a potential customer. The purpose is to promote the potential customer's confidence in your products or services. For example, a watch salesman might say to his customer, "Creekside Club has purchased a lot of these rugged stopwatches for their athletes, and they all are very pleased with the model," or, "We have sold more than twenty thousand wristwatches of this brand over the last six years, and so far, we have not received a single complaint!"

We as human beings feel secure in following others. When a product works for others, we feel confident that it will work for us as well. The thought process goes something like, "A large number of people are buying this product, so there must be something good about it; I shouldn't miss this deal as I am not at risk to lose anything."

When reasons and consequences compliment a testimonial, the offer becomes almost irresistible. For example, a car salesman might say to his customer, "This car uses less fuel, needs little maintenance, and has a good resale value. The manufacturer is considering hiking the price next month. You can check with Mr. Radcliffe and Ms. Cynthia working in your company; they both bought this model recently and are very happy with it."

However, we cannot afford to give testimonials that are not true or inaccurate; our customers' trust is of prime importance. Customers will not come back to us if they don't trust us. Our focus should be on building relationships, rather than making sales through deceit and dishonesty.

Reasons convince, consequences motivate, and testimonials sell.

QUIZ – 3: Circle the appropriate option.

1. When you suggest or recommend something to your customers, why is it important to support your talk with reasons?

    a) Reasons help your customers to fully understand the scope and context of what you say to them.

    b) Legally, you are bound to provide the reasons for what you say to your customers.

    c) Giving reasons shows that you are a subject matter expert and can impress your customers.

2. It is good to highlight the consequences of your suggestions because:

    a) The customer cannot blame you for not sharing the complete picture with them at a later stage.

    b) Highlighting consequences makes you more persuasive.

    c) You provide either reasons or consequences, never both. It only complicates the message for the customer.

3. The consequences of not taking action or following your suggestions should be emphasized to the customer:

    a) To put fear in their minds so that they listen to you.

    b) So that all details with regards to the product or service in question are fully covered.

    c) To motivate the customer to do something or refrain from doing something.

4. Testimonials are useful because:

    a) They enable the customer to see how your products/services have helped other customers.

    b) They are a guarantee that your product/service is reliable.

    c) Without testimonials, the reasons and consequences don't have any value.

5. When reasons, consequences, and testimonials are used:

    a) It is better not to use the three together, as there is a good chance that the customer will get confused.

    b) They should all be used as much as possible and in that order.

    c) All are not necessary; testimonials alone usually suffice to convince the customer.

6. You should not use fictitious or made up testimonials because:

    a) It is ethically wrong.

    b) Your competitors can sue you.

    c) Your customers will eventually find out the truth and it will ruin your business reputation.

Score:

The appropriate answers are 1) a, 2) b, 3) c, 4) a, 5) b, and 6) c.

I hope that all of your answers were correct. If your communication with your customers is not clear, they can be misguided.

Summary

1. Reasons and consequences, the self-perpetuating motivators.

2. Reasons and consequences make your communication meaningful.

3. When you give reasons, your customer understands; when you add consequences, you motivate him to take action.

4. Put yourself into your customer's shoes before enumerating the reasons and consequences to ensure complete understanding on the part of the customer.

5. Emphasizing consequences motivates customers to take action; they convince themselves.

6. Customers with incomplete information usually fill in the missing information on their own, and that often leads to misunderstandings and confusion.

7. Customers find it easier to absorb information that is presented to them in a logical, organized, and structured manner.

8. Reasons convince, consequences motivate, and testimonials sell.

Chapter 8

LEARN TO GIVE EFFECTIVE FEEDBACK

You need to know about customer feedback that says things should be better.

Bill Gates

Case Study 9:

The D'Costas lived in a small villa located in a development at the edge of the city. Both Jim D'Costa and his wife Pamela were employed fulltime, and when they returned home from work in the evening, they were exhausted. Once home, they liked relaxing in front of the television or spending time with their five-year-old daughter, Sally, playing with her or helping her with homework.

Often, they ordered dinner from a nearby restaurant that had home delivery service. The restaurant served delicious food that was affordable, and the D'Costas were quite happy with their service. This continued until the day a new deliveryman started bringing the food. He had a bad habit of ringing the doorbell three to four times, and that irritated both Jim and Pamela. Sometimes when they ordered a late-night snack after Sally had gone to bed, the repeated ringing of the doorbell woke up Sally and rattled her so much that she had difficulty falling back to sleep!

Both Jim and Pamela mentioned this to the deliveryman a number of times, but it seemed to make no difference – the incorrigible man just kept ringing the doorbell more than needed whenever he delivered food to their house. Jim casually mentioned the issue to the owner of the restaurant whenever they ran into each other, and every time, the owner promised to look into the matter, but nothing changed!

Frustrated, the D'Costas decided to stop ordering from this restaurant, and when necessary, they ordered from another restaurant located a little further away. Although the delivery took longer and the food was not that tasty, they preferred not to order from the previous restaurant because of the odd behavior of the deliveryman.

Questions:

1. Do you think the owner of the first restaurant took any action on the feedback provided by one of his regular clients?

2. How much business do you think this restaurant was losing because the owner was not sensitive to his customers' feelings and needs?

3. What could be the long-term implication of not responding to such feedback provided by customers?

Responding to customer feedback is the key to customer loyalty.

Customers don't expect you to be perfect. They do expect you to fix things when they go wrong.

Donald Porter

WHAT IS FEEDBACK?

So what is feedback? Simply put, feedback is letting others know how you feel towards them or about something, and also what they say to you in return. Feedback differentiates between what is desirable and what is undesirable. Giving and receiving feedback brings clarity to communication and the process enables us to develop better relationships with others.

Customer feedback *is communication with our customers that lets us know how they feel about us or our services.* Their feedback helps us to segregate services they prefer from services they dislike. Based on their feedback, we can do more of the things that the customers appreciate and less of what they dislike. It empowers us to provide our services in a manner that our customers appreciate so they keep coming back for more.

Consider that you send invoices to your customers at the end of every month. However, some customers prefer to process their invoices on a weekly basis, and request that you send them their invoices every week. Ideally, you should do everything possible to take advantage of the customer feedback, and arrange to send these customers invoices on a weekly basis. Not doing so would mean that your focus is on your own convenience rather than that of your customers and that is definitely not good business sense.

Further, our feedback to our customers helps them to understand our position. For example, if their purchases are dropping, and we broach the topic with the customers in time, they may explain why they are opting to deal with a competitor. Such feedback gives you the opportunity to respond to your customers' preferences in time and stop any further loss of business.

Besides, healthy business feedback encourages the customer to give us more business. When business is good and you acknowledge it with thanks, it encourages your customers to keep returning to you. Similarly, feedback to/from our colleagues helps us to understand each other. It helps in bonding as a team and working together with the sole purpose of satisfying our customers. From the above, it is obvious that feedback is essential for meaningful communication and long-lasting relationships.

Customer feedback helps us to respond to customers' needs better.

FEEDBACK & CUSTOMER SERVICE

Establishing the practice of giving and receiving feedback is essential if you want to provide excellent customer service for two main reasons:

1. Firstly, excellent customer service is a product of teamwork that doesn't happen by chance. It requires effective feedback between the service providers and support departments to give the best to their customers. For example, if the service providers at the end of a shift do not brief the incoming shift on what they can expect from returning customers, the service level will suffer. The staff in the new shift won't know the commitments made by the staff in the earlier shift or what the returning customers are expecting.

2. Secondly, constant feedback keeps misunderstandings and personality conflicts from rising. Tension and friction amongst team members is inevitable and an effective feedback process helps prevent and diffuse animosity. Feedback helps all involved to stay focused on what needs to be done and build on each other's work to provide the best possible service to the customers.

For *internal customers* (i.e., all the staff in a company/service provider) feedback keeps staff from working in isolation and encourages a team effort. Consequently, it induces a sense of belonging.

Giving effective feedback:

1. Keeps everyone informed.
2. Keeps everyone together.
3. Encourages cooperation and coordination.
4. Prevents misunderstandings.
5. Boosts productivity because of the synergy of staff working together.

6. Motivates and nurtures.

7. Makes work fun.

Feedback helps us to work more effectively as a team.

THREE CRUCIAL FORMS OF FEEDBACK IN CUSTOMER SERVICE

Appreciation, objectivity, and **assurance** are three forms of feedback that promote excellence in customer service.

Appreciation: To understand appreciative feedback, consider this analogy. Imagine you stand in front of different kinds of mirrors that show you as thin, tall, short, or fat. Would you like to go back to the mirror that makes you look tall and thin or the mirror that makes you look short and fat? If you are overweight, you would obviously like to see yourself in a mirror that makes you look taller and slimmer. *The idea is that feedback works and is welcome as long as it focuses more on positives than negatives.*

Appreciative feedback communicates good feelings, respect, and acceptance, e.g., greeting your customers, taking interest in them, listening to them intently, appreciating them, commending their choices, and thanking them, etc.

Take the case of a customer leaving your shop without making a purchase. What do you say to this customer? You can either ignore the customer because he didn't buy anything from your shop, or you can thank the customer for visiting your establishment and invite him back regardless of his lack of purchase. If you thank the customers and invite them to come back again, they will feel good about it, and there is a chance they will return to you with their business.

However, if you ignore the customers, there is little chance that the customers will remember you, and even if they do remember you, they will not take the trouble of coming back to you. They will probably knock at the door of the first establishment that can give them what they want, and completely ignore you as you ignored them!

Appreciative feedback helps to cement and foster relationships with both internal and external customers.

Courtesies of a small and trivial character are the ones which strike deepest in the gratefully and appreciating heart.

Henry Clay

Objectivity: Objective feedback, on the other hand, signifies specific and purposeful feedback that assists others to see things clearly. It advises or informs internal or external customers on what to do or not do, and is reality based as opposed to based on opinion. For internal customers, objective feedback helps them to understand each other so that they can perform a procedure accurately or even just communicate effectively with each other. For example, the nurse informs the doctor on the patient's symptoms, fever, blood pressure, etc., thereby assisting the doctor in making the proper diagnosis.

For external or paying customers, objective feedback refers to recommending suitable products or services, keeping them informed about their business transactions, or updating them on relevant issues.

Another aspect of external feedback is educating our customers so that they can take maximum advantage of our products and services.

Objective feedback must be specific and personalized as much as possible so that all our customers are encouraged to keep doing things that are mutually beneficial, and avoid doing things that don't work for them or us.

> *Objective feedback is unbiased, as it encourages customers to accept your recommendations based on valid reasons rather than opinions.*

Assurance: Assurance and reassurance is like giving a guarantee to your customers on your services and products. It also lets them know that you are there for them no matter what. Assurance can be in the form of guarantees, testimonials, and after-sales service.

Assuring customers boosts their confidence in our products, intentions, and abilities. It puts the customer at ease, and they feel secure and confident in dealing with us. When customers find it easy and reassuring to deal with us consistently, they automatically develop strong business relationships with us, or what is called customer loyalty.

"The syringe looks big – but trust me, it won't hurt a bit."

It is important to note here that assurance and reassurance are the essence of any relationship. No matter how close we are to people, we need to keep telling them again and again, either in words or actions, how much we care for them. Otherwise, the relationship wanes.

My parents had been married for over sixty years when my mother passed away a few years ago. The secret to their successful marriage was that they both kept reassuring each other many times over every day in words and deeds. *They continuously kept telling each other in so many ways that they were there for each other, no matter what.*

Assurance and reassurance are the cornerstones of any meaningful and lasting relationship, whether personal, professional, or business. It is what bonds relationships and keeps them intact. It is the same with customers; the more you reassure them, the safer and more comfortable they feel when dealing with you.

Assurance is the glue that keeps relationships intact.

IMPRESSIONS, PATTERNS, & ASSOCIATIONS

Our brain uses impressions, patterns, and associations to recognize and make sense of the world around us. In a way, it brands things in the environment to identify them easily and quickly. The upside to this is that the brain doesn't have to analyze everything it comes across to make sense of it again and again.

However, the down side is that many things that appear similar but are actually different get lumped together and recognized as the same. This phenomenon has far-reaching implications in the field of customer service. *Negative impressions have greater impact because of gestalt; they get lumped together in the customer's memory and are seldom forgotten!*

Positive experiences don't have that impact, because good service is what the customers expect, and once it is received their minds get diverted to more interesting things. To elucidate, when you receive good service, you are thankful and move on with your life; however, when you receive less than desirable service, you wallow in the experience and the impact is higher.

Customer Impression is the customer's mindset that he forms and has about a service or product, and it is mostly based on previous experience or feedback from others or media like radio, television, newspaper etc.

For example, if a customer walks into a store and has a less than desirable experience a number of times, his brain will form a negative impression about the store.

"You cowboys are cruel folks!"

If the incident is shared with friends, the negative impression becomes stronger through focus and repeated thinking about it. Once such impressions are formed, the customer will automatically remain focused on noticing the negative aspects of service at the store, rather than expecting anything good. *That is why **first impressions** are so important for winning and keeping customers*; if the first experience is good, the customer gets into a mindset (impression) that tends to notice and expect the good things received the first time. With a positive mindset about a service, the customer's brain finds it difficult to accept anything to the contrary, for the brain resists any change in impressions.

Customers usually see what they want to see, and first impressions are difficult to change!

Patterns: Patterns are similarities in different service providers that customers see as the same. The customers find it easier to recognize a pattern and be guided by their assumptions that because the shops have the same pattern, they must also be selling similar quality products or have similar levels of service standards.

"Hello - Reliable Aircrafts Inc.? This is the third time the propeller has come off while in the air!"

For example, we assume that anything sold at discount stores cannot be of high quality. Although the assumption (discount stores pattern) is generally valid, it may not necessarily be true in all cases. There could be a discount store that has some quality products.

The opposite of the above pattern would be products sold at a branded shop; here, the customer recognizes the shop to be a branded shop (a pattern) and they assume all of products therein to be of high quality, which may not be true. As stated above, all of this happens at a subconscious level.

The implications of patterns are that the overall image of your establishment counts a lot on how your customers perceive you.

Anything and everything that you do or don't do tells your customers something about you; so watch yourself from the customer's perspective and be on guard for anything that can put off your customers.

Association: Similar to impressions and patterns, association creates another set of complications that are not logical. If a customer has a bad experience because of a particular staff member's behaviour at an establishment, the establishment is also branded as less than desirable as long as the experience remains unresolved in the customer's mind.

"Like father like son, eh?"

This is because, as far as the customer is concerned, they are closely associated with one another, as one is the employee of the other. Similarly, imagine you are the sales agent of a renowned brand of mobile phones and you fail to provide the service your customer expects. Now, since the customer is dealing with you and not getting the expected service, he is likely to become apathetic towards the brand as well!

This may occur even though the customer logically knows that you are at fault and not the brand. Even a small discrepancy in the expected product quality or service standards, such as one of the service agents being shabbily dressed, could trigger the customer's association pattern phenomenon. The customer could perceive the establishment as substandard. In this case, the customer has falsely concluded on the basis of a shabbily-dressed service agent that the establishment has substandard service levels. It is interesting to note here that the shop is getting branded on the basis of one shabbily-dressed staff member!

Therefore, we need to ask ourselves what our customers think about us. We have to be aware of our behavior and the way we come across to our customers and others around us. This has a massive impact that not only affects our reputation, but also that of our employer.

If the customer dislikes you, he is likely to develop a dislike for the establishment or brand you represent as well.

WHEN TO GIVE FEEDBACK

I once read a story of a man reading an interesting article while relaxing in a lounge. His newly-acquired dog was also in the room with him, and all seemed to be well until he smelled something foul. Looking around, he realized the dog had relieved itself on the carpet! He wanted to whack the dog, but decided to put it off until after he had finished reading the interesting article in the newspaper.

A few minutes later, he rolled up the newspaper and whacked the dog with it. The dog squealed and ran to another corner of the room, looking confused. Upon being chased by the man, the dog jumped out of the window, and thereafter avoided the master whenever he had a newspaper in his hand. The dog couldn't connect what he had done on the carpet earlier with being whacked by a rolled-up newspaper. However, what the dog learned was that when the master had a rolled-up newspaper in his hand, it was time to run!

*As a rule of thumb, feedback is most effective when it is given **instantly**.*

If a customer made a significant purchase from you and you thanked her a week later, it is unlikely to mean anything to the customer or encourage her to come back to you for further purchases.

Similarly, if your colleague makes a mistake and you point out the error after a few days, it is unlikely that he will be able to relate to it in a meaningful way. However, avoid giving feedback to anyone who is emotionally worked up or physically tired. Both situations are stressful, and however constructive the feedback, it is usually not welcome in a stressed state of mind and body. In such cases, the feedback should be deferred to a later and more suitable time.

For example, if your colleague has just finished a twelve-hour shift and is dog-tired, it is not a good time to give constructive feedback and expect it to be accepted. Similarly, if the customer is upset about something, it may not be the right time to thank them for their patronage or inquire as to their views about your service levels. When dealing with internal customers (colleagues), and if time permits, feedback should be given with adequate preparation to ensure it is delivered in a palatable manner and taken in the right spirit.

Delayed feedback is like stale news; it has no value. However, constructive criticism given at an inappropriate time is even more damaging than useful.

RECEIVING AND RESPONDING TO CUSTOMER FEEDBACK

Given below are some ideas on how to receive and respond to customer feedback:

1. Ask and thank customers for their feedback on your product, company, and services; they can guide you on what they want, how, and when.

2. Ask new customers for their views. Their views will give you neutral feedback, as they are strangers to your company.

3. Don't believe everything new customers tell you as their feedback; sometimes they just say things to please you, or they make something up simply because you asked. Check and validate their feedback by asking why they are saying what they are saying.

9. Don't take negative feedback personally. Stay objective and go to the source by asking, "Why the negative feedback?" Ask them what you could do to improve their perceptions.

10. Keep yourself abreast of customer surveys, suggestions, complaints, etc. Surveys, questionnaires, assessments, and suggestion/complaint boxes are all customer feedback tools that will help you to modify your services to what the customers prefer.

11. Remember, until and unless you do something with the customer feedback, it is useless.

12. Avoid being an "order-taker" (order-takers are service providers who just answer questions asked by their customers; they take *no initiative* to find out what their customers want). Be responsive to customer feedback by using it to improve your services.

13. Facilitate and encourage customer feedback.

14. Take immediate action on customer feedback. Keep them informed as to any action being taken, and be thankful to them for expressing their concerns. Feedback not responded to discourages customers from giving valuable feedback in the future.

15. Subtly broadcast/display the positive feedback that you have received from your customers. Such feedback is good advertisement and tells other customers that you care and that you're listening.

16. Look for the negative patterns in your customers' feedback to discover any major flaws in your services.

> Your customers can teach you how to provide excellent customer service.

People don't want to communicate with an organization or a computer. They want to talk to a real, live, responsive, responsible person who will listen and help them get satisfaction.

Theo Michelson

GIVING FEEDBACK TO CUSTOMERS

Below are some ideas on the positive feedback we can give to our customers:

1. Opening and closing feedback:

    Greetings, salutations, thanks for their business, and invitations to come back are all forms of positive feedback that we can give to our customers.

2. Appreciative feedback:

    a. Thanks them for their patronage.

    b. Commend them on their choice and/or assure them that they have made the right choice.

    c. Recommend products or services and demonstrate how they will benefit by using your services.

    d. Give accurate and satisfactory answers to their queries so they can rely on you.

e. Be respectful and patiently manage their objections.

f. Advise them on market/industry situations and forecasts regarding what they can expect.

g. Do whatever is necessary to make them feel good.

3. Objective feedback:

Product information/helping the customers to make an educated choice or take advantage of your product or services.

4. Care and reassuring feedback:

Following up with customers to find out how they are doing is another effective way of showing the customer that you care and are committed to them.

It is your moral obligation to give positive feedback to your customers.

HOW TO GIVE FEEDBACK TO COLLEAGUES

Given below are some ideas on how to give feedback to colleagues:

1. Before giving constructive feedback, first establish with them that the feedback is in their interest and intended to assist them. It is advisable to obtain their permission first before giving any feedback. Any feedback that is not welcome is not only useless, but is also damaging to that relationship. If you remember, getting lectured by your parents on something when you wanted to be somewhere else was hardly productive. Further, unsolicited feedback is highly offensive and annoying. Therefore, make sure you build the necessary rapport and mood before embarking on giving feedback.

2. Be well prepared before giving any feedback. Base your feedback on facts and avoid feelings and opinions. Even if you are giving instant feedback, take a few moments to organize your thoughts on how you intend to provide the feedback,

so that it is accepted by the person receiving the feedback and is beneficial for them.

3. Start with positives. *Lavish praise and appreciation are forms of feedback that are highly motivating.* People usually live up to your expectations of them; when you point out their strengths and then mention the undesirable behavior in a non-judgmental way, you allow the person to start looking at the negative impact of their behavior.

4. Separate people from their behavior; blame the behavior in question rather than the person. For example, don't say that they are rude. Instead, draw their attention to their "unacceptable, abrasive behavior" by pointing out to them that their behavior is rude. In a way, you are telling them that they are acceptable, but their abrasive behavior is not.

5. Ask questions and let the other person realize your viewpoint on their own. This approach is preferable to the traditional approach of telling them. This coaching approach is effective, because the learning happens internally.

   For example, avoid telling your colleague that their uniform is unkempt; rather, ask them if their uniform is clean – make them think and realize.

6. Apply the **3P** principle: **Prepare** before giving feedback. Be wary of the **Place** in which you give the feedback, e.g., avoid giving feedback in front of others if it has negative elements. Be mindful of the **Person** to whom you give the feedback. For obvious reasons, although the core message may be the same, your feedback to a child would be different than that given to an adult.

7. Before you give any feedback, ask yourself the following questions:

a. Is your intention in giving the feedback morally correct and in the interest of the recipient (Or do you have a personal agenda and/or are you just venting your feelings)?

    ----

b. Do you have the other person's faith, confidence, and trust so that he or she will accept your feedback (Is your relationship with the person receiving the feedback more important than the feedback itself)?

    ----

c. Is it the right time, place, and environment for giving the feedback (Do you respect the recipient of your feedback enough so as not to embarrass him or put him in unnecessary distress)?

    ----

d. Is the way in which you plan to give the feedback the best and most effective way (Are you being sensitive to the recipient's feelings and understandings)?

Win your colleagues over by giving them lavish praise and keep misunderstandings at bay by letting them know how you feel in a way that they can accept it and not take it to heart.

HOW TO RECEIVE FEEDBACK FROM COLLEAGUES

Given below are some ideas on how to receive feedback from colleagues:

1. Don't take things personally if your colleagues have your best interests in mind. Learn to take constructive criticism with a grain of salt. Take it as an opportunity to improve from the advice given to you by peers and your supervisors who know you and are speaking from their experiences with you.

2. Don't accept anything and everything given to you as feedback. Ponder it and be ruthless in assessing yourself with reference to the feedback. Learn to separate the wheat from the chaff; accept what you find valid and discard the rest.

3. Feedback on procedures or relating to work:

   o   Look at things from others' perspectives.

   o   Build on others' feedback rather than try to force your own ideas. You don't have to reinvent the wheel; realize that there are many ways to fleece a cat!

   o   Focus on your colleagues, their feelings, and their needs.

4. Thank the colleagues who give you constructive feedback and mean well; keep lines of communication open.

Feedback from colleagues is like having eyes everywhere to know how the world sees you.

WHO NEEDS FEEDBACK?

Anyone and everyone can benefit from feedback. That includes your supervisors, colleagues, people who report to you, and most importantly, your customers. *Remember, feedback is a way of telling others how you want them to treat you.*

For example, if for some reason, you don't like your supervisor, and she approves your much-needed leave application in spite of operational constraints, would you thank her? If you do thank her, you'll have taught her that in spite of your strained relationship, you were mature enough to appreciate her approving your leave.

On the other hand, if you don't thank her, the next time you have an emergency, she may not be so considerate.

Positive feedback fosters strong and rewarding relationships. It also heals strained relationships.

CHALLENGES TO GIVING AND RECEIVING CONSTRUCTIVE FEEDBACK

Below are some situations in which giving and receiving constructive feedback can be quite a challenge (I don't like using the phrase "constructive criticism" in this context). In such situations, it is advisable to remain as objective as possible. If that is not possible, refrain from giving feedback to others or encourage others to give you feedback. You could wait until the situation is more conducive to either giving or receiving feedback.

1. Giving or receiving feedback between people who have personality conflicts.

2. Giving constructive feedback to people too close to you: peers, colleagues, or friends who could react emotionally.

3. Giving feedback to a boss who is not open to receiving feedback from a subordinate.

4. Giving or receiving feedback to/from outsiders or strangers; neither of you knows enough about the other to give any valuable feedback.

5. Giving feedback to emotionally disturbed people.

6. Receiving feedback from someone you don't trust.

Feedback is what makes or breaks relationships.

Summary

1. *Responding to customer feedback is the key to customer loyalty.*

2. *Customer feedback helps us to respond to customers' needs better.*

3. *Feedback helps us to work more effectively as a team.*

4. *Appreciative feedback helps to cement and foster relationships with both internal and external customers.*

5. *Objective feedback is unbiased, as it encourages customers to accept your recommendations based on valid reasons rather than opinions.*

6. *Assurance is the glue that keeps relationships intact.*

7. *Customers usually see what they want to see, and first impressions are difficult to change!*

8. *Anything and everything that you do or don't do tells your customers something about you; so watch yourself from the customer's perspective and be on guard for anything that can put off your customers.*

9. If the customer dislikes you, he will likely develop a dislike for the establishment/brand you represent.

10. Delayed feedback is like stale news; it has no value. However, constructive criticism given at an inappropriate time is even more damaging than useful.

11. Your customers can teach you how to provide excellent customer service.

12. It is your moral obligation to give positive feedback to your customers.

13. Win your colleagues over by giving them lavish praise and keep misunderstandings at bay by letting them know how you feel in a way that they can accept it and not take it to heart.

14. Feedback from colleagues is like having eyes everywhere to know how the world sees you.

15. Positive feedback fosters strong and rewarding relationships. It also heals strained relationships.

16. Feedback is what makes or breaks relationships.

Even breastfeeding infants give feedback to their mothers from time to time by smiling. They acknowledge the unconditional love, affection, and care that their mothers shower on them.

Mak

Chapter 9

"I kill for money, but you my friend, I'll kill you for free."

LEARN TO CARE FOR OTHERS

Too often we underestimate the power of a touch, a smile, a kind word, a listening ear, an honest compliment, or the smallest act of caring, all of which have the potential to turn a life around.

Leo F. Buscaglia

Case Study 10:

Lucy was rushing to her office, as her supervisor had expressed concerns about her habitual tardiness. As she left the driveway, she noticed an elderly man walking awkwardly on the footpath. She thought the person was drunk, and drove on without a second thought. A little farther ahead, she glanced into her side mirror and caught a brief glimpse of the person slipping on ice and falling on his back!

Lucy had two choices: keep going and make it to the office on time, or attend to the old man and be late to the office. Her head told her to ignore the old man and keep going, but her heart prodded her to stop and assist the elderly person. She slammed on the brakes, reversed the car to where the old man was lying, and got out of her vehicle to check what was wrong with him.

She found the old man unconscious and barely breathing. He had badly bruised his elbows and he was bleeding from the back of his head. She immediately called 911 for an ambulance and waited by the man's side until the ambulance arrived.

Lucy was late to the office by almost an hour, and her supervisor sternly told her to shape up or get out! Even her colleagues gave her the looks that clearly indicated that they too were concerned about her tardiness. Later on in the afternoon, Lucy's supervisor got a call from the hospital thanking her for calling the ambulance and saving a life. As was standard procedure, the ambulance staff had taken Lucy's contact information before taking the old man to the hospital.

"I didn't care if I was going to be late to the office, I just…"

A few hours later, the old man's relatives turned up at her office to personally thank her for caring enough to stop and attend to their grandfather. They thanked Lucy profusely and remarked that these days, no one had the time for strangers in trouble.

Even the local newspaper covered the incident with a brief report and printed Lucy's photograph.

Lucy's supervisor didn't have much to say about the incident, but seemed glad that Lucy had taken the trouble to stop to help an old man in need. Her colleagues were very vocal about what Lucy had done for the old man and looked up to her with respect and reverence.

That evening, Lucy had a feeling of calm and peace that she hadn't felt in years, and promised herself that henceforth she would be more helpful towards others, no matter what. With her newfound attitude, she found her life to be more meaningful and rewarding. To her surprise, she was hardly ever late to the office thereafter! Any idea why?

There is more pleasure in caring for others than in being cared for.

Beginning today, treats everyone you meet as if they were going to be dead by midnight. Extend to them all the care, kindness, and understanding you can muster, and do it with no thought of any reward. Your life will never be the same again.

Og Mandino

THE JOY OF CARING FOR OTHERS

Have you noticed people who habitually drive rashly with little concern for the safety of others? Do you come across people who block the aisles in the supermarket with their shopping cart, totally oblivious to other shoppers? Do you think that these people would make good customer service providers? It is unlikely.

People who are caring, respect themselves and respect others, no matter where they are or what they are doing. Whether these people are at home, at a social gathering, on the street, in the park, or at work, it doesn't matter; they are always caring. These people don't judge others and are always ready to listen and assist. To these people, caring comes naturally.

Most of us working in customer service don't realize the opportunity that we have in helping and serving others, whether they are external customers or colleagues. When we work from the precept of assisting others, work changes from drudgery to a joy that is deeply fulfilling.

> *Customer service is a great opportunity to care for others.*

CARE IS A BASIC INGREDIENT OF AN ENDURING TEAM

When you care for others, whether they are colleagues or customers, they reciprocate with gratitude and acceptance. This applies to the people in your personal life as well. People around you become more helpful, appreciative, and considerate towards you when you care for them.

On the professional front, this helps you gel with others in your team and feel less stressed at work. You feel worthwhile and life takes on greater meaning and is more fulfilling. A sense of belonging, common objectives, and commitment to teamwork brings out the best in people. Everyone in the team takes the initiative of helping their teammates in achieving the team's objectives.

When people work as team, there is considerable brainstorming, cooperation, and innovation. Team members take responsibility for their own work and become supportive of each other; work and communication becomes more objective-driven, and personal agendas are relegated to the background. Caring then becomes a win-win for all involved.

Let us not forget that caring people are not only happier than most other people, but they are also more creative, innovative, and energetic in whatever they do. Their outlook towards life is positive and they have more in life.

When you care for others, they reciprocate by caring for you.

I feel the capacity to care is the thing which gives life its deepest significance.

Pablo Casals

BECOME AN "EMPLONER"

"Since I'm part owner in the company, I choose to read comics at work!"

In my training classes on customer service, I often use the word **"Emploner."** It is a word that I have coined to explain the fact that, in a way, we are employees as well as owners of the business for which we work. If we do not provide excellent customer service, our customers will not return, and as a result, the business we work for will close. In other words, our source of income will cease to exist!

On the other hand, if we give our best and the business does well, it grows, giving us the chance to grow with it. From that point of view, we are also part owners of the business for which we work. Therefore, it is important that we take responsibility for the work we do and care for the company for which we work.

Don't judge the supervisor or management as unfair partakers of the business, as they are owners of the business just as we are. They have a different job to do, a higher level of responsibility, and therefore receive higher remuneration. We too can become supervisors or managers by giving our best and winning the recognition of our superiors. When that happens, we can expect to take on additional responsibilities and grow within the company.

Don't forget, in a way, it is your own business; it is up to you to grow your business and grow with it.

Summary

1. *There is more pleasure in caring for others than in being cared for.*

2. *Customer service is a great opportunity to care for others.*

3. *When you care for others, they reciprocate by caring for you.*

4. *Don't forget, in a way, it is your own business; it is up to you to grow your business and grow with it.*

Don't be afraid to give your best to what seemingly are small jobs. Every time you conquer one, it makes you that much stronger. If you do the little jobs well, the big ones will tend to take care of themselves.

Dale Carnegie

Chapter 10

PRESENT YOURSELF WITH CONFIDENCE

You must believe in yourself before you can expect your customers to believe in you.

Mak

Case Study 11:

Victor was shopping for a four-wheel drive, and he had his eyes on a Korean-made vehicle that was within his budget. The vehicle offered everything that the other expensive brands in its class offered, except that it was not as rugged. The upside was that the vehicle was within his budget and the fuel consumption was moderate. As Victor seldom went off-road, the vehicle seemed to be the ideal choice given the affordable price tag.

Not being able to decide, and yet badly wanting to purchase the vehicle, Victor decided to ask the opinion of the attending salesman. Victor inquired if the salesman considered the vehicle to be a good buy. The salesman thought for a while, and then casually told Victor that it was okay, but that sometimes the rear air conditioner didn't function so well! The salesman's unexpected response confused Victor so much that he left the showroom disappointed and never returned.

Why do you think Victor was so confused and disappointed by the salesman's response?

WHAT IS CONFIDENCE & WHY IS IT IMPORTANT?

Confidence comes from "belief in self." Belief in self is more of an attitude than anything else. Belief in self is synonymous with self-esteem or our opinions of our self-worth. People with high self-esteem have a "can-do" attitude, while those with low self-esteem feel they don't have the capability to do much, and consequently, seldom take on any challenges that come their way. Such people give up even before trying!

Over the course of our lives, we have all made little choices every now and then to cope with difficult situations. Depending on how we responded to those situations, we now either have or lack confidence in ourselves.

For example, if we accepted the challenges that life threw at us and we faced them confidently, we are likely to have grown up into confident individuals.

Similarly, if we shied away from the problems in our lives, we would have developed into a person who lives in denial and lacks self-confidence. All the little choices we kept making throughout our lives culminated into our current levels of confidence and character.

Who has confidence in himself will gain the confidence of others.

Leib Lazarow

Confidence, like any other state of mind, is highly contagious.

WINNING THE CUSTOMER'S CONFIDENCE

If you are confident, your customers feel confident in dealing with you. Similarly, if you are not confident, your customers pick up on your lack of self-confidence and avoid dealing with you. Confident service specialists win their customers' trust by providing excellent service and by being reliable. The customers feel that they are in competent hands and transact business, reassured. A high level of confidence indicates a high level of initiative and commitment that makes the service provider more dependable and persuasive in the customers' eyes. The customers become attentive and listen with interest to the service specialist.

How does it happen? It is quite simple. When you feel confident, your body language, gestures, tonality, and overall disposition show it. You become more enthusiastic, creative, and passionate about what you sell, and your customers pick up the positive vibrations in your communication and respond to them positively.

We all know that customers tend to buy more and feel satisfied with their purchases when they are in a positive state of mind as compared to when they are apprehensive.

If you don't trust yourself, your customers will not trust you!

Even if you haven't encountered great success yet, there is no reason you can't bluff a little and act like you have. Confidence is a magnet in the best sense of the word. It will draw people to you and make your daily life and theirs a lot more pleasant.

Donald Trump

HOW TO BE CONFIDENT

Belief in self as a service specialist means that you are enthusiastic about serving your customers and have the ability and resources to do so.

Such a level of confidence comes from your product knowledge, skills, and experience in managing customers. Having a thorough understanding of your products and services, customers, market, industry, and a strong sense of commitment to your customers are essential for confidence-building.

"Buy life insurance and your wife will start praying for you to go to heaven soon!"

To become an exceptionally effective customer service provider, it requires sincere effort and perpetual self-development in your area of work. You have to be in competition with yourself to do better than yourself. At the same time, observe other service agents who excel in their work so that you can emulate their winning behavior.

A high level of personal motivation and the will to exceed your own standards has to be the driving force behind all your activities.

Whatever you say, say it with conviction.

Mark Twain

BELIEVE IN YOUR PRODUCTS/SERVICES

To believe in your products or services doesn't mean that you delude yourself into believing in a substandard product. Nor do you have to have the best product to believe in it.

To believe in your product, you need to sincerely believe that your product has value. You should be able to see the positive aspects of your product that stand out in comparison to those of the competition and cater to a particular market segment. You cannot have a product that fits the needs and preferences of all customers in a market. Some products are of very high quality, and are therefore expensive. Such products attract customers who value quality and are ready to pay for it. However, other customers prefer more affordable products or services that meet their requirements.

To believe in your product, you need to sincerely believe that your product has value.

TAKE RESPONSIBILITY FOR YOURSELF & YOUR DEVELOPMENT

You need to choose to be responsible and present yourself with confidence. That means taking responsibility for your dealings with your customers, taking initiative in assisting them, and actively participating with your colleagues to ensure that your customers get the best possible customer service. When you realize that your work has a significant impact on the company's bottom line, it becomes more meaningful and rewarding. Identify areas that are common to your employer's goals and your personal goals and operate from that perspective.

If you find that you don't have the opportunity to excel, cannot express yourself by providing superior service, or that the company culture doesn't value a high level of customer service, then it may be wise to look for a better employer who will give you the opportunity to contribute more by letting you get involved and perpetually develop yourself. Remember, either you move forward or backward; you can never stand in one place. If you stand in one place, then soon you will find yourself overtaken by others as they move forward.

You have to be a subject matter expert; take responsibility for yourself and your development as a service specialist.

An expert is someone who knows some of the worst mistakes that can be made in his subject and how to avoid them.

Werner Karl Heisenberg

"Tell me, what do you see in their expressions?"

EDUCATE YOURSELF ON CUSTOMER PSYCHOLOGY & BEHAVIOR

Keep yourself updated on the latest concepts and discoveries in customer psychology, service, and behavior. If possible, take every opportunity to train and retrain yourself.

Read books and exchange ideas with colleagues on customer psychology and behavior, and keep abreast of any surveys related to customer service in your market and industry. *Get actively involved in assisting junior staff, as teaching others is the quickest way to learning something you want to master.*

Become a keen observer of service levels whenever you take on the role of a customer. Learn to observe not only the shortcomings in service standards, but also the things that make you feel good as a customer.

<u>Observe and model excellence in customer service.</u>

Be in constant contact with your customers. Make walk-in customers, major customers, principals, suppliers, and even your competitors your resources from which to learn. Your customers and competitors are your best resources to learn how proficient you are in customer service and how you can improve further.

> *Teach and learn from others to become an expert in customer service.*

WHY SHOULD YOU HAVE THOROUGH KNOWLEDGE OF YOUR SERVICES?

Have you ever dealt with a service agent who couldn't give you straight answers about a product that you were interested in, e.g., trying to understand how to operate a sophisticated cell phone you were considering buying? How did you feel about the situation, the product, or the service agent? "Frustrated" is probably the word that comes to your mind.

If, as a service specialist, you cannot field the queries of your customers, they will not have confidence in you or your services. You should be able to show your customers how the product will benefit them by making their lives easier.

For example, don't harp on about the mobile phone having a camera. Rather, emphasize how the customer will be able to take clear shots of unexpected events anytime, anywhere, without having to lug a camera around. You should have adequate knowledge about your services and that of your competitors as well. It will enable you to make an objective comparison between the two and show your customers the advantages of using your products or services.

A word of caution: *Under no circumstances should you put down your competition!* If you do, your customers will perceive you to be manipulative and biased. Understand that if your customer has a high opinion of one of your competitors, there must be a genuine reason why the customer feels that way. Respect the customer's opinion, and then move on with the benefits and advantages of your product. For example, "I quite agree with you, Elegant Electronic has an excellent line of products. With our cell phone, you will be able to surf the web from anywhere."

Knowing your products, your customers, and your market are all essential elements in an excellent customer service equation.

If we know how to create the energy of love, understanding, compassion, and beauty, then we can contribute a lot to the world.

Thich Nhat Hanh

KNOW HOW YOUR COMPANY WORKS

You also should know how your company works so that you can make commitments to your customers confidently and honor them. There is nothing more infuriating to customers than being let down on a given commitment. For example, if you need permission from higher-ups in the company to do something special for a customer, you should know from experience how long obtaining that permission usually takes.

Also, consider the chances of management approving or disapproving your request. Otherwise, you may make promises that you cannot keep. Notice that even if you have good intentions and want to help the customer; your over commitment and failure to deliver will not only disappoint the customer, but also tarnish the reputation of your company. Customers often expect a service that is different from what we can offer, and it is therefore important that we clarify what we offer. Our customers should not expect anything that we cannot deliver, as that can be immensely disappointing for them.

Another advantage of knowing your products or services well is that you will be able to manage your customers' expectations and complaints more effectively and to their satisfaction. For example, if your ability to make deliveries is constrained because some of your delivery vans are in the garage for maintenance, you will commit to your customers accordingly, and your customers won't expect immediate deliveries.

In some establishments, there are bureaucratic procedures that make it difficult for their front-line staff to give simple commitments to their customers. Often things take a bad turn when the higher-ups fail to respond to service agents either all together or in time; some of you may have had the experience of getting approval for things that you applied for on behalf of a customer only after the customer had left!

Know how your company works so you can make commitments that you can keep.

Not the maker of plans and promises, but rather the one who offers faithful service in small matters. This is the person who is most likely to achieve what is good and lasting.

Johann Wolfgang von Goethe

QUIZ - 4

This is more of an introspective exercise, and as such, you should take your time with each statement and evaluate yourself carefully. The remarks column is for you to note your strengths, areas needing development, and plans for how you intend to become more confident.

Sr. No:	Statement	Disagree	Don't know	Agree	Your strengths or how you plan to improve in areas that need development
		Tick the appropriate column			
1.	Confidence is highly contagious; when we are confident, our customers feel reassured in dealing with us.				
2.	Confident service specialists are proactive. They are committed and take initiative when serving their customers.				
3.	One of the hallmarks of confident service specialists is that they are enthusiastic about serving their customers.				
4.	Confidence in customer service requires thorough product knowledge, customer service skills, and experience.				
5.	Confidence is a state of mind that you can choose.				

6.	Confident service specialists have a "can-do" attitude that is highly empowering.				
7.	Confident service specialists take responsibility for what they feel, think, and do.				
8.	Confident service specialists keep themselves up to date on the best practices.				
9.	Confident service specialists are aware of their capabilities and the capabilities of their organization.				
10.	Confident service specialists think twice before making a commitment, and once they commit, they follow through.				

If you agreed with all of the above questions, you're probably a very confident customer service specialist, or at least a person who knows how the process works.

Summary

1. You must believe in yourself before you can expect your customers to believe in you.

2. Confidence, like any other state of mind, is highly contagious.

3. If you don't trust yourself, your customers will not trust you!

4. A high level of personal motivation and the will to exceed your own standards has to be the driving force behind all your activities.

5. To believe in your product is to sincerely believe that your product has value.

6. You have to become a subject matter expert; take responsibility for yourself and your development as a service specialist.

7. Teach and learn from others to become an expert in customer service.

8. Knowing your products, your customers, and your market are all essential elements in an excellent customer service equation.

9. Know how your company works so you can make commitments that you can keep.

Chapter 11

OFFER CHOICES OR ALTERNATIVES

The desire and ability to choose makes us human; the more choices we exercise, the greater our freedom and adaptability.

Mak

Case Study 12:

In the mid-seventies, Omar was a ticketing and reservations agent with an international airline operating out of Dhaka, Bangladesh. He was sent to Moscow for three months on temporary assignment to make up for a temporary shortage of English-speaking staff.

Omar was surprised to find that although the state provided the Russians with the basic amenities of life, they were unhappy compared to common people in Bangladesh. At the time, Bangladesh was still recovering from the ravages of the Liberation War with Pakistan; the economy was in shambles and the country was in a state of anarchy. The common man in Bangladesh suffered untold miseries and could hardly afford one square meal a day. Yet, Bangladeshis seemed to be happier than most people in Russia!

What do you think was the reason for this anomaly?

Let me give you a hint in case you're having difficulty in figuring it out. Many years ago, the municipal authorities of a large city in an underdeveloped country conducted a drive to remove the beggars from some of its main streets.

The authorities felt that the beggars were tarnishing the image of the city. Therefore, they rounded up the beggars, took them to a temporary shelter outside the city, and provided them with food and lodging in exchange for some menial work.

You'd be surprised to know that within days, the beggars got restless, and escaped from the facility that provided them with food and shelter! Please note that these people previously had no place to sleep and lived off the garbage dumps.
The authorities had to abandon the project and the beggars went back to the street, begging and sleeping on the footpaths of the city.

Why do you think the beggars passed up on such an excellent offer by the municipality?

Returning to the Russians, you may have guessed it. The Russians were unhappy because under the communist regime, they had very limited rights. Even though the state looked after their basic needs, the state also dictated what education they would acquire, what they would do for a living, and where they would live. The Russians felt that they were being stifled and didn't have any *choice*!

One of the greatly valued aspects of human existence is the right to choose. Take that away and the dignity of human existence is lost!

Mak

How does that relate to your customers?

Customers value choice and alternatives.

Customers want correct answers immediately in the medium of their choice.

Tony Adams

CUSTOMERS LIKE TO CHOOSE

"Dear Charlie, the choice is yours: either you vote for me or I let your sweet wife know about…!"

To be persuasive, offer alternatives to your customers so they feel that they can exercise their choices. Avoid any kind of hard-selling; hard-selling is manipulative and puts psychological pressure on the customer to buy. For example, don't tell your customers that an item is too expensive for them or make them feel guilty if they want to see many items and can't seem to make up their mind on buying any.

Soft-selling, on the other hand, involves first finding out what the customer wants, then providing them with what they want, and finally, providing it in the way they want it. Soft-selling makes the customer feel at home and lets them decide what they want to buy. The act of choosing gives them an opportunity to express themselves, and this act of expression gives them a sense of control. Hard-selling stifles the customer's right to choose and suffocates the customer; it forces them to go by what the seller decides for them. *Therefore, soft-selling builds relationships with customers, while hard-selling focuses on a one-time sale.*

In a way, the customer's ability to choose is closely connected to their self-worth. Self-worth or ego in turn is a by-product of imagination; imagination enables us human beings to compare ideas, things, and situations, and judge them from different perspectives. Imagination allows people to judge whether they like something, whether it is good or bad, right or wrong, and the list goes on. Judgment gives us the faculty to choose. At a very deep level, our ability to choose gives us our sense of identity. Customers shun any situation in which they cannot exercise their right to choose.

Giving the customer choices shouldn't be confused with who should be in control of the discussion between you and your customer. Giving choices means giving alternatives to your customers from which they can choose assisted with your recommendations. Control of the discussion refers to how the discussion unfolds, and it should be in your control so that you can guide the customer and help him make a purchase that is beneficial for him. Even though you're the one who should be in control of the discussion between you and your customers, make the customers feel that they are in control. Make it appear as if the customers are calling the shots.

Customers like to choose and be in control in any buying situation.

OFFER ALTERNATIVES SO THAT CUSTOMERS FEEL THEY ARE IN CONTROL

Alternatives get and keep the customer interested, and as mentioned above, make them feel in control. Their buy-ins are higher and they come up with fewer objections. Customers get involved and participate actively with you in the transaction.

"Oh, you can go by road, air, sea, ride the donkey, or even walk; which shall I arrange for you?"

Active participation brings out their imaginative side and they have a higher sense of belonging that ultimately leads to higher satisfaction. Customers then take responsibility for their decisions, and in the process, convince themselves of their choices.

Further, when customers sell the idea to themselves, they become protective about the idea. In fact, some become your strong proponents through word-of-mouth advertisement.

Alternatives provide a deeper level of satisfaction to your customers.

HOW TO PROVIDE ALTERNATIVES

Don't provide alternatives for the sake of providing alternatives. Any alternative you provide to your customer should have value for the customer; otherwise, the customer will not buy your products or services.

Not long ago, I was flying on a business trip to another city in the country. It was imperative that I flew in the evening and reached the destination the same night so I could rest. That way, I would be able to meet the staff in our branch office the next morning and prepare for the business meeting with a major client in the afternoon.

It so happened that the travel agent who issued the tickets made a mistake with my bookings. The tickets showed that I was confirmed in business class on the evening flight, but when I reported for the flight, it was apparent that I didn't have a confirmed seat!

I explained my situation to the airline representative and expected some assistance. They offered me a seat on a flight that departed the next morning, as the evening flight's business class was overbooked. Out of desperation, I asked the airline representative if there was any possibility of getting a seat in first class the same evening, and to my surprise, the representative confirmed that they could accommodate me in first class provided I paid extra!

When I asked the lady why she didn't offer me the first class seat earlier, she nonchalantly said that I did not ask for it! What an opportunity to up-sell that would have been lost if I hadn't asked for first class!

Innovate: The airline representative was taking orders and not solving the customer's (my) problem. *Effective service providers are innovative and think outside the box in trying to find a solution to customers' problems.* An innovative airline representative would have tried to book me via another route the same evening (if first class was also full) to make sure I flew the same evening and reached my destination the same night.

Innovation and thinking outside the box is the key to customer satisfaction.

Recommend: Ordinary customer service agents explain the pros and cons of each alternative they offer. Super service providers or consultants go one step further. They not only relate the pros and cons of each alternative but also *recommend* the most suitable alternative for that customer.

"I strongly recommend this plot; the prices of these plots are expected to skyrocket with the opening of the new shopping center in the area."

Relating and matching each alternative to the customer's needs enables the customer to understand the options better and make an educated choice. He can see how the recommended alternative will best take care of his problems. This obviously leads to a higher level of satisfaction.

Providing alternatives and highlighting the pros and cons of each without making a recommendation is like your financial advisor telling you the different ways to finance the purchase of a house, but failing to recommend which scheme would be the most suitable for you! *As compared to ordinary service providers, super service agents or consultants behave like subject matter experts and recommend solutions that they believe are most appropriate for their clients.*

You, the subject matter expert, must recommend an alternative or course of action for the customer to take; otherwise, the customer won't have confidence in you or your product. It really doesn't matter if the customer does or doesn't go by your recommendations; what is important is that you play the role of a specialist who works to protect the customer's best interest.

Recommend the most suitable alternative for your customer and relate the benefits of your recommended alternative.

WHY SHOULD YOU COMPLIMENT THE CUSTOMER'S CHOICE?

When you offer alternatives to your customer and recommend a course of action, it is up to the customer to either go with your recommendations or choose something else. Even if the customer selects an alternative that you haven't recommended, you should compliment their choice.

In case you feel that the customer's choice is not in their interest, bring up the issue subtly by asking questions in a way that highlights to the customer that his decision may not be in his interest. For example, if a customer opts for an imitation product to save money, you can bring up the downside of such a decision by asking them what would happen if the product didn't do what it was supposed to do, thus insinuating not only product failure, but also a waste of money and time.

In a way, complimenting the customer's choice compliments the customer and makes them feel good. They become confident and reassured about their choice and have a higher level of satisfaction. This applies particularly to situations in which the customer is spending a large amount of money to buy a product or in situations where they do not have the know-how about the product in question.

For example, if a lady buys a car and doesn't know much about motor vehicles, or if a gentleman buys kitchenware for his home and is unsure about his wife's preferences. Complimenting the customer's choice in these situations would reassure them and lead to greater satisfaction.

Complimenting the customer's choice assures him that he has made the right choice.

CROSS, UP, & DOWN-SELLING

a. Cross-sales: Cross-selling refers to offering related products or services to a customer. For example, if a customer is buying pants, you can suggest a matching shirt and tie. Alternatively, if a passenger is buying an airline ticket, you could offer travel insurance, a hotel room, or a car rental as well.

A word of caution: You can cross-sell only after the customer has finished selecting or buying the core product for which he came. Otherwise, the customer may get confused or feel pressured to buy things to which he cannot relate. In the above example, cross-sell the shirt and tie only after the customer has made up his mind to buy the pants of his preference.

b. Up-sales: Up-selling refers to suggesting higher-priced products or services to a potential customer. For example, if a customer wants to buy an economy class ticket to fly somewhere, you could suggest that he buy a business class ticket so that he can stretch out during the long journey and travel comfortably. Alternatively, if a customer wants to buy a basic computer, you might suggest another model that is faster and has a higher memory so that he can manage his work more efficiently.

c. Down-sales: When a customer finds his choices of products or services too expensive, you can offer a more affordable alternative that is within his budget. For example, if a customer wants to buy an expensive voice recorder that has a lot more features than the customer needs, you could offer an affordable model that only has the features that the customer wants.

Sometimes you may down-sell because the product or service is more appropriate to what the customer wants, and your commission from selling the product is higher than what you would earn from selling a more expensive brand. <u>However, keep the interests of your customer in mind all the time.</u>

Cross, up, and down-selling are opportunities to sell that most service providers ignore. All the techniques described above can significantly add to your revenues. Remember, it makes sense to sell to customers who are already with you or who have walked into your shop.

Up, down, and cross-sales can significantly add to your sales revenues at no additional cost or effort.

Summary

1. The desire and ability to choose makes us human; the more choices we exercise, the greater our freedom and adaptability.
2. Customers value choice and alternatives.
3. Customers like to choose and be in control in any buying situation.
4. Alternatives provide a deeper level of satisfaction to your customers.
5. Innovation and thinking outside the box is the key to customer satisfaction.
6. Recommend the most suitable alternative for your customer and relate the benefits of your recommended alternative.
7. Complimenting the customer's choice assures him that he has made the right choice.
8. Up, down, and cross-sales can significantly add to your sales revenues at no additional cost or effort.

Chapter 12

EMPOWER YOURSELF

Take responsibility for yourself, your life, and your growth.

Mak

Case Study 13:

Khalid and William worked as customer service agents for a computer hardware retailer and dealt with customers face-to-face across the counter. They both seemed to be enthusiastic and enjoyed their work. Khalid focused on his work and was interested in developing himself, both at a personal as well as a professional level. He was always on the lookout for opportunities to attend training that enhanced his skills and knowledge. He would pick up books on self-development or on customer service and devoted much of his time to learning. He was aware that to grow, he would need to set goals and work towards achieving them; it was something that one of his supervisors had impressed upon him a few years ago when he first joined the company after graduating from college.

William was also a good worker and managed his customers quite well. He, like most college dropouts, did not particularly feel the need to enhance his knowledge and skills. It was not that he didn't care; he just thought that there would be time for such things later. William was quite content with how things were and didn't plan for his future.

A few years later, Khalid had moved on in his career and become a team leader, while William remained where he was. Khalid was looking forward to his life, whereas William became negative and blamed the company for not recognizing his good work. He became despondent and the quality of his work suffered. Soon, William was no longer good at his job; he became cynical and vindictive in his overall attitude towards life. Customers started complaining about William's abrupt and impolite behavior, and he responded by blaming them!

What do you think happened with William?

If you're not moving forward, you're actually moving backwards as others move forward.

MANAGEMENT WANTS TO EMPOWER YOU

 Most managers and supervisors think twice before empowering their staff, because empowering staff involves taking risks. They are concerned that the staff could give away the shop, give in to the demands of difficult customers, and make serious mistakes that could cost the company money. The supervisor's unwillingness to empower newly-recruited staff is understandable.

The staff can make serious mistakes due to a lack of skills and experience, especially while servicing major or regular clients. On the other hand, customers want to deal with empowered staff that can provide solutions to their problems quickly and efficiently. The management has to weigh empowering staff with the risk of compromising service versus staff development. Therefore, *it is not comforting for the management to empower staff that is <u>not interested</u> in empowering themselves.*

Whether the management is willing to empower you or not, you should take initiative and the responsibility of empowering yourself. If you do so, the management will recognize your initiative eventually and entrust you with higher responsibilities.

The only way you can become an expert at customer service is by servicing as many customers as you can, and by trying to improve on your performance each time. In doing so, understand and expect to make mistakes that can be embarrassing at times. Take initiative in your work and make an effort to continuously improve your customer management skills. Making mistakes should not keep you from acquiring and improving the skills that will help you serve your customers better. Imagine what would happen if toddlers gave up trying to walk just because they kept falling down! What you can do is take responsibility for yourself and do everything possible to minimize your mistakes.

Remember, continuous improvement and development can only happen if we allow ourselves to learn from our failures, and that is empowering. Just don't take any chances with major customers, as you could make costly mistakes that are not worth the risk.

Management wants to empower you; if you don't take the initiative and responsibility to empower yourselves, who will?

WHAT IT MEANS TO EMPOWER YOURSELF

1. Take responsibility for your dealings with your customers, both external and internal, while being fully aware of the consequences of your actions.

2. Never hesitate to ask pertinent questions of others or yourself to seek clarification; be inquisitive.

3. Keep your commitments.

4. Gain the confidence, trust, and respect of your customers and colleagues alike.

5. Communicate clearly by providing appropriate reasons, consequences, and testimonials.

6. Become part of the team and be willing to work on your own when necessary.

7. Be confident and bold enough to make decisions on your feet.

8. Be willing to adapt to the needs of the situation.

9. Be creative and innovative in solving customers' problems.

10. Take pride in your work, your contributions to the bottom line of your company, and your colleagues.

11. Manage your own development and do everything necessary to improve your life; take responsibility for your actions and avoid blaming others or feeling victimized.

12. Be goal-oriented; focus on solutions rather than on winning arguments with customers.

13. Agree to disagree without feeling the need to judge others or getting annoyed.

14. Be assertive and confidently state what is unacceptable without being aggressive.

15. Try to manage demanding customers on your own rather than passing the buck to your supervisor.

16. Keep learning from experience.

17. Display sportsmanship.

Whatever you are, be a good one.

Abraham Lincoln

Empowered people are confident, motivated, focused, enthusiastic, and committed. They take responsibility for their actions and their own development.

Every day, you may make progress. Every step may be fruitful. Yet there will stretch out before you an ever-lengthening, ever-ascending, ever-improving path. You know you will never get to the end of the journey. But this, so far from discouraging, only adds to the joy and glory of the climb.

Winston Churchill

HOW TO EMPOWER YOURSELF

☐ You must know specifically what you want and the reason for it.

☐ Be able to vividly imagine what would happen if you got what it is you want and what would happen if you didn't get what it is you want.

☐ Know where you are now and have a game plan on how and when you will reach where you want to be

☐ Be absolutely ruthless in your assessment of your current capabilities and handicaps; identify what resources you need to reach where you want to go.

☐ Be fully aware that to achieve what you want, you will have to sacrifice other things that you may like for the time being so that you can focus your full attention and resources on what you want.

☐ You must eat, drink, and sleep your goal and do whatever it takes to achieve what you want.

☐ However, in applying all of the above, you must be realistic.

☐ You should be aware of your attitude, thoughts, feelings, and behaviors, and develop a positive self-image.

☐ You should develop your relationships with your key customers, whether internal or external, and be appreciative of others and their needs.

☐ You should be honest and operate from a position of integrity.

☐ You shouldn't judge your customers; learn to appreciate others without the need to analyze. Rather, be sensitive to your customers emotions.

☐ Develop and apply common sense.

- [ ] Take responsibility for your work.

- [ ] Continuously strive to enhance your effectiveness, both at a personal and professional level: read self-development books, listen to motivational tapes, and attend seminars.

- [ ] Take control of your personal growth and job satisfaction.

- [ ] Seize every opportunity for personal development and fulfillment.

Know where you stand, where you want to be, and the strategies to get there, then go for it! Live with passion.

We are the creative force of our life, and through our own decisions rather than our conditions, if we carefully learn to do certain things, we can accomplish those goals.

Stephen R. Covey

ADVANTAGES OF EMPOWERING YOURSELF

- You become more alive and responsive to your customers.

- You become aware of your environment and focus more on assisting others.

- You get to decide what to do and what not to do, be in the driver's seat, and this often leads to rapid growth, both personally and professionally.

- You can exercise a greater number of choices; people with more choices cope better with the ups and downs of life.

- You become more motivated and creative. You become committed to what you want and persist until you achieve what you want.

- You have recognition from management, colleagues, friends, and relatives. You have better relationships.

- You become more objective; you plan, take action, and optimize resources.

- You feel energetic and are more fulfilled.

- You develop patience and fortitude.

Empower yourself to live a meaningful and joyous life.

Summary

1. *If you're not moving forward, you're actually moving backwards as others move forward.*

2. *Management wants to empower you; if you don't take the initiative and responsibility to empower yourselves, who will?*

3. *Empowered people are confident, enthusiastic, motivated, and committed; they take responsibility for their actions and their own development.*

4. *Know where you stand, where you want to be, and the strategies to get there, then go for it! Live with passion.*

5. *Empower yourself to live a meaningful and joyous life.*

Circumstances may cause interruptions and delays, but never lose sight of your goal. Prepare yourself in every way you can by increasing your knowledge and adding to your experience, so that you can make the most of opportunity when it occurs.

Mario Andretti

Chapter 13

BE ASSERTIVE, NOT AGGRESSIVE!

The basic difference between being assertive and being aggressive is how our words and behavior affect the rights and wellbeing of others.

Sharon Anthony Bower

Case Study 14:

Shawn and his colleagues were frantically trying to manage a huge crowd of customers who were trying to take advantage of a year-end bumper sale at a leading electronics store.

Most of the customers were impatiently waiting their turn, standing in long queues that moved at a snail's pace. Customer patience was low and tempers flared easily. Suddenly, out of the blue, a customer barged in front of the queue that Shawn was managing and demanded immediate attention. The customer claimed that he was a high-level government official and that he didn't have the time to wait in the queue! Shawn explained to this customer that there were other customers in line before him and that they too were waiting their turn. This seemed to infuriate the customer, and soon an altercation followed that aggravated the customers in the queue, took more time to manage, and in the end, served no one's purpose!

What do you think Shawn should have done?

1. Given in to the demands of this customer and avoided any altercation.

2. Flatly refused to attend to this customer and asked him to take his turn in the queue.

3. Asked the customer to come back later at a more convenient time.

4. How would you have handled the situation?

*The customer is always right; however, sometimes in the greater interest of all other customers, you have to be **cuassertive** to right the situation.*

BE CUASSERTIVE

Cuassertive ("a" is silent) is a word that I have coined by putting together the words "customer" and "assertive." It emphasizes that sometimes, when you cannot comply with overly-demanding customers, you have to express yourself in a way that doesn't upset your customers, and at the same time conveys your message effectively.

"Mr. Smartass, for your information, we don't sell spurious products! You bought this egg somewhere else!"

For example, most companies would rightfully refuse to refund a product not purchased at their store. Instead of accusing the customer with, "You didn't buy this at our store!" you could say something like, "We cannot refund this item because this was not purchased at our store." A statement that is non-judgmental and made in an impersonal or neutral tone can avoid sounding accusatory, as if the customer is trying to refund something that they did not purchase at your store.

In the customer service context, being cuassertive goes much deeper than the above example and involves:

a. Being polite and firm, but not aggressive or submissive.

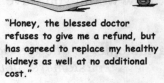

"Honey, the blessed doctor refuses to give me a refund, but has agreed to replace my healthy kidneys as well at no additional cost."

b. Explaining yourself and position without bias or prejudice.

c. Most importantly, being supportive or moving towards a solution that is acceptable to you as well as your customer.

Imagine a situation in which a customer requests a refund of a product that he purchased from your store. However, your sales policy clearly states "Goods, once sold, will not be refunded." In such a situation, you could point out to the customer that goods, once sold, are not refundable in a tone that is polite and firm, but not aggressive. You could then inquire into the reason why the customer wants a refund.

Depending on the situation and your company's policy, you could offer to exchange the product for another product in a similar price range or charge the difference. Alternatively, if the product was defective, you could arrange to have the product replaced or repaired.

The key difference between being cuassertive and being aggressive is how your customer perceives your response. *Being cuassertive helps you to respond politely, clearly, and with confidence as to what you can or cannot do, whilst acknowledging the needs of your customers.*

Furthermore, being cuassertive also means that although you cannot comply with the customer's request, you are willing to do everything possible to find an alternative that helps the customer to solve his problem. However, being aggressive is being reactive, i.e., taking things personally, blaming the customer, justifying, or feeling victimized. Becoming incensed with the idea that you are right and the customer is wrong is being reactive, and it invariably leads to aggressive behavior.

In short, being cuassertive connotes:

☐ Being able to say no to the customer politely and calmly without hurting their feelings; sometimes you have to keep doing this until persistent customers get your message.

"Now, if there is nothing else, I need to get back to the counter and assist other waiting customers. Let me know if there is anything else I can assist you with."

☐ Being honest with the customers and telling them directly what you can or can't do for them.

- Being non-prejudicial about the customers and their expectations.

- Offering to work with customers to resolve their issues.

- Managing customers who don't give us any mentionable business, and yet impose on our time, effort, and resources.

Honesty, transparency, and a little bit of tact can greatly help you manage demanding customers or situations.

WHEN DO YOU NEED TO BE CUASSERTIVE?

"Darling, I'm willing to take a step if you are. Otherwise, an amicable divorce with a befitting alimony is fine with me."

We need to be cuassertive when we are in conflict with our customers. Conflict develops when there is a difference between the customers' expectations or needs and what we did for them. Clues to such conflict can be discerned from the way customers behave with us, e.g., loud or demanding tones of voice, aggressive body language, etc.

Conflicts with customers usually happen because of two main reasons: failure to provide the service we promised, and not being able to meet customers' undue demands. In this chapter, we will discuss how being cuassertive helps in managing undue demands or in preventing such customers from twisting our arms.

Cuassertiveness helps you to resolve conflicts with your customers.

WHY AVOIDING CONFLICT DOES NOT WORK

We are always teaching others how to behave with us. Imagine one of your colleagues (internal customer), Charlie, keeps borrowing your stapler and always forgets to return it! When you need the stapler, you cannot find it and have to borrow one from another coworker. You have told Charlie many times to return the stapler after using it, but to no avail.

"Charlie, please DON'T take my stapler if you can't put it back in place after use. I can't find it when I need it."

You often think of telling Charlie in no uncertain terms that he shouldn't borrow your stapler if he cannot return it, but you never got around to telling him that because it could embarrass both of you.

Soon, Charlie starts to borrow your pens, pencils, and erasers, and it becomes extremely frustrating for you; you cannot find your stuff when you need it! Then, one day, your patience snaps, and you yell at Charlie in front of everyone in the office and tell him to keep away from your stuff. Charlie is not only surprised, but also shocked at your sudden and unexpected outburst, and thereafter, your relationship with Charlie is never the same again!

Who do you think was at fault? Was it Charlie? Or did you contribute to the souring of your relationship with him?

Do you think that if you had been assertive with Charlie from day one, you could have avoided the annoyance of not finding your stationery when needed, plus saved your friendship with Charlie?

Being assertive with Charlie would have been unpleasant for a while, but it wouldn't have cost you his friendship.

Is it not the same with our customers (external), especially the difficult and demanding customers? When we fail to advise them directly and clearly on what we can or cannot do for them, their expectations go unchecked, and they start taking us for granted.

For example, consider a situation in which a customer fails to pay you on time. You don't take up the matter with him immediately, and you continue to fulfill his orders. The customer takes you for granted and gives higher priority to paying other suppliers or diverts his resources to other business needs. Soon, he owes you a large amount of money and you take up the matter with him very strongly. When he fails to clear his dues, you respond by cutting his line of credit. To your surprise, he still delays paying you and starts a new credit line with your competitor!

Would you have tied up your money and lost this customer if you had taken the matter up with him in time and in a cuassertive manner?

Explicitly or implicitly, we teach our customers what to expect of us.

The way we communicate with others and with ourselves ultimately determines the quality of our lives.

Anthony Robbins

HOW TO BE CUASSERTIVE (A brief recap of what we have covered so far)

a. Be enthusiastic and have a positive attitude:
   • Acknowledge the customers when they come in contact with you.
   • Cheerfully greet customers to build rapport.
   • Don't forget to smile.

- Offer to assist the customer.
- Whenever possible, address them by name.

b.   <u>Put customers first:</u>
- Attend to them promptly.
- Make things easy and convenient for them.
- Bend rules where possible to accommodate their requests.
- Go beyond the call of duty and expectation in assisting your customers.
- Be sensitive to the sentiments of your customers.
- Start with the positives: focus on areas agreeable to you and your customers before moving into areas of conflict.
- Encourage the customer to work with you in finding a solution.
- If you can't resolve their problem, apologize for not being able to do so and invite them back with something such as, "We are sorry that we couldn't help you this time, but we hope to do better next time."

c.   <u>Present yourself clearly and with confidence:</u>
- Prepare for interactions with customers.
- Anticipate customers' needs, expectations, and concerns.
- Be articulate, specific, and clear about what you say to customers; communicate clearly and concisely.
- Make sure you are well-groomed and presentable.
- Validate what you communicate with reasons, consequences, examples, or testimonials as appropriate.
- Keep the customers separate from their behavior and address their behavior.
- Learn to respond to customers and refrain from being passive or reactive.
- Be very clear and specific about what you want to say, feel, or mean. Use "I" statements that are direct, but take care not to sound arrogant.

- Modulate your tone, body language, and overall demeanor to reflect your feelings and position. Use positive tones when being appreciative, thankful, or agreeing. Use neutral tones when you are being firm, decisive, or concerned. When you say no, say it in a manner that indicates no other possibility.
- Avoid reacting to customer sarcasm, manipulation, or malicious behavior as much as possible.

d.   <u>Frequently check for understanding, yours as well as your customers':</u>
- Paraphrase to check your understanding and to let the customer know you're listening.
- Check for customers' understanding by asking questions.
- Seek clarification.
- Ask the customer if there will be anything else that you can do for them.

e.   <u>Appreciate and empathize when appropriate:</u>
- Be appreciative of the customer's patronage; say thank you.
- Appreciate and praise customers for their choices.
- Appreciate anything dear to them, but stay away from flattery.
- Empathize when appropriate.

f.   <u>Behave professionally and be creative:</u>
- You should have excellent product knowledge and service expertise; you should be able to show how your product benefits your customers.
- Behave professionally. Be fully prepared to assist the customer with all necessary information and updates. Preempt their needs, communicate clearly and concisely, help customers to make an educated choice, be friendly but not familiar, and always keep your word.

- Perpetually enhance your knowledge and skills on customer psychology and the manner in which you communicate with them so you can assist customers to their fullest satisfaction.
- Think outside the box - be innovative in finding solutions to your customers' problems.

g. Focus on the customers and their needs:

- Listen, listen, and listen some more.
- If things are not clear, ask pertinent questions or paraphrase so that both parties clearly understand each other.
- Don't focus on your products/services or need to sell; rather, focus on the customer and their needs.
- Do everything possible towards building a business relationship with your customer.

h. Stay centered and keep your cool no matter what:

"I'll be mature. Even if you take my cake, I'll forgive you!"

- Whenever there is a breakdown in service or a chaotic situation, keep calm and in control of your emotions.
- Stay in control of your emotions when managing aggressive customer behavior. Staying in control and being cuassertive inhibits the buildup of tension and stress.
- Don't take things personally, and stay committed to assisting customers.
- Understand that irate customers do not know you personally, and they are angry or frustrated with the organization you represent and not you in particular.

- Stay committed to serving the customers in spite of their rude or aggressive behavior; this will enable you to win them back.
- Stay calm, as it will encourage the customer to calm down and will allow you to keep your wits under pressure.

We may be very busy, we may be very efficient, but we will also be truly effective only when we begin with the end in mind.

Stephen R. Covey

We can never judge the lives of others, because each person knows only their own pain and renunciation. It's one thing to feel that you are on the right path, but it's another to think that yours is the only path.

Paulo Coelho

i. <u>Take responsibility for your dealings with your customers:</u>
- Have open body language: be relaxed, don't frown, maintain eye contact (but don't stare), and don't cross or fold your arms.
- Empower yourself to take the necessary action in assisting the customer.
- Stay in control of your work; you are perceived by the customer as more reliable.

j. <u>Be a specialist: empathize, advise, appreciate, inform, support, rescue, recommend, etc.:</u>
- Guide the customer so that they can solve their problem in the best possible way.
- Respond to the customer's emotional needs first before giving him the product details.

- Recommend and suggest alternatives so that the customer has the satisfaction of being in control by making his own decision.

k. Don't judge customers:
  - Don't judge customers because of their race, creed, color, or religion; this can negatively influence your attitude and service levels.
  - Judging often leads to making wrong assumptions about the customer and stands in the way of developing a healthy business relationship with them.
  - When we judge customers, they in turn judge us, and the business relationship suffers.

l. Learn to say 'no' gracefully:
  - Avoid using negative words like cannot, shouldn't, will not, but, however, no, try, policy, etc. Negative words have negative connotations that trigger customers' negative feelings and emotions, even at a subconscious level.
  - Speak or communicate more in terms of what you can do for them than what you cannot do.

m. Apologize to your customers when you make a mistake:
  - Apologizing tells the customers that you care and regret the inconvenience caused to them; it is the first step to service recovery.
  - Be quick to apologize when you know that you or your colleagues have caused the service compromise; otherwise, empathize with them.
  - Use their names when you apologize; it personalizes the relationship between you and your customers.

n. When customers manipulate, bully, or pressure you to have their way, hold your ground and stay calm and neutral:

- Don't react to customers' manipulation or provocations.
- Learn to respond to and diffuse volatile situations while keeping your calm.
- When you stay calm and try to solve their problems, most customers realize that they have been unfair with you and become highly appreciative of your gracious attitude; they will stay with you!

Practice assertiveness with friends and colleagues first to develop your skills at being cuassertive with customers. However, to avoid any misunderstandings with your friends and colleagues, it is a good idea to inform them that you are practicing being assertive and encourage them to do the same with you.

Remember, being cuassertive costs nothing but has many benefits. It will make you more persuasive and effective in your dealings with difficult customers, and in the long term, they will rely on you and like you for it.

Take responsibility for the way you communicate with your customers, internal or external.

CUSTOMER RIGHTS

a. Customers have the right to change their minds about what they want or prefer.

b. Customers have the right to make statements without having to justify them.

c. Customers have the right to accept or ignore anything you say to them, even if it is for their own good.

d. Customers have the right to feel and express emotions, both positive and negative, without feeling guilty about it.

e. Customers have the right not to understand or empathize with your problems, genuine or not.

f. Customers have the right to reject your services without providing any reasons whatsoever.

g. Customers have the right to judge and criticize your product or services even though they may not be fully justified.

h. Customers have the right to leave your store in a huff and return later, expecting to be received, served, and treated like any other valuable customer.

i. Customers have the right to do all of the above and more without giving reasons or feeling guilty because they pay hard-earned money for our products/services, and we are there to serve them.

Customers have rights too; honor them to build customer loyalty.

TEST YOUR CUASSERTIVE QUOTIENT (CQ)

(Self-Assessment – 3)

Sr. No:	Cuassertive Criteria	High – Medium – Low (5 marks for High, 3 for Medium, & 1 for Low) Tick ✓			Why? (To be filled in only if your score is 1)	What are you going to do to improve on this attitude or behavior?
		High	**Medium**	**Low**		
1	You are **enthusiastic** and have a positive attitude towards your customers.					
2	You always put your **customers first.**					
3	You present yourself **with confidence and communicate clearly.**					
4	You frequently **check if you understand** your customers and vice versa.					
5	You are **appreciative** of your customers' patronage and **support.**					
6	You are a **specialist** or **subject matter expert** in your area of work and **behave professionally.**					
7	You focus on the **needs of your customers and care about how they feel (empathize).**					
8	You stay centered and **keep your cool** during any crises.					

9	You **do not take things personally**, and you stay committed to your customers no matter how they treat you.					
10	You take **responsibility for your dealings** with your customers.					
11	You are **always there for your customers:** to guide, advise, support, rescue, empathize, recommend, etc...					
12	You **don't judge** your customers.					
13	If you have to say no to customers, **you do so gracefully.**					
14	You say **thank you** to your customers and **do not hesitate to apologize.**					
15	You hold your ground without being emotional or adversarial; *you aim to resolve any conflict through a win-win negotiation.*					
Your total score:						

Assessment: Marks

0 – 15   This score strongly suggests you take action to improve on your CQ. Otherwise, ask yourself if you really want to make your career in customer service.

16 – 45   Work deliberately on improving your CQ. Select the skills that need to be improved and work on them one at a time so you can pace and measure your progress.

46 – 75   Excellent! Service providers like you give a good name to this profession. Keep up the good work!

Summary

☐ The basic difference between being assertive and being aggressive is how our words and behavior affect the rights and wellbeing of others.

☐ The customer is always right; however, sometimes in the greater interest of all other customers, you have to be cuassertive to right the situation.

☐ Honesty, transparency, and a little bit of tact can greatly help you manage demanding customers or situations.

☐ Cuassertiveness helps you to resolve conflicts with your customers.

☐ Explicitly or implicitly, we teach our customers what to expect of us.

☐ Take responsibility for the way you communicate with your customers, internal or external.

☐ Customers have rights too; honor them to build customer loyalty.

A customer is the most important visitor on our premises; he is not dependent on us. We are dependent on him. He is not an interruption in our work. He is the purpose of it. He is not an outsider in our business. He is part of it. We are not doing him a favor by serving him. He is doing us a favor by giving us an opportunity to do so   .

Mahatma Gandhi

Chapter 14

EDUCATE YOUR CUSTOMERS

We and our customers are partners in progress.

Mak

Case Study 15:

Michael was checking-in for a flight to his dream destination, Dubai in the Middle East. For him, there was nothing more relaxing than lazing around with friends in the sun and sand of the United Arab Emirates. However, Michael had one concern; he was tall (6' 9") and was carrying considerable carry-on luggage. He wondered how he would manage the six-hour flight squeezed into an economy-class seat! Restricted legroom was a perpetual problem he experienced whenever he travelled by air.

To his surprise, the lady at the check-in counter told Michael that since he was tall, she had checked to see if a bulkhead seat (i.e., seats in the front of the cabin where there is ample leg room in an aircraft) was available. She wanted Michael's concurrence to reserve the seat for him. She also advised Michael that for his future trips, he had the option of requesting a bulkhead seat when he made the reservation, and subject to availability, most airlines would honor his request. She suggested that Michael make his reservations as early as possible, because that way his chances of getting a bulkhead seat would be better.

Michael expressed his gratitude to the lady and boarded the aircraft literally dancing with joy! Once on the aircraft, Michael relaxed, stretched out his legs, and wondered why no other airline staff had educated him on requesting a bulkhead seat or the fact that he could increase the chances of getting such a seat by booking early. Michael was very pleased with the airline, and resolved to educate some of his basketball cronies who were as tall or taller and had the same problem.

Which airline do you think Michael preferred to travel with after this incident?

Educate your customers on how to get the best out of your products or services.

WHAT DOES EDUCATING THE CUSTOMERS MEAN?

Educating your customers means telling them how they can get the maximum benefit from using your products or services. Educating your customers should be one of your main priorities if you want your customers to keep returning to you. Failing to tell your customers, implicitly or explicitly, how they can get the most out of your products is nothing but negligence. Properly educating your customers requires that you become an expert in your field. To become an expert in your field or industry, you have to constantly educate and update yourself.

Read everything you can get your hands on that relates to your products or services, including anything related to your market, industry, or competitors.

Remember, we are in the information age. People want and need information that will help them get the best for their money. Providing our customers with information, suggestions, or guidance on how they can benefit from our products or services makes them feel cared for and enhances the value of our services.

Customers don't buy a product they don't understand, even if they have heard rave reviews about it.

No matter what your product is, you are ultimately in the education business. Your customers need to be constantly educated about the many advantages of doing business with you, trained to use your products more effectively, and taught how to make never-ending improvement in their lives.

Robert G. Allen

HOW TO EDUCATE YOUR CUSTOMERS

Demonstrating, showing, explaining, and above all, giving the customer a good experience educates them. For example, you may show your customer how easily she can write a document in Microsoft Word and convert the same file to a PDF format that looks professional. Once you have demonstrated the process, you can let the customer try converting the same file from Microsoft Word to PDF on her own. *In doing so, you've in fact given her an experience of success with the software.*

"See, this one will remind your husband of the alimony every ten minutes and deter him from divorcing you!"

Thereafter, she would keep coming back to you whenever she required software or related products.

Any form of product or service updates falls under the gamut of educating the customers – it could be through written material, like newsletters, product briefs in the media, recorded messages over the telephone, or face-to-face discussions. What is important is that you educate your customers on how they can access and use your products and get the maximum benefit without having to pay an arm and a leg for it.

Do not expect customers to know what your products or services can do for them unless you take the time to educate them. Customers look to us for guidance that will help them to choose the best possible solution to their problems. They look to us as specialists to protect their interests.

Educate your customers by demonstrating or letting them sample your product, so they know and experience how to benefit from it.

STEPS TO EDUCATING YOUR CUSTOMERS

Think about the last time you purchased a product and couldn't understand the directions on how to use it. This frequently happens to me when I buy electronic gadgets. For example, I find it difficult to figure out how to operate electronic recorders; especially if they are loaded with features that I don't understand! In hindsight, I have noticed that I gravitate to electronic shops where the attendants are electronic-gadget savvy and capable of explaining things to me.

Do customers appreciate being educated? <u>Yes, as long as it is done with respect and they are not made to feel ignorant or small.</u> Listed below are some pointers that can help you educate your customers without making them feel inferior:

Seek permission: Seek permission before embarking on educating your customers (e.g., "Mr. John, would you like me to show you how you can take photocopies on both sides of a page so you can save on paper?").

Emphasize & clarify the benefit: Whenever you educate a customer, always link the education to how they can benefit from applying the information you are sharing. For example, show the customers how they can reduce the maintenance expenses on their motor vehicles, or how they can save on heating bills by using your insulation products.

Respect their learning capabilities & styles: Even if a customer is slow in understanding your explanation, be patient with them. Not everyone has the aptitude to understand mechanical things. Make sure your manner is not condescending or condemning.

Information:

☐ Tell the customers what they don't know and what they need to know. First, establish what pertinent information the customers are unaware of before you educate them. Otherwise, the customer may feel offended or bored.

☐ Product updates and other pertinent information can be displayed at cash registers or notice boards or disseminated through emails, newsletters, and other media sources.

Price: If the price is high, explain to the customer why the price is high. Similarly, if the price is low, tell them why. For example, if the price is too high, you could explain that the product has a full guarantee for so many years inclusive of labor and parts for repairs. If the price is low, explain that there is a sale or promotion on the product for a limited period.

The customer should perceive your effort to educate them as an effort by you to benefit them.

Mak

Listed below are some of the positive things that can happen when you educate your customers. When properly done, educating your customers also helps in developing a bond with them that is of immense value; it keeps the customers coming back to you.

Advantages of educating your customers:

1. Your customers will perceive you as being more caring than your competitors.

2. They will have a positive experience using your product and develop confidence in you.

3. They will tell their friends and acquaintances, and you are likely to get referrals or word-of-mouth business.

4. You can update current and potential customers on your products and services.

5. Your customers will be willing to pay a good price for your products or services because they will see the value in it.

If you don't have the time to educate your customers on your products or services, they won't take the trouble to educate themselves.

Negative: (If you don't educate your customers)

1. Your competitors will win your customers over by offering products that may be inferior to yours.

2. Some potential customers will shy away from your products because they find them too complex to understand or too cumbersome to operate.

3. When they fail to get the desired result from your product because they don't know how to operate it, they will believe your product to be defective or of inferior quality.

4. Customers will perceive your products to be overpriced because they won't be able to see the value in them.

5. Customers will not know how your products have improved over time, or that they have added features and benefits.

The sole purpose of educating your customers should be to make it easy for your customers to access, use, and benefit from your products.

WHEN TO EDUCATE YOUR CUSTOMERS

Where possible, educate your customers before the transaction or purchase is completed; otherwise, the customer will feel cheated. Don't say, "Next time, please do this so you can take advantage of this scheme…" Rather, offer the scheme first and then let the customer know how they can access the scheme to their benefit in the future. However, this shouldn't stop you from demonstrating the full use of the product after the sales if you feel the customer will benefit from it.

When you give the extra service or benefit and educate the customer, he goes through a "wow" experience and appreciates being educated.

HOW TO FACILITATE YOUR CUSTOMERS' EDUCATION

1. Refer customers to websites, call centers, or information desks that your customers can contact at their own convenience to get information they need.

2. Invite clients to promotional events or product demonstration sessions to educate them about your products. Events like road shows, breakfast sessions, and seminars are all excellent ways of educating customers.

3. Leave brochures and leaflets at vantage points.

4. Publish write-ups on your products in local magazines, newsletters, etc.

Make provisions to educate customers' at all possible customer contact points.

Summary

1. We and our customers are partners in progress.

2. Educate your customers on how to get the best out of your products or services.

3. Customers don't buy a product they don't understand even if they have heard rave reviews about it.

4. Educate your customers by demonstrating or letting them sample your product so they know and experience how to benefit from it.

5. The customer should perceive your effort to educate them as an effort by you to benefit them.

6. If you don't have the time to educate your customers on your products or services, they won't take the trouble to educate themselves.

7. The sole purpose of educating your customers should be to make it easy for your customers to access, use, and benefit from your products.

8. When you give the extra service or benefit and educate the customer, he goes through a "wow" experience and appreciates being educated.

9. Make provisions to educate customers' at all possible customer contact points.

Chapter 15

This service agent just completed a sixteen-hour shift!

MANAGE YOUR STRESS LEVELS

The wise adapt themselves to circumstances as water molds itself to the pitcher.

Chinese Proverbs

Case Study 16:

Janice was a good employee and did well at her job as a cashier. On this occasion, it just so happened that that she was working the second night shift of fourteen hours at a restaurant located at the airport. The night before last, it was her boyfriend's birthday and they had partied the whole night long. Prolonged lack of sleep had exhausted her and she appeared haggard and worn out. To make matter worse, there was a considerable rush of customers due to the impending Christmas holidays; people were traveling to their hometowns to be with their near and dear ones.

Barely awake, Janice somehow managed to finish her shift at 0800 hours the next morning and planned to go home and hit the sack. As she counted the cash to reconcile the night's sales, she was horrified to notice that she had short-collected an amount that was more than a week's salary! The supervisor on duty was furious and all of her colleagues stared at her as if she had committed an unforgivable crime.

To Janice's surprise, not even her boyfriend was sympathetic towards her plight. He said, "I knew something like this would happen eventually!" Janice was very disappointed – she had lost money, sleep, and her credibility. She swore to herself that she would never let something like this happen again.

Do you think she could have avoided the stress caused by sleepless nights without giving up participating in her boyfriend's birthday celebration?

Leading a stress-free life requires forward planning.

WHAT IS STRESS?

Stress is the emotional or physical discomfort that we feel when subjected to pressures from our environment and/or events that we go through in life, and how we choose to perceive them.

In the service industry, front-line staff usually suffers from stress because of work pressure, difficult customers, and, at times, problems with immediate supervisors. Stress saps energy, motivation, and attention, and robs the service staff of their ability to attend to their customers effectively. Under stress, they do only what is necessary, and at times, snap at customers. Stressed staff members tend to argue with customers, and often get into shouting matches with demanding customers. Stressed staffs make more mistakes and prolonged stress leads to staff burnout.

Prolonged stress can adversely affect your productivity and wellbeing.

GOOD STRESS VERSUS BAD STRESS

We all know that stress is bad, but what is good stress? Small amounts of stress that enhance your will to succeed can be good. For example, short-term tensions like being nervous before an exam, making a presentation, participating in competitive sports, or managing a difficult customer can increase your stress levels, but they also can improve your performance.

Please note that such stressors are relatively shorter in nature and create a "can-do" attitude. They boost energy levels that enable you to do your best in important or critical situations. In fact, it would be impossible to be happy and content without challenging short-term stressors that spur you on to strive for things that you want in life.

Such positive stress helps you to face life challenges and live up to your potential. A life devoid of positive stress would be so dull that you would hanker for some excitement!

However, if stress gets out of control, it can harm your health, your relationships, and your mental wellbeing. Long-term stressors like constant worry, anxiety, or fear can wear a person down, both mentally and physically.

When long-term stress remains unaddressed, it drains you of energy, focus, motivation, and patience. Such a state adversely affects your productivity, and eventually, it can severely compromise your immune system. Prolonged stress often leads to life-threatening diseases like cancer, hypertension, tumors, cardiovascular complications, diabetes, etc. Therefore, understanding and moderating your stress levels is extremely important to leading a productive, meaningful, and balanced life.

The first step to managing your stress is to be aware of it.

YOU DON'T HAVE AN EASY JOB

Customers nowadays are more educated, more demanding, and more aware of their rights. Working at the front-line is not as easy as it used to be, especially if you are relatively inexperienced and awaiting your turn to train.

More often than not, we have people above us who are focused on completing tasks at hand, rather than coaching or mentoring us on how to become efficient service providers. Lack of the requisite knowledge about the products or services, little experience, and poor skills in managing and building relationships with our customers lead to high stress levels. This, at times, also culminates in a negative attitude towards our jobs as well as our customers.

An attitude that is less than enthusiastic keeps us from enjoying our jobs and being innovative. This, in turn, makes our supervisors doubt our intentions and abilities. The domino effect is that they avoid entrusting us with more responsibility and this lack of trust or empowerment further hampers our learning process.

In the end, the business suffers (i.e., everyone, including customers, the business owners, and all who are employed by the business). The point is that you as a customer service agent don't have an easy job, and the manner in which you adapt to your work can impact your service levels. We have to satisfy the customers, operate within bounds laid down by the company, and keep our superiors and colleagues happy, all at the same time–a difficult job, isn't it?

Customer service can be a stressful profession; if you don't deliberately manage your stress levels, you could compromise your service levels and your health.

SOURCES OF STRESS AT WORK

In general, the source of stress at work for the front-line staff falls under one of the following broad categories:

1. Work pressure and long working hours
2. Lack of product/service knowledge and skills
3. Shift work and extended hours
4. Conflict and disagreements with colleagues, supervisors, or customers

Because of the competitive nature of most businesses, the stress categories mentioned above exist in most businesses the world over.

There is very little that you can do to alleviate stress from any of the above at work; _however, you can considerably reduce the impact of each by changing the way you respond to them._

Every job involves stress; you have to manage it by developing coping strategies that work for you.

SYMPTOMS OF STRESS – MENTAL OR PHYSICAL

Given below are some of the common symptoms of stress at work:

Mental:

1. Constant tension without any specific reason
2. Irritation and snapping back at customers
3. Inability to focus on anything for a reasonable period of time
4. Constant lethargy
5. Propensity towards negative thoughts and expecting the worst

Physical:

1. Pounding heart
2. Nervousness
3. Stomach upset
4. Sweating – especially the palms (for some)
5. Dry mouth and thirst
6. Tensed muscles
7. (In extreme cases) difficulty breathing

HOW DOES STRESS WORK?

Whenever we perceive stress, our brain puts us into a state commonly referred to as the "fight or flight" response. The fight or flight response is our body's primitive, automatic, inborn response that prepares the body to "fight" or "flee" from perceived dangers or threats to our survival.

 Stress from internal anxiety or external threats triggers this survival instinct that prepares us to either fight the source of stress, or if we find it prudent, escape the source of danger. It helps us to flee the situation quickly.

When our fight or flight response is activated, the brain releases a cocktail of hormones commonly referred to as sympathetic hormones into our bloodstream that make us alert and resourceful, both mentally and physically. These hormones cause our body to undergo a series of dramatic changes almost instantly. Our respiratory and heart rates increase, and blood flows away from our digestive tract to the skeletal muscles that require extra energy for fighting or fleeing the predator. Our pupils dilate to see better, and our overall awareness intensifies. The fight or flight response primes us both physically and psychologically so we can deal with the source of danger by fighting it or fleeing from it. In this state, we tend to see everyone and everything as a possible source of danger. We think in a distorted manner and react to the slightest provocation with sarcasm, skepticism, vindictiveness, or just plain aggression.

The fight or flight responses helped us when we roamed the jungles, where dangers from wild animals and the elements lurked around every corner. At the first evidence of danger, the fight or flight response helped us to take action almost instantly, as every second counted for survival; we could either fight our best fight, or flee the scene as fast as possible.

Exertion uses up the sympathetic hormones in the bloodstream

However, today life has changed dramatically. We have buildings to live in that protect us from the elements, antibiotics to keep disease at bay, planes to travel long distances within hours in comfort and safety, automobiles to commute comfortably, and media and the Internet to keep us informed. Generally, we no longer have to worry about wild animals or mortal harm from fellow human beings, as we also have the protection of the law.

However, we now have difficult bosses, demanding spouses and customers, restless teenagers, and traffic jams that give us stress, none of which we can fight or flee without facing severe consequences! The problem is that our lifestyles have evolved, but our body, specifically our brain, has not!

The curious thing to notice here is that as primates of the jungle, whether we fought or fled the danger, it involved considerable exertion that metabolized the sympathetic hormones that originally triggered the response. In the jungle if the wild animal ate us, the story ended! On the other hand, if we managed to either successfully fight or flee from the danger, another set of hormones called parasympathetic hormones took effect that brought our bodies back to normal (i.e., the original state of rest prior to the appearance of the danger). However in prolonged states of fight or flight, we lose the ability to relax and enjoy the moment. We live from crisis to crisis and remain constantly vigilant; burnout becomes an inevitable outcome. Moreover, if the situation goes on unchecked, our immune system gets exhausted and the stress begins to manifest itself as one of the life threatening diseases mentioned earlier.

Burnout is like a car in neutral gear with its engine roaring on full throttle–soon, the fan belt, bearings, or something else gives way!

Mak

ARE YOU PRONE TO STRESS?

(Self-Assessment – 4)

1. Do you feel stressed at work?

    ☐ Most of the time   ☐ Sometimes   ☐ Never

2. Do you get good and restful sleep?

    ☐ Most of the time   ☐ Sometimes   ☐ Never

3. Do you stay energetic enough throughout the day?

    ☐ Most of the time   ☐ Sometimes   ☐ Never

4. When something undesirable happens, are you the kind of person who can let it go easily?

    ☐ Most of the time   ☐ Sometimes   ☐ Never

5. Would you say you are an organized person both at work and at home?

    ☐ Most of the time   ☐ Sometimes   ☐ Never

6. Do you find it easy to make routine decisions like what to wear, what to eat, or where to go?

    ☐ Most of the time   ☐ Sometimes   ☐ Never

7. Can you prioritize or focus on one thing at a time?

    ☐ Most of the time   ☐ Sometimes   ☐ Never

Charlie worked hard every day from 8 a.m. to 10 p.m. Of course, he died early, leaving his hard-earned money to his dear wife and her second husband to enjoy!

Mak

8. Can you find the balance between work and home without fretting about it?

   ☐ Most of the time   ☐ Sometimes   ☐ Never

9. Do you have friends that you look forward to meeting and spending time with?

   ☐ Most of the time   ☐ Sometimes   ☐ Never

10. Do you take time out for yourself – on your own and away from family or friends?

   ☐ Most of the time   ☐ Sometimes

   ☐ Never

11. Do you get involved in a physical activity or some sort of exercise at least three times a week?

   ☐ Most of the time   ☐ Sometimes   ☐ Never

12. Can you sleep on problems?

   ☐ Most of the time   ☐ Sometimes   ☐ Never

13. Do you make it a point to finish today's work today?

   ☐ Most of the time   ☐ Sometimes   ☐ Never

14. Do you get away and take a vacation once or twice a year?

   ☐ Most of the time   ☐ Sometimes   ☐ Never

15. Are you involved in some sort of social work?

   ☐ Most of the time   ☐ Sometimes   ☐ Never

16. Do you pray?

   ☐ Most of the time   ☐ Sometimes   ☐ Never

Mr. Faith, Ms. Patience, and Ms. Choice joined hands and kept the bad Mr. Stress out of town for good.

___ *Mak*

17. Do you have family and friends with whom you get together at least once a week?

☐ Most of the time　　　☐ Sometimes　　　☐ Never

18. Do you care for, look after, and spend time with a pet?

☐ Most of the time　　　☐ Sometimes　　　☐ Never

19. Do you participate in a hobby like gardening, painting, or cooking – something that allows you to be creative?

☐ Most of the time　　　☐ Sometimes　　　☐ Never

20. Can you do nothing and just relax without feeling guilty?

☐ Most of the time　　　☐ Sometimes　　　☐ Never

21. Do you make it a point to keep away from your stressors – social and situational?

☐ Most of the time　　　☐ Sometimes　　　☐ Never

22. Can you appreciate other people and their views without analyzing them too much or judging them?

☐ Most of the time　　　☐ Sometimes　　　☐ Never

23. Can you say no to others without feeling guilty?

☐ Most of the time　　　☐ Sometimes　　　☐ Never

24. Do you enjoy daydreaming?

☐ Most of the time　　　☐ Sometimes　　　☐ Never

25. Can you adapt to unexpected situations?

☐ Most of the time   ☐ Sometimes   ☐ Never

26. Can you easily forgive and forget?

☐ Most of the time   ☐ Sometimes   ☐ Never

Scoring: Give yourself points:

3 for - ☐ Most of the time

2 for - ☐ Sometimes

1 for - ☐ Never

Your total score: _ _ _ _ _

ASSESS YOUR SCORE:

65 and above: Excellent disposition! You're content with yourself and have a practical and down to earth approach to life. You are the kind of person who does not let stress buildup in the first place.

45 to 64: You're on the border of being stressful. If you work at it, you can stop stress from building up, and if you don't, there is always the chance that you could slide downwards into being stressful!

26 to 44: You're stressful. It may be a good idea to get some guidance on how to reduce stress and relax more. Consult a specialist on stress management. Exercise, take up a hobby, meditate, and restful sleep can greatly assist.

Holding on to anger is like holding on to a hot coal with the intent of throwing it at someone else; you are the one who gets burned.

Buddha

HOW TO KEEP STRESS FROM BUILDING UP

Practical stress relievers in the office:

1. **When customers get upset with you, don't take things personally:** The customer hardly knows you and is probably upset about some unmet expectations or some service compromise.

2. **When customers become upset, they become critical and difficult to satisfy:** In such situations, try to keep cool and close the gap between the customer's expectations and the service provided. It is a world of give and take; when customers find out that you're trying to resolve their problems, they reciprocate by being more accommodating towards the solutions you propose.

3. **When you start your shift, resolve that you'll stay in control of your mood:** Customers like to deal with service providers who are calm and composed. Besides, when you deal with your customers in a professional manner, it takes less time and effort to manage them and their needs.

4. **Keep stress from building up:** Whenever it becomes more stressful at work, spend more time at home to relax. Similarly, when faced with extraordinary stress at the home front, take a break from work. Remember, you're literally no good at managing customers when you are in a stressful state; you could do more harm than good when you are tense.

5. **While at work, take short breaks to stretch yourself:** When possible, move away from your seat or counter and share a few moments with a colleague over tea or coffee.

6. Don't take life so seriously: Learn to laugh often and share lighter moments with others. Focus on assisting others. Caring for others increases your threshold to manage stress – the satisfaction from caring for others makes serving others less stressful.

7. Divert your attention: Frequently get away from your computer and defocus your eyes; prolonged reading from the monitor screen engorges the eyes with blood and can cause headaches. Take a five-minute break from reading the monitor every two to three hours.

8. Stress-busters: Given below are three stress-busting techniques that are effective at keeping stress at bay when applied properly.

- **Power-naps:** Take power-naps (mini-naps of ten to fifteen minutes where you completely let go of everything and just slump into a comfortable chair, sofa, or cot).
  Power-naps are a quick way of replenishing your energy. Stress specialists in the health community have carried out studies indicating that people who are in the habit of taking power-naps during long hours of work live healthier and longer lives.

- **Three-minute meditation:** If it is not possible to take a ten to fifteen-minute power-nap, then three minutes of meditation can also alleviate stress quite effectively. Get away to a private and quiet place and sit in a chair with your eyes closed. While in

that state, take some deep breaths, slowly inhaling and exhaling, focusing completely on how the air is entering and leaving your nostrils, and just be.

☐ **Relax tensed muscles:** The mind follows the body and the body follows the mind. Normally, when you feel stressed, the body sends negative feedback to your mind, and the mind in turn responds by amplifying the negative feedback received and sends it back to the body. Soon, this pattern becomes a negative spiral that keeps going downward until it hits the threshold of stress.

However, if the cycle of feedback between the body and mind is broken, stress dissipates rapidly. The trick is to focus the mind on how the tense muscles in the body feel and let go. Focusing on the tense muscles helps the muscles to relax and in this way, the mind is kept occupied with focusing on tense muscles. The mind, once busy, cannot send stress signals to the body and the body becomes progressively relaxed. The body then has no chance to send negative feedback to the mind; soon, both relax and stress dissipates.

☐ **Isometric exercises:** If you're someone who works long hours at a desk, then isometric exercises can be very effective in warding off stress buildup. Isometric exercise is a form of resistance training in which the participant exerts a force (e.g., pushing or pulling) against an immovable object (e.g., the arm of a chair or a table) for a set duration of time and without much movement of the joints. Look up isometrics on the Internet for more details on this form of exercise.

- **Drink ample water:** Keep a bottle of water at hand and keep sipping from it whenever you get a chance. The bottle should preferably be made of glass and not plastic, as plastic containers leach harmful chemicals into the water they hold. Sip water every now and then before you become thirsty; doctors say that by the time you're thirsty, your body is already depleted of water!

  Drinking water in air-conditioned environments becomes more crucial, as air-conditioned air is very dry and leads to dehydration. Dehydration can cause a host of health problems. Even mild dehydration can cause excessive thirst, fatigue, headache, dry mouth, dizziness, constipation, etc.

- Moderate the use of coffee and tea: Say no to soft drinks and carbonated drinks like Coke or Pepsi with sugar, artificial flavoring, and preservatives.

- Stop using intoxicants: Stop smoking and avoid alcohol, even the night before work!

- Avoid high calorie food, refined carbohydrates, or excessively spicy food.

STRESS RELIEVERS WHEN AT HOME

1. Exercise – more aerobic then anaerobic (e.g., walking, jogging, swimming, cycling, etc.)

2. Hobbies – especially gardening

3. Socializing

4. Looking after pets

5. Meditating

6. Praying

7. Listening to music

8. Restful uninterrupted sleep for six to eight hours everyday

9. Reading

Stress is an ignorant state. It believes that everything is an emergency.

Natalie Goldberg

CONSERVE & MODERATE YOUR ENERGY AT WORK

As a customer service facilitator, I habitually notice the service levels at various shops and stores that I visit for our day-to-day consumables. Frequently, I notice that service agents are more accommodating and cheerful towards their customers at the beginning of their shift and become progressively detached and snappy towards the end of their shift. I noticed the same thing at airports, where the service agents are very helpful at the beginning of their shift; however, as time passes by, they became less enthusiastic in assisting passengers. For example, if you were to ask one of the airport attendants to direct you to the restroom at the beginning of their shift, chances are that they would cordially walk you to the restroom. However, six or seven hours into a shift, they would probably give you directions from where they are. If you happened to approach them in the last hours of their shifts, some are likely to ask you to follow the signs, barely hiding their irritation!

I believe that such a contrast in attitude and behavior happens because of fatigue that builds up with time during a shift; the further you are into a shift, the more irritated they become. However, the fatigue can be minimized if you, as a service provider, understand the process; simply conserve your energy and make an effort to spread it evenly throughout your shift and also keep stress from accumulating.

Simply speaking, don't overstress yourself in the beginning of a shift such that you have no energy left to manage the later part of your shift. Beware that as you work longer hours, you deplete your energy and tend to become irritable.

Take mini breaks, drink water frequently, stretch from time to time, and take at least two to three 'ten to fifteen minute power-naps' during a twelve to sixteen hour shift to manage your stress levels. Such habits can go a long way in preventing stress from accumulating.

Stress builds up drop by drop, like water dripping into a bucket; make sure you keep draining the stress so it doesn't build up to a level that makes you uncomfortable.

SUMMARY

1. The wise adapt themselves to circumstances as water molds itself to the pitcher.

2. Leading a stress-free life requires forward planning.

3. Prolonged stress can adversely affect your productivity and wellbeing.

4. The first step to managing your stress is to be aware of it.

5. Customer service can be a stressful profession; if you don't deliberately manage your stress levels, you could compromise your service levels and your health.

6. Every job involves stress; you have to manage it by developing coping strategies that work for you.

7. Burnout is like a car in neutral gear with its engine roaring on full throttle—soon, the fan belt, bearings, or something else gives way!

8. Holding on to anger is like holding on to a hot coal with the intent of throwing it at someone else; you are the one who gets burned.

9. Stress is an ignorant state. It believes that everything is an emergency.

10. Stress builds up drop by drop like water dripping into a bucket; make sure you keep draining the stress so it doesn't build up to a level that makes you uncomfortable.

When you find yourself stressed, ask yourself one question: Will this matter in 5 years from now? If yes, then do something about the situation. If no, then let it go.

Catherine Pulsifer

Chapter 16

LEARN TO NETWORK

It's not what you know but WHO YOU KNOW that makes the difference.

Anonymous

Case Study 17:

Jim was a mediocre staff member working at an airline call center located somewhere in the Middle East. There were more than a hundred and fifty reservation and telesales-agents working in shifts at this twenty-four/seven call center. The call center's main functions were to accept bookings, handle inquiries from passengers and local travel agencies, and also to coordinate special services requests with back office service departments and other airlines.

Often, problems arose because of miscommunication. For example, a passenger's booking would be cancelled by the reservation system automatically because the passenger or their agent failed to provide the ticket number purchased within the given time limit. Many such passengers claimed that they were not informed of the time limit. The reallocation of seats to such passengers closer to flight dates was sometimes difficult, as the flights were filled up by then and there weren't any seats left to offer.

Similarly, there were requests from local travel agents who issued tickets to their customers but undercharged them by mistake. The deficit amount had to be written off; otherwise, the issuing agent would be debited for the amount under-collected. Other problems came from passengers making special requests at the last minute, such as special meals, specific seats, medical attention, wheelchairs, etc. Arrangements for special requests take time, and sometimes arrangements can't be made last minute. For example, a passenger requests a vegetarian meal a few hours before the flight, and catering can't provide a meal requested at such short notice. If you know the chef in catering, then it would be a different matter. In such a situation, any discerning passenger would wonder how you managed their meal request at such short notice - a "wow" level of service!

Some of the above-mentioned discrepancies had to be resolved in favor of the customer or travel agent because of the volume of business they generated; after all, they were the airline's major customers. Whenever resolution of such discrepancies came to an impasse, Jim was summoned, and he somehow managed to resolve the most difficult and impossible cases promptly. Jim just made some calls to his colleagues and associates in other departments or friends in other airlines, and more than often, the matter would be resolved. Although Jim was no better than any other telesales-agent in other aspects of work, Jim was an expert at resolving such issues.

How do you think Jim resolved such issues quickly and amicably? Why was the other staff at the call center not able to do the same?

Excellence in customer service is not something that you can provide alone; rather, it is a product of networking and teamwork that leverages your ability to serve and solve your customers' problems promptly.

NETWORKING & BENEFITS

To reiterate, serving customers and resolving their problems is not something that you as a service agent can do alone. It requires the assistance of all of your other colleagues in the back offices and your suppliers who assist you in serving the customers as well as resolving their problems.

*You are a **contact point** for the customer who gets what they need through you.*

I have seen many service agents who have excellent product knowledge and are skillful at managing their customers; however, sadly enough, they don't have any network established with key people in their back offices that could assist them in resolving their customers' problems promptly! Contrary to such enlightened lone rangers, there is another breed of service agents that have relatively little product knowledge, but have excellent networks.

They understand that things cannot always be done by the book, and that to be effective they have to seek the assistance of key people in other departments who can help them to help their customers better.

Imagine you need to raise a requisition for replenishment of stock (a product), but don't have the time as the customer is already in front of you. What if you could just pick up the telephone, request your **key contact** in the store, and seek his assistance in rushing you the necessary replenishment? You could explain that you would send the paperwork or requisition later. Your contact obliges by prioritizing your need and rushes you the replenishment without the paperwork just because you have a close relationship with him.

Networking leverages your ability and effectiveness in managing customers because you have the combined effort and assistance of key people in the organization working for you. Sometimes, your colleagues in other departments are working to make your job easier after working hours even as you sleep! *In fact, networking is the single most effective strategy that you can use to advance in your career as well as build and maintain personal and business relationships.* Learning the skills for effective networking is worth the time and energy it requires, since it's such an important aspect of your life and work. Networking is all about building relationships with key people around you, people who can assist you and vice versa. The more effectively you network, the more effective you become in achieving what you want, because you're not alone and others (who are experts in their field) are there to assist you.

You could be a genius, but without a network, no one will know you; you will be a nonentity who has no means of applying his skills in assisting others!

The successful networkers I know, the ones receiving tons of referrals and feeling truly happy about themselves, continually put the other person's needs ahead of their own.

Bob Burg

NETWORK WITH YOUR COLLEAGUES

As stated earlier, you cannot produce and deliver the services that you provide to your customers all by yourself. You need the assistance of your colleagues in your section and other support departments all working together before the services become deliverable. You need to work as a team, and that means that you should have an excellent understanding with all the colleagues in your company, especially the colleagues that contribute to the development and delivery of the range of products and services you provide. For example some of the key people in your organization that you should network with are described below.

Seniors and bosses:

The seniors and bosses in your own and other departments are the movers and shakers in the organization. Network with them so that you can get your job done through them quickly and efficiently.

Keep this kind of network informed on relevant business issues and you'll find that all your communication with them is treated with priority.

Just make sure that while you deal with this kind of a network, you don't approach them with your customer problems only. Always have a set of possible solutions or alternatives that you can suggest. That way they won't have to work out a solution for you, rather choose and approve a course of action suggested by you. You're providing the service; you know your customer's problems better, so solutions suggested by you are likely to be more effective.

Colleagues and key people in support departments:

Customers usually have to go through a number of stages to access our service, and the service levels at all such stages has to be perfect before the customer experiences a "wow" level of service. We cannot provide excellent customer service on our own, and need the help of our colleagues within our department as well as those in the support departments. For example, when you travel by air, you make a reservation, buy the airline ticket, check in for the flight, fly onboard the aircraft, disembark at your destination, and finally, collect your bags. If the service is excellent throughout all the stages, you feel wonderful, but if you discover that one of your bags is missing on disembarkation, then the whole experience gets muddled up! To make things worse, if the staff at baggage services is not helpful, the whole experience can become a nightmare!

Have you noticed how one shortcoming in the service could compromise all other aspects of a trip that otherwise went so well? Is it any wonder that you need the support and assistance of your colleagues, and in some cases, even external suppliers to make your services stand out?

To provide effective customer service to external customers, you first need to network with internal customers.

CHARACTERISTICS OF AN EFFECTIVE NETWORK

1. Mutually beneficial: Effective networkers build mutually beneficial relationships with key people in their lives and at work; their motto is, "I scratch your back, you scratch mine." An effective networker selects the key people carefully, based on their necessary expertise and compatibility. It may seem a bit self-serving and egocentric; however, it is not so because the networker also benefits the key person in one way or another.

For example, you could develop an excellent relationship with your IT department manager, who could assist you with any problems related to your computer or use of software. In return, you could assist her with something you are good at. If you're in sales, you could help her to understand the sales perspective so that she could assist others in positions similar to yours better.

It is important to note here that you need not always be of a benefit to the other person professionally, as just developing a close relationship and keeping in touch can suffice; friends don't mind helping each other. Appreciation, gratitude, and the seeking of assistance can keep a network alive and benefit both parties.

Everyone in a network benefits from each other, - regardless of the extent of benefit.

2. Empowering: Both parties in a network benefit from this mutually beneficial relationship, and they empower each other to become more proficient at their work.

Let us take the example of the graphics on the first page of this chapter. The ticketing agent is getting the assistance of the key person in reservations to get her client a seat when the flight is relatively full. The ticketing agent in this case has empowered herself to assist a valued customer, and the key person had the opportunity to make a difference in the services the company provides to a regular client.

Now, you may ask, "How does the key person in reservations benefit?" or, "How can the ticketing agent reciprocate the favor received?" As stated above, there are numerous ways that the ticketing agent can appreciate the key person's assistance. For example, she can:

1. Be appreciative of the assistance received and provide feedback to the key person on how his assistance has helped the organization to retain the patronage of a major client.

2. Assist the key person's friends, relatives, or referrals with planning their itineraries and bookings for flights, hotels, and rental cars etc.

3. Maintain and nurture the relationship through other forms of appreciation, such as sending birthday cards, season's greetings, taking interest in the key person's hobbies, occasionally socializing with them, and so forth.

More business decisions occur over lunch and dinner than at any other time, yet no MBA courses are given on the subject.

Peter Drucker

3. Relationships: Network members do not keep count of how many times they help each other. It is not as if you can expect to receive help from others only as many times as you have helped them; networkers don't keep a tally of favors done or received.

Both parties keep in touch and seek each other's assistance when required. The assistance is provided more because of the relationship between them than any obligation, and they don't hold each other accountable. If one cannot assist the other, the other doesn't take it to heart; he simply trusts and accepts the key person's inability to assist implicitly.

Some of the biggest challenges in relationships come from the fact that most people enter a relationship in order to get something: they're trying to find someone who's going to make them feel good. In reality, the only way a relationship will last is if you see your relationship as a place that you go to give, and not a place that you go to take.

Anthony Robbins

4. Brainstorm: Network members can benefit immensely from each other by brainstorming for problem solving and other work-related issues; two or more heads are better than one.

5. It affords the individuals of a networking group different perspectives and ideas on how to approach the problem. Frequently, networkers help each other to solve each other's problems.

The best way to get a good idea is to get a lot of ideas.

Linus Pauling

Position yourself as a center of influence - the one who knows the movers and shakers. People will respond to that, and you'll soon become what you project.

Bob Burg

HOW TO BUILD YOUR NETWORK

Effective service specialists are always on the lookout for contacts amongst their colleagues in other departments. Listed below are the simple steps to building your network effectively and quickly:

1. First, establish what you want to achieve by networking with someone.

2. Second, identify the key people/colleagues in the back office or other departments that can assist you with your work/purpose:

   ☐ Make sure that you can get along with these people; compatibility is essential for a network relationship to sustain.

   ☐ Make sure that you have similar interests.

   ☐ Make sure that these people are reasonably accessible.

3. Determine the best way and time to make contact; a written plan with deadlines is highly recommended. That way, you will be able to structure your contact approach for establishing the network.

4. Make contact.

5. Follow up to develop and sustain the relationship.

Networking is an ongoing process that needs to be applied consistently to be of any benefit to anyone.

NETWORKING TIPS

1. BUILD RAPPORT - take interest in your key contacts:

☐ When possible, attend key contacts work-related meetings and conferences.

☐ While attending such gatherings, circulate and get acquainted with as many key contacts as possible.

☐ Let the key contacts know who you are, what you do, and your achievements without bragging or putting them off.

Rapport? You mean like, 'You run as fast as you can, and I'll throw it as far as I can'?

Jeff Kemp

2. BE OBJECTIVE - when requesting something from your key contact, be objective:

☐ First, make a simple mental strategy as to how you'll explain what help you're seeking; your reasons and

"How shall I present this to William so he can easily understand what I need?"

consequences will provide a compelling picture and context to your key contact.

- ☐ Be specific and get to the point. Be clear about what you want from your key contact

- ☐ Listen and do not interrupt to impress them; this is where things go awry.

- ☐ If they cannot help, ask if they know anyone who could.

- ☐ Never ever forget to thank them for their assistance and time.

When you have an important point to make, don't try to be subtle or clever. Use a pile driver. Hit the point once. Then come back and hit it again. Then hit it a third time - a tremendous whack.

Winston Churchill

3. **FOSTER RELATIONSHIPS** - focus on developing the relationship:

"This doctor is the best cosmetic surgeon in the country; I'll give you his contact information."

- ☐ Be appreciative of their assistance and always give positive feedback.

- ☐ Go out of your way to assist them when they ask for help.

- ☐ Converse normally without being apologetic or too excited.

- ☐ Keep in touch, especially with something that they find interesting and useful, or something that cheers them up.

It's all about people. It's about networking and being nice to people and not burning any bridges.

Mike Davidson

SUMMARY

1. It's not what you know but who you know that makes the difference

2. Excellence in customer service is not something that you can provide alone; rather, it is a product of networking and teamwork that leverages your ability to serve and solve your customers' problems promptly.

3. You could be a genius, but without a network, no one will know you; you will be a nonentity who has no means of applying his skills in assisting others!

4. To provide effective customer service to external customers, you first need to network with internal customers.

5. Everyone in a network benefits from each other, regardless of the extent of benefit.

6. More business decisions occur over lunch and dinner than at any other time, yet no MBA courses are given on the subject.

7. Some of the biggest challenges in relationships come from the fact that most people enter a relationship in order to get something: they're trying to find someone who's going to make them feel good. In reality, the only way a relationship will last is if you see your relationship as a place that you go to give, and not a place that you go to take.

8. The best way to get a good idea is to get a lot of ideas.

9. *Networking is an ongoing process that needs to be applied consistently to be of any benefit to anyone.*

10. *Rapport? You mean like, 'You run as fast as you can, and I'll throw it as far as I can'?*

11. *When you have an important point to make, don't try to be subtle or clever. Use a pile driver. Hit the point once. Then come back and hit it again. Then hit it a third time - a tremendous whack.*

12. *It's all about people. It's about networking and being nice to people and not burning any bridges.*

Chapter 17

"Imagine, you'll be the <u>first and only bloke</u> in the whole of Antarctica to own a fridge!"

FEATURES VS. BENEFITS

Customers don't buy products or services; they buy what the product or service can do for them. Similarly, you don't sell products or services, <u>but what your products or services can do for your customers.</u>

Mak

Case Study 18:

Years ago, I was responsible for a field sales team that covered a large region. The sales executives used company cars almost daily to travel to far-flung areas to meet our agents. Subject to the wear and tear on the cars, the sales executives were entitled to change them for new ones every two years. I was on the committee that decided on the purchase of replacement vehicles, and for that reason, the automobile sellers in town kept in touch with me.

One day, I read in the newspaper about one Mr. Suhail, who was declared the best car salesman of the year in the country. It came to me as a surprise, as I was well acquainted with this gentleman; he was one of the car sales executives who kept in touch with me in the hopes of winning the car replacement orders mentioned above. From what I knew about this person, I found it difficult to believe that he was the best car salesman in the country. However, when I read the number of cars he sold to individual clients, I was impressed. According to the newspaper, he sold one and a half cars per day on average – and the figure didn't include the cars that he sold to corporations like ours! Somehow, it did not add up, and I had my doubts about the statistics presented.

A few months later, when my wife got her driver's license, we decided to purchase a second car. While shopping for a medium-sized car, we ended up at a car showroom where Mr. Suhail was the sales manager. I introduced my wife to Mr. Suhail, and with a little sarcasm, I cautioned her. I told her that Mr. Suhail was the car salesman of the year and that he could sell any car to anyone! Mr. Suhail just smiled and proceeded to show a Japanese car to my wife.

He told my wife that in addition to being stylish, the car was very safe, sturdy, spacious, easy to maintain, low on fuel consumption, and best of all, it had a high resale value. Up until that moment, I was not impressed by Mr. Suhail and wondered how he managed to sell so many cars.

Anyway, as we talked about the car, a young man entered the showroom and showed interest in the same car at which we were looking. Mr. Suhail excused himself to attend to this customer while we considered the payment options.

We could overhear Mr. Suhail's sales pitch to this young customer, and he said things to this customer that he hadn't told us! He asked the young man to notice the sporty design of the steering wheel, and the thick wheels and low center of gravity of the car, which meant that it could negotiate curves at high speeds. He told him that the engine output was a formidable 185 horse power and it had two carburetors; the second carburetor kicked in when the car reached speeds over 100 km/h (kilometers per hour). He also told him that the car could accelerate from zero to 100 km/h in less than nine seconds.

We were surprised that he gave two sets of information to two different clients; and yet from the car's manual, we knew that he was telling the truth. For your information, Mr. Suhail sold one car to us and another to this young man!

Can you figure out why Mr. Suhail was good at selling cars?

The features of a product are the functions it can perform, whereas the benefits are the features in the product that appeal to a particular customer. In the above example, my wife, a housewife, was predominantly focused on safety, durability, and resale value, whereas the youngster wanted speed, power, and maneuverability.

FEATURES, BENEFITS, & ADVANTAGES

Features: All characteristics of a product are referred to as its features (e.g., a wristwatch has hour, minute, and second hands, an alarm, a stopwatch, countdown facility, is waterproof and shock-resistant, etc.)

Benefits: Benefits, on the other hand, are what the customer gains from one or more of the features. For example the alarm could be a beneficial feature to a busy executive who has to keep many appointments every day. It reminds the executive of the meeting and helps him to get ready in time.

Similarly, there could be another customer who is a 100-meter sprint runner and the stopwatch feature in the same watch becomes a benefit to the runner; it helps him to measure the time he takes to run 100 meters. Likewise, another person who goes scuba diving will benefit from the waterproof feature of the watch. As it is waterproof, the watch will not malfunction under water. In simple terms, the features are the attributes, functions, or different aspects of a product or service, and the benefits are what these features can do for a particular customer.

Therefore, the same product with many features can have different benefits for different customers.

Benefits are what customers pay for.

Advantages: Advantages are statements about what a product or service can do, and they are not directly linked to a particular customer's need. *The difference between advantages and benefits is that while the customer may see some advantage in a product, she will not necessarily buy the product based on the advantage alone.* For these customers, the advantage is good to have, but they wouldn't necessarily pay for it. For example, a grocery store located next to your house may give you the advantage of saving time when commuting for groceries. However, you wouldn't shop there only because of its proximity; if it doesn't provide the quality and bargain you want, you may decide to shop somewhere else.

Therefore, advantages are the extra features of a product or service that the customers may appreciate, but for which they wouldn't necessarily pay.

Another good example of advantages can be seen in mobile phones. Many adult mobile phone users appreciate electronic games in their phones; however, for many customers, it is not a criterion on which they will base their buying decision. The games function will add some value to the phone, but the customers may not perceive it as a necessity.

Features tell,

Advantages are good to have, &

Benefits sell!

WHY SELLING FEATURES DOESN'T WORK

When you as a service provider embark on extolling the features of a product, the customers get bored. They get bored because not all the information that you give out regarding the product relates to them, and they cannot see how the product will benefit them. At best, they appear to be attentive, but get distracted. They switch off and their minds wander off to other things they find more interesting. In fact, in certain situation, the customer can develop apathy towards you and anything you have to offer!

Further, once the customer stops listening to you, there is hardly any chance that they will buy from you. When they stop listening to you, they cannot link your solution to their problems. Additionally, because they cannot see the solution in your product, they may find it irrelevant or overpriced.

Mr. Feature and Mr. Benefit both went to town. While Mr. Feature said, 'Hi' to everyone in town, Mr. Benefit made a few close friends.

Mak

Customer cannot relate to features; they are interested in the benefits that help them to solve their problems.

WHY SELLING BENEFITS WORKS LIKE A CHARM

When you sell benefits, you have your customers' complete attention and they take interest in what you say to them. Benefits tug at the customers' emotions and emotions move the customer to buy. It is worth repeating that when you sell benefits, you link the solution in your product to your customers' problems.

You may find the manner in which your solution benefits the customer obvious, but the customer has a million things on their mind and they seldom make the connection on their own. Assuming that they can connect the benefit in the product with their problems is taking things for granted. Remember, when you assume, you make an "ass" out of "u" and "me!" When you present the benefits to your customers properly, they can see clearly how your products will benefit them and they seldom raise any objections. Your product appears to be a good bargain, and price becomes less of an issue.

Benefits make it a bargain for your customers.

BENEFITS & OBJECTIONS

A customer who is totally disinterested in your products or services is likely to walk away without asking any questions. However, if the customer is interested in your product, but has some concerns about it, then there is a high probability that he will raise objections to clarify his concerns. *From that point of view, objections are benefits that your customers cannot see.*

Objections are usually the result of benefits not properly explained or understood by your customers. For example, if you are selling a computer to a customer who seems to be asking a lot of questions or raising objections, it may mean that the customer is interested in the computer, but has some concerns that are stopping her from buying it.

The customer may not be consciously aware of her concerns, but she will be uneasy about something. She may have concerns because you have not explained the benefits to her properly; in other words, she hasn't fully understood how the computer will benefit her.

Therefore, you should first verify what your customers need, then make them consciously aware of those needs. Once you have established their needs, you can then relate the benefits of the product that satisfy those needs. *When you make your customers consciously aware of their needs and then show them how your product will meet those needs, the customer's objections simply vanish in thin air.*

Nevertheless, you should preempt all possible objections and prepare accordingly. Being prepared for customer objections will help you to field them effectively.

When customers object, it's more than likely that they are interested in your product/service but have not fully understood the benefits to them.

"It's a cozy and compact house that is easy to maintain... your wife will love it!"

USE BENEFITS TO RESOLVE OBJECTION

Sometimes, when customers raise objections that do not make sense or do not relate to any benefit that they have not understood, it is best to:

- ☐ Ask questions to identify from where the objection is coming. Identify the reason for the customer's objections and then take care of it by explaining the related benefit/s. For example, ask "What exactly is your concern that is stopping you from considering this product?"

- ☐ When the source of the objection is not identifiable, the best thing to do is back up and again enumerate the benefits. Start at the beginning of the list of benefits and go through each, making sure that the customer understands and sees value in them; you may want to check from time to time if the customer is with you.

- ☐ Customers also object when they cannot make a decision on their own or when they don't want to purchase because of financial constraints.

In the first case, arm the customer with ammunition so that he can justify the purchase to the person who is the decision maker. For example, if the product in question is a microwave oven and the main decision maker is the customer's wife. In situations where the customers do not have enough funds to purchase the item now, show them items that are more affordable; failing that, thank them for their interest and invite them to come back again when convenient.

Benefits and objections are inversely proportional.

CONVINCE ALL THE STAKEHOLDERS

One of the mistakes that salesmen make is to talk only to the decision maker and ignore others who are stakeholders in the product or service. Remember, those with access to the decision maker can positively or negatively influence the buying decision. This happens quite often in corporate sales and with personal purchases involving large investments such as property, motor vehicles, jewelry, etc.

More than often, the salesman sells the idea successfully to the decision maker – say, the "man of the house" and completely forgets that the customer is inevitably going to discuss the possible acquisition with his better half. Moreover, if the better half doesn't see the value in the purchase, then the idea can go back to the drawing board! You must neutralize the objections that can come from the other stakeholders, especially those to whom you have limited access. Otherwise, things could go wrong unexpectedly and they could undo all your hard work. Therefore, it is crucial that you arm the decision maker with benefits not only relevant to them, but also to the stakeholders, such as wives, husbands, other managers, etc. When you have all stakeholders on your side, your position becomes extraordinarily strong and you can expect to make the sale without a hitch.

Years ago, when I was looking after the field sales team of an airline that had installed personal video systems on their aircrafts, we approached the schools and sold the idea to children, saying they could watch cartoons or play video games while traveling by air. We then told the parents that they would be able to travel in peace, as they wouldn't have to chase after their children running around in the aisles all over the aircraft. The idea worked so well that our flights were almost full despite the fact that our prices were much higher than those of our competitors. It was a win-win for all.

Another advantage of enumerating all the benefits for the decision maker and the stakeholders is that it can keep the competition at bay.

Appoint the decision maker as your spokesperson; arm them with the benefits for all of the stakeholders.

SUMMARY

1. Customers don't buy products or services; they buy what the product or service can do for them. Similarly, you don't sell products or services, but what your products or services can do for your customers.

2. The features of a product are the functions it can perform, whereas the benefits are the features in the product that appeal to a particular customer. In the above example, my wife, a housewife, was predominantly focused on safety, durability, and resale value, whereas the youngster wanted speed, power, and maneuverability.

3. Benefits are what customers pay for.

4. Features tell, advantages are good to have, and benefits sell.

5. Customers cannot relate to features; they are interested in the benefits that help them to solve their problems.

6. Benefits make it a bargain for your customers.

7. When customers object, it's more than likely that they are interested in your product/service but have not fully understood the benefits to them.

8. Benefits and objections are inversely proportional.

9. Appoint the decision maker as your spokesperson; arm them with the benefits for all of the stakeholders.

Chapter 18

"Dear Sonia, can you imagine how badly you could be hurt if you lost control of the car at such a high speed?"

PUT THE CUSTOMER INTO THE PICTURE

Mankind is governed more by their feelings than by reason.

Samuel Adams

Case Study 19:

Imagine the police gave your teenage sister a ticket for rash driving. The incident is disturbing, and you are concerned that if she continues to drive recklessly, she could end up in an accident that could be fatal for both her and others! There are two approaches open to you. One, you tell her in no uncertain terms that rash driving is unacceptable. Alternatively, you try to make her realize that the risks involved with reckless driving are not worth it. The question is, which approach do you think is likely to work?

We as human beings are usually critical of being told to do or not do something; such input is usually blocked subconsciously. This is because the idea is coming from someone else and our psyche perceives it as an imposition. However, when the ideas, thoughts, or intentions are our own, we are not so critical of them. Let us elaborate more on the above so that we have a clearer understanding of the effectiveness of making others realize as compared to telling others.

Telling:

In the above incident, if you were to tell your sister not to drive recklessly, you would probably do so in a stern manner that could be perceived by your sister as a rebuke, something like, "Your rash driving is endangering your own life and the lives of others. This is unacceptable. Please drive safely."

Your sister may accept what you say to her on a logical level, but on an emotional level, she may not feel so good about you telling her that her driving is rash. In her thoughts, she could be saying, "My dear big brother, you always worry too much!" Or, if she is the extrovert type, she may say to herself, "It is my life and my car, and I know what is right and what is wrong. Save the speech for someone else!"

Making others realize:

The other option would be to try to make her realize the hazards of reckless driving. You could do this by asking her how fast she drives. Show understanding to build rapport by saying something like, "I know at your age the excitement of driving fast is almost irresistible; when I was your age, I too sometimes couldn't control myself and gave in to the temptation of driving fast." Build rapport with your sister so that she listens to you and is more accommodating.

Then, ask her what the chances of fatalities at such a high speed are. Ask about the possibilities of permanent disability and what life would mean to her if she were to become permanently disabled. Ask how she would justify the loss of lives or severe injuries to innocent others due to her negligence, e.g., bystanders, others in her vehicle, or those in other vehicles. Make sure that you give your sister a chance to ponder or answer each of your questions so that she thinks about what you say to her.

In this case, your sister would have to think about an accident to process your questions. She would have to conjure up an accident scene in which she would see herself lying in the mangled wreck of her car, bleeding helplessly. In her imagination, she would see a ghastly bloodbath, torn flesh hanging loose, or broken bones sticking out of bodies. Not a pleasant sight, is it? In a way, she would have gone through the accident, but only in her mind, and chances are that the imagined scenario would make her drive more responsibly.

Which of the two approaches do you think would be more convincing?

Don't tell your customers; rather, put them in the picture. They will convince themselves.

HOW PHYSICAL SENSES HELP US PERCEIVE

We have five senses. We have the ability to see, hear, taste, smell, and touch. These senses allow our brains to make sense of what is happening around us. In other words, we perceive our world through these senses.

The depth of our perception depends on how many senses are <u>involved simultaneously in perceiving something</u> and the <u>intensity of each sense involved</u>.

For instance, if we see a silent black-and-white movie clip of someone cooking our favorite dish, it probably would not be so appealing. Now, if we were to add the sizzling sound of the food frying, it would probably have more impact. Then, if color were added to the clip, you would probably start drooling. However, we could, make it even more effective if we were to see someone physically cooking the dish instead of just a movie clip. In this case, you would be able to see, hear, and smell the aroma of the dish in real terms, and if someone offered you some of that food to taste, you would use your fingers to pick up the morsels (touch) and savor (taste) it.

Is it any wonder why shrewd car salesmen insist that their customers test-drive the car? By letting the customer test-drive the car, they increase the customer's motivation to buy it. While test-driving the car, the customer feels the smooth operation of a new car, notices the quiet hum of the engine, sees the immaculate upholstery, and smells the pristine scent of new leather. These are all positive signals from four different senses, and the impact of their synergy can make the car irresistible!

Sensory input strongly influences customers to buy, so where possible, let customers sample your products.

PHYSICAL SENSES MAKE ALL THE DIFFERENCE

Most service agents don't make any significant impact on their customers because they just tell their customers about the product or service in question. A few take the trouble of showing the product, which is more effective than telling; a picture is worth a thousand words! *However, service agents should try to make their customer feel.* That is, give the customers an experience of the product by appealing to all their senses simultaneously. The more senses involved, the higher the level of persuasion. Service agents that make their customers feel have more success at winning them over. *They not only tell, they show, and most important of all, they make their customers feel good.*

For example, consider ladies who are buying dresses. The shopkeeper lets the customers touch the fabric, put it on, and look at themselves in a mirror, and when appropriate, remarks that the fabric really suits them, appealing to their senses of touch, sight, and hearing.

"You are a rage in that dress!"

Besides making the customers feel good, the above technique can also make the customers like you, the beginning of a relationship or customer loyalty. Although the customers may not know why they like you, they would definitely notice that for some reason, they find it more pleasurable dealing with you.

Don't merely tell or show, better yet, make your customer feel it.

WHY FEELINGS ARE MORE EFFECTIVE

Let me ask you two very simple questions. First, what did you eat for dinner eleven days ago? Second, do you remember how it felt when you kissed for the first time? Or the day you got married? (Your first marriage, that is, of course!☺)

In all likelihood, you wouldn't be sure of what you ate eleven days ago. At best, you would struggle to answer the question. On the other hand, it is likely that you would be able to provide a detailed answer to the second question! Do you have any idea why you easily could recall what happened years ago and yet had difficulty in recalling things that happened just a few days ago?

Well, our memories depend on the intensity of the emotions we feel during an incident; the more emotional we are (feelings) during an incident, the longer we can remember it, and vice versa. For example, events like our first kiss, a horrific accident, our wedding day, getting fired, or a fight with loved ones can be emotionally charged, and it is unlikely that we will ever forget them. Further, the effect of one sense plus another sense doesn't merely double the level of perception or depth of memory, it increases it many times over. When three senses are involved in perceiving something, the intensity of the perception becomes even greater. The synergy of many senses working together increases the perception or feelings exponentially!

Your first kiss and your wedding were significant moments in your life, and at significant moments like those, all your senses and emotions worked overtime to capture the moment. When all the senses work together, they complement each other, and because of the synergy involved, the intensity of each sense automatically rises.

Consider another example where students preparing for exams the night before read aloud and pace up and down to concentrate. They are seeing and hearing what they read aloud and the pacing up and down is physical movement that becomes associated with the other two senses to form stronger memories.

In other words, the higher the intensity of each sense we feel and the number of senses we use in processing an incident, the more powerful and indelible the perception or memory of that incident becomes.

Therefore, telling the customers how good your product is isn't effective, as the customers can only hear you. Showing them a picture is better, as sight is a more powerful sense than hearing for most people. However, letting the customers sample your products is by far the most effective method. In sampling your product, they not only see the product, but also feel it by using a number of other senses.

Remember, intense perceptions lead to long-term memories, and when long-term memories are played back repeatedly, they create strong attachments that lead to powerful emotions. That is why you miss your loved ones so much when they are away and have such ecstatic reunions with them when they return.

In the context of customer service, when you induce positive feelings in your customers, they feel good and keep returning to you for more. When this process is repeated a number of times, they become attached to your product or services.

Make your customers feel the excitement and have a positive experience in using your services, and they will keep coming back for more.

The positive effect of kindness on the immune system and on the increased production of serotonin in the brain has been proven in research studies. Serotonin is a naturally occurring substance in the body that makes us feel more comfortable, peaceful, and even blissful. In fact, the role of most anti-depressants is to stimulate the production of serotonin chemically, helping to ease depression.

Research has shown that a simple act of kindness directed toward another improves the functioning of the immune system and stimulates the production of serotonin in both the recipient of the kindness and the person extending the kindness.

Even more amazing is that persons observing the act of kindness have similar beneficial results. Imagine this! Kindness extended, received, or observed beneficially impacts the physical health and feelings of everyone involved!

Wayne Dyer

WHAT ABOUT INTANGIBLE PRODUCTS?

When you're selling a car, it is practical to invite the customer to test-drive the car. However, what if you sell intangible products or services? Say you sell life insurance, ocean cruises, or vacations. These products or services are intangible; how would you make your customers feel the excitement when there is nothing to see, touch, hear, taste, or smell? For vacations, you could probably show some pictures of the exotic destination, but how do you sell life insurance? Surely, you cannot ask the customer to die and sample how quickly their nominee is given the assured sum!

The key is to make the customers _imagine_ the thing or situation that you are trying to sell.

For example, make them imagine how nice it would be to go on a vacation to the clean beaches of Puerto Rico. **_Ask them to imagine_** the clean and open beaches that extend for miles, the wet sand under their feet as they walk on it, or the sound of crashing waves on the rocks. Asking appropriate questions will induce your customer to visualize what you are trying to tell him, and in the process, your talk will have a greater persuasive impact.

When customers visualize what you tell them, they can see, feel, smell, touch, taste, and hear the beach in their mind's eye. It is the same process if you were to close your eyes and think about squeezing a fresh and ripe lemon into your mouth. Most people start to salivate in spite of the fact that there is no lemon and it exists only in their imagination.

Imagination triggers the five senses because the brain doesn't experience the world around it directly. It experiences the world around it by deciphering the electrical and chemical signals that the five senses provide. For example, the eyes send the visual signals through the optic nerves deep inside the brain where the signals <u>get</u> <u>interpreted</u> into something meaningful. Inside the brain, it is totally dark; the brain cannot see on its own.

The customer's does not analyze the product you sell to him, rather he responds to his perception of the product you present to him.

POSITIVE IDEAS SELL WHILE NEGATIVE IDEAS DWELL!

"When you die..!"

There's an old story about two salesmen selling life insurance. One of the salesmen was in his fifties and had more than 33 years of experience in selling life insurance. The other was new at selling life insurance and was barely 20 years old.

They would both go to the weekly bazaar and take turns making their sales pitches while standing on an empty wooden crate. The senior of the two would make his sales pitch first, and usually within a short while, a large crowd would gather to listen to what he had to say. At the end of the speech, a large majority of the crowd would pick up the application forms so that they could apply for a life insurance policy. The new recruit then would wait for a while and take his position on the crate to make a small speech to a scanty crowd. On certain days, he would be lucky if someone from the small audience would come forward and pick up an application form. Yet, at the end of most months, the younger salesman with relatively no experience was selling more life insurance than the much wiser and experienced partner!

Do you have any idea what was going on here?

You may have guessed it: the experienced salesman used to create a morbid picture by asking the audience to imagine that they had moved on to the next world and what would happen to the families that they left behind? Who would feed and clothe them? The idea terrified most of the audience members, and they picked up the application forms, intent on buying a policy to protect their families after their demise. However, by the time they reached home, they avoided the thoughts connected to their death and the plight of their families thereafter, for they had other, more appealing things on which to focus.

However, in the case of the younger salesman, he would ask the audience members what their wives would think of them when they showed them the insurance policy in the evening.

Wouldn't their wives be appreciative of such caring husbands? Wouldn't their wives cook their favorite dish for dinner that evening? Not to mention the scenario after lights out! What about the next day? Wouldn't their wives be boasting to the neighbors, "My husband really cares for me. See, he bought a life insurance policy for me and little Charlie; do you guys have life insurance?"

"You know, my Georgee cares so much, he bought a life insurance policy yesterday, just in case...!"

Good news sells, and the closer you bring the benefits, the more persuasive you become.

SUMMARY

1. Mankind is governed more by their feelings than by reason.

2. Don't tell your customers; rather, put them in the picture. They will convince themselves.

3. Sensory input strongly influences customers to buy, so where possible, let the customers sample your products.

4. Don't merely tell or show, better yet, make your customer feel it.

5. Make your customers feel the excitement and have a positive experience in using your services and they will keep coming back for more.

6. The customer's does not analyze the product you sell to him, rather he responds to his perception of the product you present to him.

7. Good news sells, and the closer you bring the benefits, the more persuasive you become.

Ask your customers **good questions** that <u>help them to imagine</u>, when they **imagine**, they **feel**, and when they feel, <u>they are **convinced**</u>; telling only falls on deaf ears!

Mak

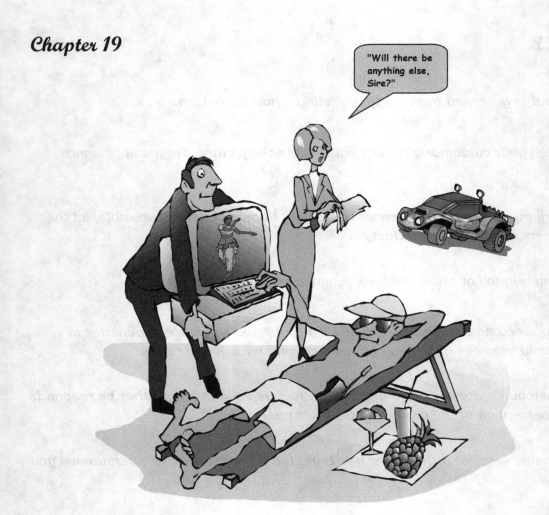

Chapter 19

ROMANCING YOUR CUSTOMERS

Customer service is about perceptions, feelings, and emotions. Emotions like excitement, joy, love, desire, and passion, etc., give customers a memorable experience.

Mak

Case Study 20:

Once upon a time, there were two real estate salesmen working in a large city that was going through intense development. The government was building new roads, bridges, and flyovers. The private sector was busy developing housing projects in every nook and corner of the city.

One of the salesmen was an expert in the technical aspects of the real estate business and the other was new to the business and just had a working knowledge of the industry. However, the inexperienced salesman was an expert with people; he could persuade his customers with relative ease.

Both were selling three to four properties per month on average. The only difference between them was that the salesman who was the technical expert usually had to work harder and took longer to sell the properties. The other salesman, the people expert, hardly ever went out of the office, and when he did, it was mostly to show a property to one of his potential clients.

The manager of the real estate company noticed that the technical expert's clients usually wanted to see the property more than three to four times, but that the people expert's clients seldom requested a second look. The manager found the pattern intriguing and wanted to get to the bottom of it. He thought that if both could copy each other's strengths, then both could increase their productivity – a win-win for everyone.

What do you think the real estate manager found out?

You guessed it: *the technical expert was selling houses whilst the people expert was selling homes!*

Don't sell products or services, sell dreams.

"I'll never make you cry. I'll never hurt you, & I'll always be there when you need me...!" ♫

Legend has it that Mary Ann never returned home to her family after that concert!

THE POWER OF EMOTIONS

Memories, beliefs, attitudes, and thoughts all make up and influence our emotions, and our emotions drive our behavior. Compared to emotions, logic, on its own, is a poor motivator. When there is a tie between emotions and logic, emotions eventually dictate the choices we make.

Emotions influence customers more than logic. *However, if we can trigger the emotions of our customers and provide logical reasoning that supports that emotion, then our argument becomes extremely persuasive.* On its own, logic can seldom move customers to buy. Logic is based on facts, and facts are dry statistics that seldom move people.

Emotional patterns take years to form and operate through feelings. Feelings are the strongest of motivators. That is why advertisers frequently resort to feelings of joy and fear to make their advertisements compelling. Mobile telephone manufacturers sell the joy of talking to distant family from anywhere and anytime. Internet advertisers' work on the customer's fear of losing a good deal that "expires today," and yet the next day, the same advertisement still reads "expires today!"

Note that the emotional buildup of men, women, and children differs significantly. For example, chocolates, flowers, and jewelry influence most women profoundly. Men, on the other hand, usually like to make strong statements with flashy cars, cigars, and expensive suits. Children inherently like games, toys, and storybooks.

Appeal to customers' emotions to be more persuasive.

Dreams and fantasies: In every one of us, there lives a dreamer, and all of us have fantasies. Our dreams and fantasies generate powerful emotions in us.

We, as customers, relate better to products or services that help us to materialize our dreams or live out our fantasies. It is for this reason that customers buy without resistance when they find that they can live out their dreams or fantasies through a product or service.

Imagine you are buying a suit and the shopkeeper says to you, "This is the latest design, and the material is durable too." Alternatively, he could have said, "The suit makes you look sophisticated and elegant. I'm sure the ladies would appreciate your choice." Which statement is more appealing? Probably the second, right?

Emotionally and positively charged customers not only buy more and do so readily, they also feel good about their purchases.

Hot buttons: Emotional triggers can be described as the emotional values or hot buttons of customers. Different customers have different preferences or hot buttons, for example, while one customer may prefer powerful and rugged vehicles like four-wheel drive automobiles, another may prefer style, luxury, and safety over anything else, along the lines of something like a luxury sedan.

Imagine you're selling a property to an old-timer as opposed to selling the same property to a young man. What aspect of the property do you think will tug at the emotions of the old-timer? Additionally, what would tug at the emotions of the younger customer?

Do you think the old-timer would be more interested in open spaces in and around the property where he could go for walks, do some gardening, or even frolic with the grandchildren? The younger person could be more interested in the romantic patio where he could witness the sunset with his wife over a bottle of ice-cold champagne and the investment value of the property.

The next time you buy something of emotional value to you (e.g., something like your dream car) notice the extent to which you are ready to stretch your finances to own the product and how you feel after having made such a purchase. Alternatively, if clothes, fashion, and appearance are high on your list of priorities, notice how readily you pay for designer clothes that make you look young, smart, and chic.

Find out the hot buttons of your customers before trying to win them over.

"I strongly believe it is morally and ethically wrong to eat old men! Besides, in case you didn't know, I have lioneukemia!"

Our beliefs: We don't question our beliefs and values; we take them for granted. As explained earlier, they reside in the deeper recesses of our minds. We hardly ever are consciously aware of them, and anything that matches our beliefs and values is easily accepted. We find it easy to make decisions that are in line with our beliefs and values. For example, you may not want to spend money on yourself, but if you spend the money on your near and dear ones, you may do so with pleasure because you believe in doing so.

However, the moment that there is a conflict between our actions and our beliefs, we become uncomfortable, frustrated, and at times, angry. In fact, we are so blind to our beliefs and values that when adequately provoked, we even give our lives without asking any questions.

That is why, as service providers, we have to make sure that anything we do or say is in line with the customer's beliefs and values and not contrary to them.

Imagine how you would feel if a salesman condemned a competitor whose products you were using. Alternatively, if as a customer, you value honesty, how comfortable would you be with a salesman who forgets to tell you the drawback of a product you were contemplating buying?

Make sure you don't contradict the beliefs and values of your customers directly or indirectly.

Conditioning: Conditioning can be defined as forming a habit or developing a taste for something as a result of repeated use. For example, you may prefer a particular brand of tea just because your family has been using it since your childhood. Habits and preferences result from conditioning, and because they take a long time to form, they are difficult to break. Newspapers often try to get you habituated and comfortable with their publication by offering you "free" copies over extended periods.

In the service industry, another name for this kind of conditioning is "customer loyalty." The only way to wean customers from such conditioning is by making extraordinary offers that are more appealing and personalized than the products or services that the customer is currently using. The extraordinary offer could be in the form of reduced price, better quality at the same price, higher quantity, or any other form of additional services that the customer finds attractive or useful.

You can terminate conditioning only by making your offer extraordinarily appealing.

WHAT ADVERTISERS HAVE KNOWN FOR A LONG TIME

Have you ever seen advertisements like the one shown here, a beautiful young lady standing next to a luxury car? What are the advertisers trying to convey?

Advertisers know that human beings are far more emotional than logical. Does the advertisement subtly suggest that a car like this will give you access to such pretty women? I don't have to tell you how effective such advertisements are. They may not appeal to you consciously, but on a subconscious level they are nothing but brainwashing!

Therefore, appeal to your customers' emotions, make them feel the emotional benefits of your product, and then support their emotional buying decisions with logic or reasons.

Years ago, just after I received my driving license in 1980, I went shopping for a car in Dubai, United Arab Emirates. At the time, I was working for an airline as a reservation and ticketing agent. With a small salary to feed a family of four, I barely had the financial resources to buy and maintain a small car. However, the salesman at the car showroom had different ideas. He recommended a luxury car that was way beyond my meager income! Not only did he recommend the car, but he also took me for a test-drive.

While I savored the luxury and comfort of this eight-cylinder American beauty, he casually mentioned how my life could change if I owned this car – how my colleagues and friends would envy me and how people would look up to me!

There was no doubt that he had me thinking about buying the car. However, when I pointed out that I couldn't afford such an expensive vehicle, he gave me all the reasons why I should go for it. He said that the banks in Dubai would arrange for me to pay in easy installments and that the petrol prices were the cheapest in Dubai. Besides, insurance on luxury vehicles was minimal in the United Arab Emirates, and there was no income tax... If I didn't take advantage of such opportunities, especially in my youth, when was I going to avail myself of them? He even suggested that I keep the car for the next three days, free of cost! Reluctantly, I accepted.

What do you think I did when I drove off with the car? You guessed it right. I went straight home and coaxed my family into the car for a drive. To my relief, my wife seemed pleased with the vehicle, but after a while, she started asking questions about price, running and maintenance costs, and about the resale value, etc. I, of course, repeated what the car salesman had told me verbatim.

On returning home, my wife jolted me out of my trance by saying, "Nice car, either it stays or I stay!" We still have a good laugh about the incident whenever the subject comes up.

Appeal to your customers' emotions before enumerating the logical benefits.

When dealing with people, remember you are not dealing with creatures of logic, but creatures of emotion.

Dale Carnegie

HOW CAN YOU FIRE UP YOUR CUSTOMERS' EMOTIONS?

The trick is to ask the customers carefully devised questions that trigger their imagination and makes them feel or have emotions that are highly compelling. For example, if you merely tell the customer the consequences of using spurious and cheap spare parts for his car, it is unlikely that you will be able to make any significant impact. However, what if you were to ask him what would happen if he were driving with his family on the highway and the spurious part gave way in the middle of nowhere?

Now, to process your question, the customer has to imagine himself in the car with his family, having a breakdown on the highway in the middle of nowhere! In his imagination, he can feel the negative consequences of buying spurious or imitation spare parts. This way, the customer is likely to take your advice and go for the original and reliable spare parts, even though they are more expensive than the imitation spares.

Given below are some sample questions/comments that can trigger your customers' imaginations:

a. What could happen if your house is not insured against theft, fire, or any other natural calamity?

b. How much money will you save if you buy this product that is three times more durable than the other one, not to mention the hassles of replacement and increased prices due to inflation?

c. Can you imagine how heads would turn if you entered a party wearing this dress?

d. What would your wife think if you handed her the life insurance policy this afternoon? Wouldn't she think of you as a caring and responsible husband?

e. With the way the cost of property is spiraling upward, what do you think this property would fetch you in ten years' time?

f. Do you think it would be wiser to travel in business class and in comfort on such a long flight? The difference in the fare is worth it, is it not?

g. Imagine what you could be doing with this camera when you and your family picnic this weekend!

h. Can you feel the comfort and restful sleep this mattress will provide you and your wife?

i. Do you have any idea how much you will save on heating bills every month if you invest in this insulation?

j. Can you imagine you and your granddaughter running around the spacious garden of this villa?

Remember, the brain doesn't understand the difference between what is real and what it vividly imagines.

Near Versus Far:

Present your product in a manner that enables your customer to relate to it. They should be able to see, feel, and understand how your product can benefit them ***immediately*** or ***in the near future.*** When the benefits appear to be in the distant future, they don't influence your customers, as they see the benefits as too remote to be of any value to them.

For example, if I say to you, "Give me a loan of $1,000 and I will give you back $100,000 after sixty years," I doubt you would agree to such a proposition, even if you trusted me.

Any number of things could happen in the span of sixty years; therefore, the proposition is not viable. However, if I had offered to pay you back a lesser amount of only $1,500 after a month's time, you would probably loan me the money.

In other words, you need to speak in a manner that influences your customers' feelings in the near future and makes them expect good things to come.

Mak

Add color and sound to your description. Make the picture clearer and brighter by bringing it closer, so that your customers can clearly imagine, see, and feel your product in their mind's eye.

> *Present your product to the customers so that they can clearly imagine it as if it were real and immediately accessible.*

Memories:

The brain retains any significant incident or experience for future reference.

Memories are impossible to change; there are only two options. Either you wipe out the memory (i.e., forget or suppress it), or you change your response to the memory and stop reacting to it.

"Kicked out on the very first day at work – I'm afraid I shall never forget this moment!"

When it comes to your customers, you cannot wipe out or suppress their memories. What you can do is ensure that you do everything possible to imprint positive memories in your customers' psyches in the first place. It is no wonder that first impressions are so important when it comes to customer service.

However, if the customer had a negative experience with us, we can reduce its effect by compensating the customer with something extra for the inconvenience that was caused. Compensating the customer is like adding a new positive memory to their mind that negates the previous negative memory.

Compensating and winning the customer back can be hard work and expensive, both in terms of money and time.

Formation of Beliefs:

Memories precipitate into judgments and judgments ultimately consolidate into beliefs. Imagine you fly to London frequently on business, and whenever you fly on X airlines, something or the other goes wrong. After this happens a number of times, you recognize the pattern (judge), and instinctively avoid traveling on X airlines! In other words, you have formed a belief about X airlines, namely that their services are unreliable.

Beliefs, as mentioned earlier, reside very deep in the recesses of our psyche, and we are hardly aware of them. They constantly influence our thoughts and behavior and we never question their validity, as they operate from a subconscious level. In fact, we are, at times, even protective of our beliefs, so much so that when someone tries to question them, we react strongly.

Beliefs take a long time to take root and are very difficult to eradicate. For example, you may believe that German cars are sturdy and durable. It would be inadvisable to try to change that belief. What would be advisable is to induce another belief and reinforce it so much that the newer belief overshadows the previous belief. In this instance, you could induce a new belief in your customer's mind. For example, some Japanese cars are as sturdy and durable as German vehicles and come with the advantage of an affordable price tag.

Beliefs are difficult to change. It is easier to induce parallel beliefs that are weightier; however, that takes time and effort.

Desires & Emotions:

Our desires and emotions directly influence our behavior. From the perspective of influencing customers' behavior, you would agree that if both the customers' desires and emotions are favorable, the customer would readily buy. The problem arises when the customers' desires and emotions contradict each other. For example, if a customer had incurred heavy losses by investing in the property market in the past, he may become apprehensive about investing in property again. Logically, he would be able to relate to the positive forecasts based on statistical trends; however, emotionally he may still be apprehensive about investing in property again because of his previous negative experience.

In a situation like this, you would have to address his negative emotions associated with investing in properties before trying to fuel his desire to make money by investing in a buoyant property market. Dissect the apprehension the customer has developed concerning investing in property and show him how things have changed. Show the customer that he can expect to have better returns because of the prevailing increase of demand in the property market that is likely to continue.

Help the customer to understand why his previous attempts failed at making money by investing in property. Once he can see the reasons why he lost the money by investing in property the last time, he will be able to combat his fears. His reasons would replace his fears and apprehension, and he would be willing to have positive thoughts on investing money in the property market again.

Combat customers' fear and apprehension by showing reasons.

Focus on Positive Emotions:

Help the customers to focus their attention on the core benefits that induce positive emotions (e.g., the core benefits of purchasing a property: investment value, safe locality, amenities, etc.). Let the customers see in their mind's eye how much they will benefit from your proposal. Negative emotions are powerful, but they put the customer into a negative frame of mind that dampens their spirits, which is usually an impediment to buying.

Negative emotions are useful in preventing customers from doing something, e.g., convincing a customer not to use spurious spare parts for his car.

Exceptions are rare and happen when customers fear that they will lose an opportunity to buy something that is in short supply. For example, a lack of availability of bottled water because of short supply could motivate you to hoard bottled drinking water to tide over the period of the short supply.

Be more persuasive by focusing on the positive aspects of your products or services and soon customers will be returning for more.

Provide testimonials:

Support and validate your arguments by showing how others are benefiting from your products or services. Customers infer that if your product works for others, it will work for them as well. Apart from the apparent logic mentioned above, there is also an element of emotional solace that the customer feels. The emotional solace from a testimonial says to the customer, "You're not alone; there are others who have also taken the risk and benefited."

Testimonials give emotional and logical support to the customers and make it easier for them to buy.

STEPS TO ROMANCING YOUR CUSTOMER

Step 1: First, find out your customer's hot buttons; hot buttons are things that your customers are emotional about. For example, women generally are emotional about flowers, men easily get excited by gadgets or cars, grandparents are emotional about their grandchildren, and so forth.

Step 2: Then, make your customers imagine the benefits of buying your product. Make the imagery so real that they feel the benefits through their imagination.

In case you run into resistance from the customer, check for problems in the following areas and rectify them before you proceed:

    a.   Your rapport with the customer.

    b.   Customer beliefs that may be hindering the customer from imagining what you're telling them. If the customer's belief is the problem, represent your arguments in a way that doesn't contradict his beliefs.

           For example, if a lady considers maintaining a large car extravagant (because of some conditioning – her dad was thrifty and probably drove a smaller car), focus on a new perspective (e.g., she has a large family that often travels long distances, a bigger vehicle will not only be more comfortable, but will be safer as well).

    c.   You're not asking the right questions to trigger the right imagination in your customer's mind.

Step 3: Support and fortify the customer's emotional need to buy the product by providing justifications that are logical and relate to that particular customer's needs. For example, if you are selling cars, start by appealing to the emotional needs of your customers. Start with the status conveyed, luxury value, etc. (the emotional needs), and then focus on maintenance, durability, resale value, etc. (the logical reasons that support their decision to buy).

When you romance your customers, they become excited, and excitement is the positive experience customers crave.

Mak

SUMMARY

1. Customer service is about perceptions, feelings, and emotions. Emotions like excitement, joy, love, desire, and passion, etc., give customers a memorable experience.

2. Don't sell products or services, sell dreams.

3. Appeal to customers' emotions to be more persuasive.

4. Emotionally and positively charged customers not only buy more and do so readily, they also feel good about their purchases.

5. Find out your customers' hot buttons before trying to win them over.

6. Make sure you don't contradict the beliefs and values of your customers directly or indirectly.

7. You can terminate conditioning only by making your offer extraordinarily appealing.

8. Appeal to your customers' emotions before enumerating the logical benefits.

9. Remember, the brain doesn't understand the difference between what is real and what it vividly imagines.

10. Present your product to the customers so that they can clearly imagine it as if it were real and immediately accessible.

11. *Compensating and winning the customer back can be hard work and expensive, both in terms of money and time.*

12. *Beliefs are difficult to change. It is easier to induce parallel beliefs that are weightier; however, that takes time and effort.*

13. *Combat customers' fear and apprehension by showing reasons.*

14. *Be more persuasive by focusing on the positive aspects of your products or services and soon customers will be returning for more.*

15. *Testimonials give emotional and logical support to the customers and make it easier for them to buy.*

16. *When you romance your customers, they become excited, and excitement is the positive experience customers crave.*

Chapter 20

Mr. Pain   Mr. Pleasure

THE PUSH & PULL TECHNIQUE

Alone, we can do so little; together, we can do so much.

Helen Keller

Case Study 21:

George was a station manager for an international airline operating in and out of Nairobi. He was quite happy with his life, as he had a good job and a good family; he was looking forward to what life had to offer. William, his only son, was a civil engineering student in his second year at one of the best universities in Nairobi and was doing well with his studies. Both George and his wife had great expectations for their son and were looking forward to his employment in one of the Western firms as soon as George got his bachelor's degree.

Their dream was shattered when William came home from the university one day and announced that he was going to take a break from studies for two years. He said that he needed the break so that he could dedicate himself to learning to play the guitar. According to George, most guitarists working with famous rock bands were making more money than any civil engineer could ever dream about. Besides, joining a rock band would give him the opportunity to go on international tours and see the world!

George and his wife tried everything under the sun to convince their son to give up on the idea and concentrate on his studies, but it was to no avail. They threatened to throw him out of the house, cut his allowances, coaxed him with kind words, hired psychiatrists, and even resorted to sessions with local sorcerers, but nothing seemed to dissuade William from his idea of joining a rock band as a guitarist.

Not knowing what to do, George resorted to a persuasive technique that he had picked up at a training session on effective communication that was sponsored by his employers a few years ago.

George called his son one day and told him that although he was not comfortable with his idea of joining a rock band as a guitarist, he would let William decide on his career. After all, it was William's life and he should decide what to do with it.

George instructed William that if he was going to pursue his dreams of becoming a musician, he should do it properly. He gave William some money, suggested that he join a music school immediately, and told him to strive to be the best guitarist in Kenya.

William was a little surprised at George's sudden change of mind and was skeptical about his father's intentions. However, after joining the music school, he realized that his father was only trying to help him advance in life. Soon, father and son became quite accommodating of each other and everything reverted to normal at home. There were no long, one-sided lectures from his dad, and William's mom reverted to being a doting mother.

A few days later, George informed William that their neighbors were looking for a groom for their eldest daughter, Susan. To William's surprise, his dad seemed to know that Susan and William were in love and had dreams of their own. In a casual manner, George mentioned that he had tried convincing their neighbor to consider Susan's betrothal to William, but the neighbors had flatly refused. The neighbors said that they wouldn't knowingly betroth their daughter to somebody like William who had given up on his studies. They agreed that William was a good person, but questioned how many guitarists made it to the top.

William was totally crushed and became severely depressed; he seldom ventured out of his room and avoided talking to anyone. Soon, his health deteriorated to the point where he lost considerable weight and developed black patches under his eyes from sleepless nights. At this point, George called his son once again and suggested that he go back to his studies so that he could convince their neighbors to reconsider giving their daughter's hand to William.

George also suggested that William continue his music lessons in tandem with his studies, so he could complete his studies as well as follow his heart's desire of becoming a musician. That way, he had a better chance of winning Susan's hand and would have a safety net of finding a good job to provide for his family if things didn't go according to plan on the music front.

William seemed to ignore the idea at first, but after a few days, he reluctantly agreed to go back to the university. Soon thereafter William was engaged to Susan and he continued learning music in the evening classes without giving up on his studies.

What do you think happened here? Why was George successful in convincing William to go back to his studies?

We cannot convince others; we can only help others to convince themselves.

Mak

Tact is the art of convincing people that they know more than you do.

Raymond Mortimer

WHAT IS THE PAIN & PLEASURE TECHNIQUE?

The purpose of everything we do in life is either to avoid pain or to move towards pleasure. Pain and pleasure dictate everything we do. It explains why we did what we did in the past and predicts what we are going to do in the future.

For example, if you eat, it could be because you want to avoid being hungry (pain) and want to enjoy a good meal (pleasure). Alternatively, if you dress well, it is because you want to avoid being ostracized as a badly dressed person, and at the same time, want to be more confident about how you look and feel. In short, pain and pleasure are the two basic motivators that dictate all our actions.

Show your customers the pain they will go through if they don't use your services and the pleasure they will receive if they do.

Mak

BOTH PAIN & PLEASURE MOTIVATE

Both pain and pleasure are strong motivators. For example, if you work during the day and want to go to college in the evening to further your studies, you will have the pain of going to college after a long day's work. On the other hand, you will have the pleasure of knowing that should you acquire the degree, you will have a good chance of getting a better job than your current position. If the pain you experience turns out to be greater than the pleasure, you would probably keep postponing your studies. However, if the pleasure you experience is greater than the pain of going to college in the evening after work, then you would complete your studies.

Of the two, pain is more powerful provided it is perceived as imminent. Our physiology by nature is programmed to avoid it, whereas pleasure is something that we can consciously choose to experience. In short, when there is a tie between pain and pleasure, pain usually wins. However, notice that the pain, in the above example, is more certain than the pleasure – if you go to the evening classes, the distress will definitely be there. However, getting an academic degree may not ensure a better job. Besides, as stated earlier, the good job is something you can only expect years later and not immediately.

For the purpose of using this concept in customer service, we shall refer to pain as "push" and to pleasure as "pull;" therefore, we will refer to the concept as the **'Push and Pull Technique'**.

HOW DOES THE PUSH AND PULL TECHNIQUE WORK?

The push and pull technique creates contrast between a customer's perception of pain and pleasure; together and on the same side, they become formidable motivators.

Mak

Now, you might be wondering what this concept of push and pull has to do with customer service. The push and pull technique is a very effective and useful technique in customer service and sales; it can be used to convince customers more effectively. By inducing the two motivators in a certain sequence, you can make your communication with your customer more persuasive.

The idea is quite simple. Suppose you provide genuine spare parts for motor vehicles, and because they are genuine and original, they cost more than the spurious and imitation spares available in the market. Your customer finds your products expensive and doesn't see any reason why he should pay more for your products when he can buy the cheaper ones elsewhere. Here you have an ideal situation in which you can use the push and pull technique.

Push: First, you need to ask your customers questions that push or induce pain in their minds by making them aware of the possible negative consequences of buying spurious products. For example, you could say, "What will happen if the spurious part fails to function? Do you think it is likely that you could meet with an accident?" You could increase their pain by pushing harder. Ask another question that brings even worse consequences to their mind. For example, you could say, "What could happen to your family if they are there with you at the time of the accident?" If you think that this is too harsh, you could ask pain questions that refer to frequent breakdowns that point to considerable inconveniences and additional expenses.

Pull: Once you are sure that you have raised a big question mark in your customer's mind, you then can start focusing on providing the solution. Ask a different set of questions that pull the customer, or induce pleasurable thoughts. For example, show the customer how he is going to benefit from using your product even though it is more expensive than the imitation. You could ask questions like, "Can you imagine the pleasure of driving with the confidence of not having any breakdowns?" or, "Can you put a price on the safety of your family and others on the street?" Alternatively, you could say, "Don't you think you could end up spending less because our products are guaranteed to last more than a year?"

Notice that you have pushed the customer away from what he thought was good for him, and at the same time, pulled him towards what is more beneficial for him – **double whammy, eh?** Unlike selling only benefits, you have doubled the impact by un-selling other products and then selling your product. In other words, you have increased the value in your product so the customer is more likely to buy from you.

Caution: Pain is a powerful motivator, and if not equalized with the opposing pleasure, it can lead to frustration, inaction, and loss of customers. Never leave the customer in pain.

Pain and pleasure are powerful motivators, and when both point in the same direction, the synergy makes them even more powerful.

Mak

SUMMARY

1. *Alone, we can do so little; together, we can do so much.*

2. *We cannot convince others; we can only help others to convince themselves.*

3. *Show your customers the pain they will go through if they don't use your services and the pleasure they will receive if they do.*

4. *Pain and pleasure are powerful motivators, and when both point in the same direction, the synergy makes them even more powerful.*

Chapter 21

"I don't know...it still feels too wide in the shoulders!"

HOW TO MANAGE CUSTOMER OBJECTIONS

An objection is not a rejection; it is simply a request for more information.

Bo Bennett

Case Study 22:

Josephine was a travel agent specializing in selling vacations.

One day, a customer came and wanted to buy a vacation to the Far East for himself and his family. As usual, Josephine asked relevant questions to find out the needs and preferences of the customer before offering a wide range of vacations that suited his requirements.

"Just because we are offering a heavy discount on this product, doesn't mean it is cheap!"

The customer seemed to like a number of options, but kept asking many questions that didn't make sense. Sometimes the questions related to security issues, sometimes to food and hygiene, and at other times, to cultural issues.

Josephine was confused as to what the customer really wanted. She explained the features of the vacations in detail, and yet the customer seemed to shy away from committing to a vacation! After a long discussion, the customer left, saying he would have to discuss the alternatives with his wife before making a firm commitment. Josephine was disappointed and didn't know how she could have done better.

What do you think happened here, and what do you think Josephine should have done?

Customers often like a product, but cannot tell why they stop themselves from buying it.

MANAGING CUSTOMER OBJECTIONS

Selling across the counter or over the telephone is not always easy. You are sure to meet objections from customers more often than you expect. Therefore, it is important to be prepared to deal with objections that your customers raise. Many service providers think of customer objections as price-related and believe that the only way to handle such situations is to reduce the price before the customer walks away. Considering high price to be the major reason for customers' objections is a myth that costs companies millions of dollars that could have been part of their profit margin.

Just think about it; if it were true that price is the major determinant why customers buy or don't buy, wouldn't all the sellers with lower prices be dominating every market? To put the question another way, why would customers buy expensive products when there is a whole range of products or services available at rock-bottom prices in every industry everywhere in the world? But the facts are that high priced products also sell and such products have a sizable portion in any market.

It is important to understand that customers raise objections for a variety of reasons and price objection is just one of them. *Customers object when they are not sure if what you are offering them is really going to satisfy their needs.* They could be objecting because they need more information or are concerned about certain aspects of the product, or they just need assurances that what they are buying is the right thing for them.

The good news is that you can turn objections to your advantage. As explained earlier, most customers who raise objections do so *because they are interested in your products or services and have some concerns that stand in their way of purchasing them.* All you have to do is manage their concerns and the sale goes through.

The first thing to do is to ensure that you have developed a good rapport with your customers. More often than not, developing good rapport with walk-in customers involves the ability to listen patiently to your customers without being judgmental. The more rapt attention you give, the more the customer bonds with you. Rapt attention and being non-judgmental means that you are able to look at issues from the customer's point of view and resolve those issues.

With regular customers, developing a relationship becomes critically important, as you want your customers to keep coming back to you. Building relationships with your regular customers requires that in addition to being sensitive to their needs, you win their trust, build credibility, and show them that you are there for them in their time of need. One technique that helps in managing customers' objections and building relationships with them is thinking in collaborative and cooperative terms rather than seeing your customers as adversaries.

When customers object, they are usually interested in your products and have some concerns that need clarification.

COMMON CUSTOMER OBJECTIONS

There are many kinds of objections. Listed below are some common objections that are typical of most industries. Remember, customers raise objections because they do not understand the benefits in your products or services.

1. Insufficient information - customers cannot relate to the benefits in your services or products

2. Customer's particular circumstances - previous negative experience with similar services or products

3. Opinions of friends and relatives - customers influenced by others

4. Other stakeholders - customer not the sole decision maker

5. High price - usually because the customer cannot see the value/benefit in your products or services

6. Issues related to service flexibility - restrictions of any kind (e.g., delivery times, payment terms, etc.)

7. Procrastination - customer keeps delaying the decision to buy for various reasons (e.g., the hassle of product installation, the drudgery of learning to operate it, or complicated formalities of acquiring the product that are too cumbersome, etc.)

8. Budgetary constraints - customer doesn't have the money to buy.

Note: *Never avoid or argue with the customer when dealing with their objections.* To the customers, their objections are valid issues and they expect you to deal with them in a courteous and helpful manner. Arguments will simply destroy your relationship with your customers and make them more difficult to convince.

Customers raise objections because they don't fully understand the benefits in your products or services.

ESTABLISH THE REAL CAUSE

Identify the real cause of the customer's objection. Once you have identified the real cause, it becomes relatively easy to manage the objection by going over the specific benefit connected to the customer's concern.

"Jane, are you refusing to marry me just because your parents don't approve of me?"

As stated earlier, the first step to managing customers' objections is to listen intently to what they say and don't say, so that you can uncover their concerns. Given below is a guideline that could be useful:

1. Listen to objections intently and try to understand from where the customer is coming.

2. Paraphrase - restate the objections with emphasis so that the customer is encouraged to confirm or clarify your understanding. For example, "Are you saying that this model is too complicated?" The chances are that the customer will then either confirm your understanding or correct you by stating what exactly is bothering him.

3. If none of the above proves effective, then ask probing questions that may reveal the real cause of the customer's objection. For example, you could ask, "Do you have any concerns that I may assist you with?" or, "What exactly is stopping you from considering this product?"

    Ask test questions like, "Would you be willing to consider buying this product if I were to offer free maintenance for the first year?" or something similar. This and similar options, though viable, are not advisable until and only when absolutely necessary. By making the product or service more attractive (putting more value into it, e.g., free maintenance for a year), you could be incurring substantial additional costs that could eat into your profit margins!

Listen carefully and ask questions to understand the real concerns in the customer's objections.

HOW TO MANAGE PRICE OBJECTIONS

Apart from budgetary constraints and supply and demand considerations, price objections usually arise because the customers cannot equate the benefits in the product to their needs. Also, customers readily pay more for something that they need or like and refrain from buying products that don't fit their needs or preferences, even when the quality of the product in question is beyond doubt.

Most service providers try to manage price objections by giving discounts or by throwing in something extra. Basically, by reducing price or giving something extra, they enhance the relative value of the product in the customer's mind, and the customer perceives the purchase as a bargain because of the lowered price. This practice eats into profit margins that are already depleted in most markets because of the current economic slowdown, increased cost of production, distribution, and intense competition, etc. Therefore, it should be avoided as much as possible.

This propensity to discount and win customers comes from the mindset of many service providers and operates subconsciously. They basically equate customers' buying power with their own, and don't believe that there are many customers who can afford to pay higher prices if they see more value in the product in question. Regrettably, they make minimal effort to protect their profit margins, and eventually, this works to the detriment of the business for which they work.

If lower price were the sole reason customers purchased, then products at the higher end of the price spectrum hardly ever would sell. However, the reality is that there is a vast multitude of factors that dictate customers' purchase behavior. Factors like reliability, accessibility, value, ease of use, status the product confers on the customer, price, durability, and a host of other similar reasons dictate customers' behavior when buying.

Price is important; however, it should not be the first or core strategy for convincing customers to buy. From the context of price, there are two ways of winning customers: one is by reducing the price of a product as described above, and the other is by enhancing value in the product so the customers feel the deal is a bargain. Enhancing value could be as simple as making sure the customer understands how the product is going to solve her problem. The first eats into the profit margins, whereas the second protects the profit margins as well as satisfies the customer, a win-win for all.

We, as service providers, have to realize two things about customer behavior as it relates to price:

1. Customers readily pay higher prices for products they perceive as having higher value and vice versa.

2. All products have their own niche market or clientele; no product fits all markets. Keeping other things equal, generally customers with more money go for higher-end or quality products, whereas customer with lesser buying power go for affordable products.

Therefore, increasing the value of the product in the appropriate customer's mind is a sound strategy in convincing customers to buy.

For instance, if the customer says, "This watch is very expensive!" you could respond by asking why the customer thinks so.

The customer would probably draw parallels with other cheaper watches on the market. Then, you could agree with the customer and highlight the watch's benefits to justify the higher price.

You could say something like, "Yes, this watch is more expensive than the others you mention, but unlike them, this is waterproof up to 300 meters and ideal for your scuba diving. Plus, it comes with a three-year guarantee on maintenance, repairs, and parts, all included in the price."

Loathe to give discounts and passionately sell value; it will precipitate into a relationship that both you and your customers will appreciate.

WHAT TO DO WHEN THE CUSTOMER REJECTS

"I just hope this fellow doesn't give up!"

Sometimes, no matter what you do, the customers are not ready to buy. What should you do when the customer rejects your offer?

Customer rejection does not mean that the customer will never buy your product. It only means that *he is not willing to accept your offer at that moment in time.*

It is likely that when you approach him again and when he is in a different frame of mind, he may become interested. Don't take customer objections personally, as the customer hardly knows you. The same customer often

"Oh Abdullah, how can you propose at a time like this?"

accepts the same offer at another time when he is in a more accessible frame of mind. Just thank the customer for their interest and invite them back. Effective service providers avoid hard-selling and keep their relationships with their customers intact to ensure they keep coming back.

Customer rejections only mean that, at that moment, the customers are opting out from buying.

SOME MORE EXAMPLES OF CUSTOMER OBJECTIONS AND HOW TO MANAGE THEM

If the customer says, "I will have to think about it," say something to the customer such as, "I can appreciate that you would like to think it over. What it says to me is that you are interested. I just want to make sure that I have explained everything properly. Would you mind telling me which particular aspect you would like to think over?"

- To the customer who says, "I can't afford it," say to the customer:

"I do understand what you mean. We can work together and find a solution that may suit your budget." (Down-sell)

- If the customer says, "I will come back later," say something such as:

"No problem. Would you like me to send you more information about the product by fax, or would you like me to call you?"

The idea is to keep the communication lines open with your customer so that you can close the sale at a more opportune moment.

SUMMARY

1. An objection is not a rejection; it is simply a request for more information.

2. Customers often like a product but cannot tell why they stop themselves from buying it.

3. When customers object, they are usually interested in your products and have some concerns that need clarification.

4. Customers raise objections because they don't fully understand the benefits in your products or services.

5. Listen carefully and ask questions to understand the real concerns in the customer's objections.

6. Loathe to give discounts and passionately sell value; it will precipitate into a relationship that both you and your customers will appreciate.

7. Customer rejections only mean that the customers are opting out from buying at that moment.

Chapter 22

HOW TO CLOSE THE SALE

Selling isn't closing. Closing is the key to every successful business and failure of any business can be attributed to a lack of learning this valuable skill.

Stephen J. Young

Story 1:

A long, long, long time ago, in the city of Romantica, there used to live a boy and a girl who were neighbors, and they grew up together. They spent a lot of time together and even went to the same school, college, and university. The boy's name was Dumio and the girl's name was Juliet.

As they grew up, they became very fond of each other, and people used to say that they were made for each other. While at the university, Dumio fell in love with Juliet and everyone could see that Dumio was very possessive and protective of Juliet. Juliet, on the other hand, was very considerate and receptive towards whatever Dumio had to say or do. It was everyone's guess that soon Dumio would propose to Juliet and they would get married.

However, fate had different plans, as Dumio never had the courage to either express his love for Juliet or to ask for her hand. Juliet kept waiting for the day when Dumio would ask for her hand, but alas, that day never came. Although Dumio never failed to bring Juliet flowers and gifts with or without reason, he never could propose to Juliet. This confused Juliet, and after a while, she was saddened to think that Dumio was just a close friend and a well-wisher!

Soon, another young man came into Juliet's life and swept her off her feet. It seemed like love at first sight, and the next day, the young man proposed; he was so insistent that Juliet couldn't refuse. They were married the next week and no one could believe how quickly it all happened.

Fifty-five years later, Dumio is still a bachelor and Juliet's a widow. Rumor has it that Dumio still loves Juliet, but cannot bring himself to express his love for her. Poor Juliet wishes that Dumio had told her how much he loved her!

How do you think things would have turned out if Dumio had asked for Juliet's hand when they were in the university?

WHAT IS "CLOSING THE SALE?"

To successfully close a deal, you have to invite the prospect to buy.

Why? Because most customers find it hard to commit or part with their hard-earned money. In other words, you have to prod, invite, and coax the customer, implicitly or explicitly, to buy. Closing the sale process is very simple, and all that you need to do is learn a few simple closing techniques that prompt customers to buy.

Building rapport, connecting with customers, becoming a credible seller, and giving valuable options and friendly service all go a long way in closing the sale successfully. However, you have to watch the customer's body language, his or her tone, and overall disposition etc., to make out if the customer is interested in your services. If the customer displays any of the signs or buying signals mentioned below, as they are popularly known in selling, than it is time to ask for the sale, or in other words, close the sale.

Watch for the buying signal, and when you notice one or more, like the customer seeking clarifications, raising minor objections, or displaying positive body language, you can stop selling and invite the customer to buy. Otherwise, the customer's buying impulse may wane and you could lose an opportunity to sell. Contrary to popular belief, customers seldom buy based on benefits alone!

If the above works, you have made the sale. If it doesn't work, then you can continue with your sales pitch. Frequently check to ensure that the customer sees the value in the service being offered. It is a good way of convincing the customer to buy.

Besides, frequently checking gives you the opportunity to address any objections or doubts in the customer's mind as and when they arise. Remember, if you leave any doubts unaddressed as you continue your sales talk, the customer may become disinterested and switch off or avoid buying by making excuses.

If you don't ask for the sale, your competitors will cash in on your hard work of convincing the customer and take your sale!

Ask, and it shall be given to you; seek, and you shall find; knock, and it shall be opened unto you. For every one that asketh receiveth; and he that seeketh findeth; and to him that knocketh, it shall be opened.

Matthew 7:7-8, Bible

BUYING SIGNALS

Customers give buying signals that indicate that they are interested in our products. Buying signals are usually in the form of body or spoken language that tells us that the customer is interested in buying. When the customer does any of the following, they indicate that they are interested in our products or services:

a.   Increases eye contact.

b.   Leans forward and listens to you intently.

c.   Attentively listens to your sales spiel.

d.   Seeks clarification on minor issues (e.g., "When can it be delivered?" "What kind of guarantee is offered?" "Will someone show me how to operate this?").

e.   Confers or discusses your offer with another accompanying person, like a family member or friend.

f.   Smiles at you and nods their head as if they agree with you, etc.

Watch your customers' body language and listen to their verbal cues. With a little practice, you'll be able to determine if they are with you.

WHEN IS THE RIGHT TIME TO CLOSE THE SALE?

Several times during the sales process:

1. Right in the beginning if the customer is interested and eager enough to buy.

2. In-between the sales discussion by checking if the customer will buy.

3. At the end by highlighting the benefits to the customer.

A good time to close the sale is anytime and all the time; it's whenever the customer gives off buying signals or is eager to buy.

"The close really starts in opening," says Neill MacMillan, president of Toronto-based sales training and research firm Communicare Inc. "A successful sale is the result of small commitments gained from the prospect throughout the sales process," he says. [The close] is not some magical question asked at the end of the sales call."

AVOID HARD/PRESSURE CLOSING TECHNIQUES

Don't push the customer to buy; rather, invite the customer to buy. Pressure techniques do work sometimes; however, the customers feel uncomfortable about the purchase because it robs them of their choice. They feel manipulated or disrespected and are not likely to return to you for another purchase!

"Of course you can have your fish and chips; the cuisine I suggested is only appreciated by the upper class!"

Some examples of "pressure closing" that you should avoid:

i. "Shall I issue the tickets now?"

ii. "Only people with taste buy these suits!"

iii. "You will regret it if you don't buy this…"

iv. "I don't think you can afford to buy this product."

v. "I can understand this is too advanced and complicated for you."

vi. "We are closing within the next ten minutes, so please make up your mind if you want to purchase or not!"

vii. "Everybody is buying this stuff; I don't see why you are having difficulty in making up your mind!"

viii. "Do you really want to buy it, or are you just window shopping?"

ix. "I know this is the product you should buy."

x. "Whatever you do, don't even think of buying any other product."

Customers don't like being forced into buying or making a decision.

SOME USEFUL CLOSING TECHNIQUES:

i. **Direct Close:** "Now that all arrangements have been made, subject to your approval, I would like to issue the tickets."

ii. **Alternative Close:** "Would you like to wait so we can put the items in your car, or shall I have them delivered to your office/residence by noon today?" Or, "Will you be paying in cash or with a credit card?"

iii. **Opportunity Close:** "The price of this property can go up without notice; I suggest you make the down payment and lock in the deal."

iv. **Demonstrate:** "Why don't you test-drive it before you make up your mind on purchasing this beauty?"

v. **Testimonials:** "Mr. George and Mr. Ali from your office also have purchased this product and they are very satisfied with it." Testimonials given by third parties (e.g., other customers) are very convincing; the customers feel that if other customers have benefited from this product, it should be okay for them as well.

vi. **Focus on the End Product:** "Just imagine...by buying this package now, you could be enjoying your holiday with your family on the lush green valleys of...by next week."

vii. **Objection Handling**: In the case of objections, ask questions to uncover their concerns and address them appropriately.

Not closing the sale is like a lost opportunity in making a sale.

SOME REASONS WHY CUSTOMERS DO NOT BUY:

a. The customer is not the decision maker (e.g., a housewife wanting to consult with her husband to make sure a larger-than-planned refrigerator is affordable).

b. The customer wants to make sure that other stakeholders in the purchase will be satisfied with the product/service (e.g., a husband buying a cruise; the husband in this case would want to discuss the trip with his wife and children before making the purchase).

c. The customer doesn't fully comprehend the benefits of the product.

d. The customer cannot afford the product - *at the moment*.

e.   The customer finds the product too complicated.

f.   There is a lack of availability of spares, maintenance facilities, or a proper guarantee.

g.   The product is of inferior quality.

h.   The product is too expensive for the purpose that the product serves (e.g., high fidelity equipment that has superfluous functions or refinements).

i.   The delivery time is too long.

j.   Legal considerations (e.g., a property that the customer likes but decides against due to the property being in a foreign land with ownership laws that are not transparent).

One word of caution, though: Don't celebrate closing a sale, celebrate opening a relationship.

Patricia Fripp

SUMMARY

1. Selling isn't closing. Closing is the key to every successful business and failure of any business can be attributed to a lack of learning this valuable skill.

2. If you don't ask for the sale, your competitors will cash in on your hard work of convincing the customer and take your sale!

3. Watch your customers' body language and listen to their verbal cues. With a little practice, you'll be able to determine if they are with you.

4. A good time to close the sale is anytime and all the time; it's whenever the customer gives off buying signals or is eager to buy.

5. Customers don't like being forced into buying or making a decision.

6. Not closing the sale is like a lost opportunity in making a sale.

7. One word of caution, though: Don't celebrate closing a sale, celebrate opening a relationship.

Chapter 23

LOOK AFTER YOUR CASH COWS

80% of your business comes from 20% of your clients!

Pareto's Law

Case Study 23:

Nancy was the manager of a busy call center somewhere in the Far East that sold cosmetics and toiletries for both men and women all over the world. She had sixty-eight telephone agents working in shifts taking calls twenty-four hours a day, seven days a week. Each agent had a monthly revenue target to meet, and most agents had to work hard to meet their targets.

At the end of every week, Nancy would review the number of calls handled by each agent, the business generated, and the average time taken for each call. What perplexed Nancy was that there were agents that managed a large number of calls but produced less business than a few others who handled fewer calls and yet produced significantly larger volumes of business. She decided to find the underlying cause of this phenomenon and started listening to the recorded calls handled by agents in both categories. Soon, a pattern emerged.

The agents that were producing more business in spite of handling fewer calls were closing more sales to returning customers, customers that had their business profile in their database and regularly purchased from them. The other set of agents, on the other hand, were handling a larger number of calls, mostly from new customers, and yet produced less business.

What do you think was the reason for the above phenomenon?

Returning customers give us more business than new customers.

Major customers are those customers who provide us with a large volume of business on a regular basis. They are the mainstay of our business, and as such, have significant impact on our business and growth. Our major customers are happy with our services and that is why they keep returning to us.

PARETO'S PRINCIPLE

In 1906, an Italian economist, Vilfredo Federico Damaso Pareto, observed that 20 percent of Italians owned 80 percent of the land in Italy. This noteworthy ratio seems to apply to business as well as many other aspects of our lives. For example, 80 percent of our troubles in life are caused by 20% of the people we know, and similarly, 80% of our joy in life comes from another 20% of people in our lives. Over time, this concept became popularly known as the **Pareto Principle** or **The 80/20 Rule.** So, what does the 80/20 rule have to do with major customers?

Well, the 80/20 rule also applies to customers; according to the 80/20 rule, ***80% of your business revenue comes from 20% of your customers,*** and generally, it is true for any business anywhere in the world! It may vary a little; for example, 75% of your business may come from 25% of the clients, or the ratio may even be closer to 70% to 30%. The important thing to note here is that a major chunk of your revenue comes from a smaller chunk of major clients who give you business regularly.

> *80% of your business comes from 20% of your clients!*

WHERE SHOULD WE FOCUS OUR ATTENTION?

The question then arises, should we lay out our servicing resources on all of our customers equally, or allocate them to customers according to the amount of business they give us? In other words, should we give more attention to customers who give us more business?

"This is on the house - a token of our appreciation for your kind patronage."

Let us consider this from a major customer's point of view. Suppose you are a major customer; would you expect a higher level of service from the service provider you deal with, or would you be content being treated like any other customer?

Obviously, you would like to be treated as a preferred customer. That is why we need to provide *a more personalized service* to our major customers that generate more than 80% of our revenue, as compared to the rest of customers who give us a mere 20% of our business. *Personalized service, as the name implies, is a service that is customized and tailored to the requirement of that particular customer.*

Notice that when we apply this strategy i.e., when we focus on our major customers, we reduce our workload significantly and make our business more manageable. We have fewer customers to concentrate on and get comparatively more business per customer for our effort, time, and attention.

Provide personalized service to your major customers so you can retain their patronage and get more business for your time and effort.

AREN'T WE SUPPOSED TO TREAT ALL OF OUR CUSTOMERS EQUALLY?

Yes, we are supposed to treat all of our customers with courtesy and respect. All customers, no matter how much business they give us, deserve our attention and assistance. However, imagine once again, you're a major customer for a service provider and you provide them with over $ 2,000,000 worth of business every year, while most other customers provide only $ 20,000 worth of business. Would you like to stand in a queue with other customers and wait your turn, or would you like to be treated with some priority? To put it another way, if this company doesn't give you priority treatment, would you stay with them? Would you prefer to move to another service provider that does give you priority over other customers? My guess is that you would move to another company that gives you priority treatment.

If you're still not convinced, have you ever wondered why the airhostesses draw the curtains between first, business, and economy class while serving meals on an aircraft? They don't want the economy class passengers to feel bad about the higher level of service provided to business class passengers, and similarly, between business and first class. *The rule of the thumb is that although <u>all customers are to be treated with courtesy and respect,</u> the major customers deserve extra and personalized attention.*

The personalized attention facilitates their business transactions, acknowledges their patronage, and also shows our appreciation.

We should be courteous and helpful towards all our customers; however, we should provide a more personalized service to our major clients, recognize them as major customers, and validate their patronage.

DO YOU KNOW WHO YOUR MAJOR CUSTOMERS ARE?

It is likely that you have, if nothing else, a vague idea of who your major customers are. However, vagueness is not something that you can afford to depend on in business. As emphasized earlier in the book, one of the main objectives of customer service is to develop an excellent business relationship with your customers, especially your major customers.

"You're the only girl in town that always cared for me. I cannot imagine life without you."

Therefore, if you don't know who your major customers are and how much business they generate, you should ask your immediate supervisor for the information. Your supervisor should be able to advise you on this or point you in the right direction to where you could access the information.

In some companies, though, you may get a brush-off attitude from your superiors. They may ridicule you as to why you want to know who your major customers are, and they may advise you to just do your job! Such an attitude usually indicates that the supervisor doesn't want to take the trouble of finding out the information.

If you don't know how much business I give you, how can you value my patronage?

Mak

However, in some cases this happens because the company doesn't want to share such sensitive data. It is understandable that data on major customers could inadvertently wind up with competitors and that could spell disaster. Nevertheless, you can ask for indicators that help you to identify major customers so you can respond to them appropriately.

If you want to give excellent service to your major customers, you need to track their business. Any increase in business should be appreciated and any drop in business flagged, so that you can take steps to remove any kinks in your services to such clients.

Get more involved with what you do for a living and make it more meaningful by doing your best in developing excellent business relationships with your major customers. Feel good in knowing that you are effectively contributing not only to the bottom line of the company for which you work, but also to the assistance of your major partners (major customers) in progress.

Identify your major customers, develop excellent business relationships with them, and give them your best.

KEYS TO WINNING AND KEEPING MAJOR CUSTOMERS

Business from major customers is guaranteed business, and therefore we need to win and retain their patronage. If we are to retain their patronage, we need to foster strong business relationships with them.

All relationships, whether of a personal or business nature, have the same foundation; they require trust and commitment, understanding, and common objectives to proliferate and sustain.

a. **Trust & Commitment:** Our major customers have to trust and feel that we are totally committed to protecting their business interests and are fully reliable. Such a commitment is possible only when we take interest in them and find our self-worth in assisting them. Being enthusiastic, of selfless conduct, and showing thoughtfulness and the right attitude are external manifestations of an inner state of mind that shows our customers how much we enjoy serving them. Don't we display similar dedication and loyalty in our close relationships?

In a way, our near and dear ones are like our major customers –they expect more from us; when we live up to their expectations, they give to us with an open heart, and when we don't, they are gravely hurt.

Mak

b. **Communication and understanding:** For any relationship to sustain, understanding between the two parties is essential and crucial. Understand gives meaning to communication and keeps positive energy flowing between the parties. To understand our customers we need to know more about them, their markets and businesses, priorities, preferences, background, and so forth.

Again, is this not similar to what happens in personal relationships as well? What happens to a relationship when the understanding and communication between two friends break down?

c.　　**Common goals:** *Benefit* is the common goal for both parties in a relationship. In the customer service context, we want the benefit of their patronage, and the major customers want the benefit of our personalized service. Therefore, it is a mutually beneficial relationship, as we and the major customer are partners in progress.

We help our major customers to focus on their core business so they can do well. They delegate parts of their business to us that we are good at running for them, and so they reward us for our assistance. Remember, just like in personal life, two people cannot have an ongoing relationship if they don't subscribe to a common goal.

To be successful, you have to be able to relate to people; they have to be satisfied with your personality to be able to do business with you and to build a relationship with mutual trust.

George Ross

Work diligently at understanding, building, and maintaining business relationships with your major customers.

WHY IS REPEAT BUSINESS ESSENTIAL?

We all know that the key to survival and continued progress for any business is repeat business. When we have regular customers who keep using our services, we don't have to spend so much money on advertisement and promotion.

These days, one of the major expenses corporations have is advertisement and promotions targeted at new customers. It may come as a surprise to you that getting new customers is at least five times more expensive than keeping an existing customer. That is why it is more cost-effective to give priority to repeat customers rather than chase new customers.

By analogy, building relationships with major customers is similar to getting married, while chasing new customers is akin to dating. Imagine you date beautiful women; you take them out to expensive restaurants, go to movies, buy them flowers and gifts, and so forth. This all costs you an arm and a leg! ☹

On the other hand, when you marry one of them (major customer), you don't have to take her out to restaurants or buy her expensive gifts as often, and yet, she is loyal to you, helps you make a home, and is there beside you no matter what. ☺

Spend a lot of time talking to customers face-to-face. You'd be amazed how many companies don't listen to their customers.

Ross Perot

ADVANTAGES OF HAVING MAJOR CUSTOMERS

Loyalty:

Major customers stand by your side in times of market depression and are not easily lured away by competitors. *Besides, when we make mistakes, they are more tolerant and forgiving towards us.* Don't we do the same in close personal relationships?

I remember an incident during the first few days of my career as a ticketing and reservations agent at an international airline in Dhaka, Bangladesh. It was actually my second day at work at the airline office, and I was not familiar with airline ticketing or reservation procedures. To cut a long story short, an elderly lady, the wife of a British high commissioner, came to purchase a return ticket to Calcutta.

For the purpose of this discourse, let us call her Mrs. Winston. Mrs. Winston wanted to travel to Calcutta in the morning and return the same evening. Mrs. Winston used to travel to Calcutta often to meet friends and do some shopping there.

While in the process of writing out her ticket, we casually talked and discovered that we both loved swimming; I loved swimming to keep fit, and it seemed she loved the swimming pool because it gave her relief from arthritis. Furthermore, we both loved horticulture and enjoyed pottering around in a garden. Even though this was our first encounter, we somehow liked each other.

By mistake, I issued her a ticket for Calcutta on a day when there was an outbound flight in the morning but no return flight in the evening. Poor Mrs. Winston had to be put up in a hotel and return on a flight the next evening. Finding suitable accommodations in a good hotel in Calcutta at short notice was quite a challenge those days!

The British high commissioner was furious and had every reason to be. On her return they came to our office to lodge a complaint. The high commissioner demanded that I be sacked, and I probably would have been if it weren't for Mrs. Winston's intervention. She accosted me by asking me if I knew what I had done, and once I apologized, she calmed down. She told her husband in a very stern tone that she would take care of the matter herself and he needn't bother with it.

To my surprise, she even bought a necktie for me as a souvenir from Calcutta. I still have the tie and bless Mrs. Winston whenever I remember her for teaching me such a valuable lesson–*one of the hallmarks of caring is to forgive even before being asked to be forgiven.* She bought the necktie for me even before I had the chance to ask for her forgiveness.

When we make little mistakes, our loyal customers are forgiving and less critical.

Word of mouth advertisement:

Word of mouth is the most effective form of advertisement and doesn't cost a penny. In simple terms, word of mouth advertisements are the good things that our customers have to say about our products or services to their friends, relatives, acquaintances, or associates.

Usually, it is our regular/major customers who recommend our products to others, and it is effective because they recommend them to their friends or relatives who trust their word. The best thing about word of mouth advertisement is that it doesn't cost a dime, and yet, it is one of the most effective forms of advertisement. It is referred from person to person and spreads very quickly.

Word of mouth advertisement is the most effective and affordable publicity you can get.

If you do build a great experience, customers tell each other about that. Word of mouth is very powerful.

Jeff Bezos

Approach:

Your approach towards your major customers should be such that they find it difficult to make out if you're working for them or the company that employees you. Protecting the interests of your major customers should be one of your prime concerns, second only to protecting the interests of your employer.

What we have to understand is that our major customers entrust us with their business because they think that we have the ability to deliver what they want and that they can depend on us.

One of the best ways to approach the subject of major customers is to realize that we have to take all their headaches concerning what they entrust us with so that they can focus on their core business. In practical terms, this means that we have to find ways to add value to what we provide to our major customers. We have to deal with them in a manner that is <u>convenient to them,</u> and at the same time, beneficial for their business.

For us, our most important stakeholder is not our stockholder, it is our customer. We're in business to serve the needs and desires of our core customer base.

John Mackey

WHAT MAJOR CUSTOMERS APPRECIATE

1. **Follow-ups from their suppliers** – You should check regularly with your major customers to make sure that all is well, and that they are happy with what you're doing for them.

    Top service providers make it their business to be invited to the marketing or regional conferences of their major accounts to better understand the pulse of their customer's business. It gives the service providers insights as to how they can better assist their customers.

2. **Thoroughness of service, information, and guidance** – Give correct, timely, and pertinent information.

3. **Information and willingness to share information** – Provide information on markets, product innovations, and new developments so the customers are always in the picture and there are no surprises.

4. **Feedback on performance** – Provide feedback on sales, returns, and complaints, etc.

5. **Sensitivity and respect for their way of doing business** – Use diplomacy in dealing with customers and tie up all loose ends.

6. **Provide concrete reasons for dealing with us** – Provide major customers with comparisons of your products and services and those of your competitors to highlight the advantages of dealing with you.

7. **Keep in touch** - Both on a professional as well as a social level (when and where appropriate).

Make it your business to help your major customers so they can concentrate on their core business.

WHAT SHOULD YOU KNOW ABOUT YOUR MAJOR CUSTOMERS?

Everything!

If you have a good relationship with your customer, the business process flows that much more smoothly.

Richard Pratt

Make sure you are up to date on the information regarding your major customers' business, industry, and overall position in the market. You don't have to go into confidential or personal information; however, things like their overall market standing, future plans, any competition they are facing, and more importantly their feelings towards you. Isn't that what we do with people who are close to us? Don't we keep ourselves informed on their preferences, likes, dislikes, beliefs, and future plans?

We mostly do this subconsciously, and the more we know them the closer we can be to them. *We can respond to them in a manner that is more appropriate, and this works both at personal as well as in the business world.*

What amazes me is that many companies fail to inform their front-line service staff about their major customers and the business they generate, and yet expect them to provide super service to such customers! It is therefore important that you obtain basic information about your major customer, for example:

1. How much the major account holder purchases on a monthly basis.

2. Whether their purchases are moving up or down as compared to a corresponding period last year.

3. Other purchase trends (e.g., seasonal or any other relevant trends).

4. How they conduct business, their priorities, and what they values or wants.

5. Key people in major accounts that you should know, as they can facilitate your business with them.

6. Know the history of their business with your company concerning buying patterns, sales, complaints, etc., so you can attend to him in a way that is more than satisfactory to them.

7. Who else do they deal with and why.

In obtaining all of the above information, it is essential that we also know our side of the business in full (e.g., our strengths and weaknesses as compared to those of our competitors, how we conduct our business, our overall position in the market or industry, etc.).

You can only assist others if you know what they want, and deliver your assistance in a way they prefer.

SOME IDEAS ON HOW TO MANAGE MAJOR CUSTOMERS

Listed below are some ideas that can help you to maintain and develop a mutually beneficial relationship with your major customers:

1. Personalize your services as much as possible.

2. Agree as to how you will communicate: set up procedures, contact persons, regular meetings, etc.

3. Keep in constant contact with your major customers:

    - [ ] Season's greetings

    - [ ] Birthdays wishes

    - [ ] Gifts and tickets to social and community events

    - [ ] Information on new products and developments through simple and brief newsletters, web sites, and blogs etc.

4. Provide Feedback:

    - [ ] Conduct periodic checks to ascertain if things are okay.

    - [ ] Find out what else you can do.

    - [ ] Acknowledge, validate, and appreciate when their business goes up, and find out the reason for drops to take appropriate corrective action.

5. Keep in touch at a social level, if possible; invite them to your annual and promotional functions, get-togethers, and similarly, try to obtain invitations to theirs, if possible.

6. Educate your major customers about your procedures, systems, and how to access your services easily. Invite them to presentations and demonstrations on new products.

7. After-sales service – make sure that your major customers get the right priority and attention when they access after-sales services.

8. Service recovery – in case of a service compromise, ensure immediate correction or replacement of the product, and do all you can to make up for the inconvenience caused.

9. Keep key people in your organization and support departments informed as to relevant information (e.g., new developments, major inquiries, purchases, or even complaints).

10. With their permission, give them publicity in your infomercials (when appropriate).

> *Communicate effectively with your major customers.*

DOS AND DON'TS

<u>Dos:</u>

Act promptly, provide accurate information, and offer quick service. Every member of the major account is precious; each service provider must take personal responsibility to manage the major account to the best of his/her ability.

> *Your customers expect your entire operation to revolve around them.*

Don'ts:

1. Don't discuss your personal or company problems with them.
2. Don't discuss politics, religion, or sexuality with them.
3. Don't react to demands from major customers – as much as possible, give them what they want, and do so quickly.
4. Don't break promises or commitments, complicate procedures, expect the major customers to be fair, or retaliate for any shortcoming on their end.

We have to remember that managing major customers is more of a team effort than individual work. Below are some thoughts that could make the team or service provider perform more efficiently.

- Team members should display a high level of skills at whatever they do for the major customers

- Multitasking
- High level of trust amongst the team members
- Mutual support and cooperation amongst the team members
- Flexibility and adaptability
- High standards of excellence in behavior and performance
- Openness to feedback
- Effective communication structure
- No conflict between common and individual goals
- Unified commitment to results
- Good and appreciative guidance – leadership

Everyone on the team needs to understand that their purpose is to satisfy major customers, retain their patronage, and when possible, to increase business with them.

SUMMARY

1. *Returning customers give us more business than new customers.*

2. *80% of your business comes from 20% of your clients!*

3. *Provide personalized service to your major customers so you can retain their patronage and get more business for your time and effort.*

4. *We should be courteous and helpful towards all our customers; however, we should provide a more personalized service to our major clients, recognize them as major customers, and validate their patronage.*

5. *Identify your major customers, develop excellent business relationships with them, and give them your best.*

6. *Work diligently at understanding, building, and maintaining business relationships with your major customers.*

7. *Spend a lot of time talking to customers face-to-face. You'd be amazed how many companies don't listen to their customers.*

8. *When we make little mistakes, our loyal customers are forgiving and less critical.*

9. *Word of mouth advertisement is the most effective and affordable publicity you can get.*

10. *For us, our most important stakeholder is not our stockholder, it is our customer. We're in business to serve the needs and desires of our core customer base.*

11. *Make it your business to help your major customers so they can concentrate on their core business.*

12. *You can only assist others if you know what they want, and deliver your assistance in a way they prefer.*

13. *Communicate effectively with your major customers.*

14. *Your customers expect your entire operation to revolve around them.*

15. *Everyone on the team needs to understand that their purpose is to satisfy major customers, retain their patronage, and when possible, to increase business with them.*

Chapter 24

MONITOR YOUR SERVICE STANDARDS

You have to perform at a consistently higher level than others. That's the mark of a true professional. Professionalism has nothing to do with getting paid for your services.

Joe Paterno

Case Study 24:

A telephone service provider's offices were loaded with state of the art gadgets, and the staff therein was one of the best qualified and trained in the country. The service provided by the company consistently exceeded the services provided by other telephone companies in the country. This was true with the exception of one of its offices, where recently the manager had retired and was replaced by a relatively inexperienced manager recruited from outside the company. The new manager had an excellent track record in sales and the management had hoped that his appointment would give a boost to the much needed revenues from this office. However, since the appointment of the new manager the revenues were showing signs of improvement, but the number of complaints had skyrocketed!

According to regular customers the service from this office fluctuated like the unpredictable weather; one moment, everything seemed to be smooth, and the next, the service levels went berserk for no apparent reasons! Customers served by this unit were confused, and over a period of time, they started leaving for other service providers in the area. The managing director of the company hired external consultants to address the inconsistencies in service levels of this unit and the consultants conducted a thorough investigation. They came up with a set of elementary recommendations based on their findings.

What do you think the consultants found?

You may have guessed it right again! The unit in question did not impose or monitor their service standards as rigorously as before, because with the appointment of the new manager, their focus had shifted from maintaining a high level of service standards to acquiring new business.

You need to continuously compare your service levels with a benchmarked level of service to provide a high level of customer service and consistently.

WHAT ARE SERVICE STANDARDS?

Service standards are a set of comprehensive service benchmarks against which the current levels of services can be compared to establish if the current service levels are satisfactory. For example, in a contact center, the service standards could be as follows:

1.   Calls should be picked up by the third ring.

2.   No customer should have to hold for more than 30 seconds.

3.   Calls to complaint ratio should not exceed 1.5%; that is, there should not be more than three complaints for every two hundred calls answered.

Amongst other factors, service standards are usually set based on the following considerations:

☐   The standard of service level the company wants to reach and maintain,

☐   The existing service levels in the industry (i.e., best practices in the current market),

☐   Accepted service levels expected in the industry worldwide, and

☐   A minimum set of service levels required by the law of the land.

Most businesses and service organizations have service standards in place to monitor their own service levels. However, there are others who, in addition to monitoring their service levels, also let their customers know what the customers can expect from them. Setting and publishing service standards moderates the customers' expectations and brings about a sense of trust and transparency for the customers. For service standards to be effectively pursued and applied by staff in a business or service enterprise, the staff must understand the standards.

They have to work towards a common vision, the vision that tells them where they want to go and how implementation of the service standards would help them to achieve the vision. For service standards to be taken seriously, <u>they must be agreed upon by everyone in the organization.</u> Agreed upon doesn't mean that every staff member in the company will agree with the standards, but that all staff should be consulted; after all, the service standards will be implemented by them and their say is important and valuable. The standards should also be linked to their performance reviews or any other feedback machinery or appraisal.

Therefore, service standards are not arbitrary rules that you write on a piece of paper and circulate; rather, they are forms of culture that are adopted by people at all levels in an enterprise. Imagine for a second that one of the service standards is that the telephone must be answered by the third ring. It so happens that while all the call agents are busy, a call comes in. The supervisor in the area rushes to take the call before it rings for the third time and without any hesitation – he sets an example that promotes a culture that honors the service standards. The important thing is that all members of the enterprise own the service standards and apply them with gusto. It is therefore important that service standards are:

1. Written out clearly and concisely.

2. Observable and realistic.

3. Objective, specific, and measureable. As opposed to, "The calls should be picked up quickly," it is better to state, "The calls should be picked up by the third ring."

4. Distributed to everyone in the company and made easily accessible.

5. Owned and agreed upon, and therefore developed with inputs from all staff that are expected to apply the standards; service standards that are imposed usually have a very limited life span and are hardly ever practiced.

6. Actively monitored and supported by the management.

7. Reviewed periodically to tweak or remove standards that no longer apply to the contemporary business requirements.

In most medium and small-sized business organizations, the service standards do not exist. If they exist, often they are outdated and there only for the sake of having service standards! If you want to check and see if a company has an operational service standard, all you have to do is ask one of the front-line staff at a customer contact point. If they have service standards that they live by, they will tell you about their service standards with a lot of enthusiasm. Otherwise, you would know from the blank expressions on their faces that the service standards are either not there or are not being applied.

This raises the question: What if you don't have service standards in place? The answer is simple: inform your supervisors of the need for an agreed set of service standards to benchmark all of your activities, especially those involving your customers. In case your company or supervisor doesn't respond to your suggestions, it is a good idea to develop a set of personal service standards against which you can measure your own performance.

Service levels have to be specific, measureable and agreed on by all involved in providing the service.

AN EXAMPLE OF SERVICE STANDARDS

Given below is an example of a set of service standards published for customers of a general trading company.

1. We will always introduce ourselves by giving you our name.

2. We will always be helpful and treat you with utmost courtesy.

3. We are always glad to welcome you to our premises – regardless of whether you buy from us or not.

4. When you come to us in person, we will attend to you within 15 seconds of finishing servicing the previous customers.

5. When you call us over the telephone, we will attend to your call within 15 seconds.

6. We will acknowledge your mail and emails within twenty-four hours.

7. Where possible, we will resolve your complaints on the spot, and if not, we will let you know when you can expect your complaint to be resolved.

8. None of the personal information that we may request while servicing you will be shared with anyone else.

9. We will send you the latest status on your account once every fortnight by email or post.

Service standards are sets of agreements or understandings amongst the service staff that help them to provide their best to their customers.

WHY DO WE NEED SERVICE STANDARDS?

As the name implies, service standards are benchmarks that remove any ambiguity from what a service level should be. Without service standards, there cannot be any consistency in the levels of service applied by staff, as each staff will apply their own standards according to their own understanding, convenience, or mood.

Service standards make the measurement of service levels specific, objective, and concise, and remove all subjectivity from such measurement. For example, a service standard that states, "The telephones should be picked up quickly," is weak and can be interpreted differently by different staff (e.g., "quickly" could mean five rings to one staff member and seven rings to another). Service standards help us to assess how we are doing and give us the opportunity to keep service levels from slipping. They enable us to maintain consistency in our service levels and ensure that our service levels are monitored objectively.

A service level that cannot be measured is not worth a standard, as it cannot be applied consistently.

PERSONAL & PROCEDURAL SERVICE STANDARDS

Service standards can be classified as follows:

1. **Personal Service Standards:** These refer to your grooming standards, personal and professional hygiene, dress code, etc. The manner in which staff members wear their hair, the ornaments they use, and the manner in which the workplace is organized falls under the gamut of this standard.

2. **Procedural or System Service Standards:** As the name implies, this category of service standards refers to procedures that need to be applied in managing customers. For example, when a complaint is received, the following steps have to be applied:

   a. Complaint details have to be captured in a given form.

   b. A written acknowledgment has to be given to the complainant immediately.

   c. The completed form then has to be forwarded to the customer affairs department under copy to the shift supervisor within twelve hours of receipt of the complaint.

   d. The customer affairs department must respond to the complainant within one week with an appropriate resolution or an indication of the time by which the complainant can expect a resolution.

Effective service consultants apply the agreed-upon service standards to consistently maintain a high level of customer service.

HOW TO DEVELOP SERVICE STANDARDS

If you do not have any service standards, or if the service standards are redundant, you may want to take up the matter with your supervisor and help her/him develop an effective set of service standards. Given below are the suggested steps to developing service standards:

1. Research the existing service standards of:

   o Your company - if there are service standards.

   o The service standards of competition.

- o The service standards that your suppliers apply.

- o The service standards in the general market, and particularly in your industry.

- o The best practices in your service industry worldwide.

2. Find out what your customers want in context to service standards through some kind of a survey or customer feedback mechanism.

3. Check and verify what your organization wants to achieve in terms of service standards.

4. Involve all staff that directly service customers by incorporating their relevant inputs.

5. Draft a set of service standards and have it vetted by all front-line staff and other departments who are directly or indirectly involved with customer service (e.g., advertising, promotions, customer affairs, quality control, etc.).

6. Have the management ratify the draft service standards to formulate the final copy of service standards.

Development and implementation of effective service standards is a process that requires everyone's participation: the front line, the support departments, the customers, the suppliers and the management.

Service standards keep rising. As competitors render better and better service, customers become more demanding. Their expectations grow.

When every company's service is shoddy, doing a few things well can earn you a reputation as the customer's savior. But when a competitor emerges from the pack as a service leader, you have to do a lot of things right.

Suddenly achieving service leadership costs more and takes longer. It may even be impossible if the competition has too much of a head start. The longer you wait, the harder it is to produce outstanding service.

William H. Davidow

Note: After the service standards have been agreed upon and ratified by the management, make sure that they are circulated, understood, and applied by everyone in the company. Breaches of service standards don't have to be pointed out by superiors only; they are best monitored by colleagues in an amicable manner, and better applied through encouragement, a sense of co-operation, and assistance, rather than imposed.

USE AND IMPLEMENT SERVICE STANDARDS AS A GUIDE TO MAINTAINING EXCELLENT CUSTOMER SERVICE

Steps to an effective implementation of service standards:

- Set the standards and arrange to display them at vantage points.
- Make the standards an integral part of your business.
- Perpetually compare your service standards with those of your competitors.
- Check what your customers have to say: complaints, compliments, customer service surveys, and consensuses.

Obtain feedback from the front-line staff and make it easy for the front-line staff to express their views. Assign the responsibility of reviewing the feedback to a senior member of the management who is empowered to take necessary action and takes service standards seriously.

Put a system in place that periodically reviews the service standards to keep them up to date. Be willing to challenge and change service standards that are not practicable or redundant. Keep raising the bar to ensure the very best possible service levels. Encourage everyone to apply and police the agreed upon service standards.

You'll never have a product or price advantage again. They can be easily duplicated, but a strong customer service culture can't be copied.

J. Fritz

SUMMARY

1. You have to perform at a consistently higher level than others. That's the mark of a true professional. Professionalism has nothing to do with getting paid for your services.

2. You need to continuously compare your service levels with a benchmarked level of service to provide a high level of customer service and consistently.

3. Service levels have to be specific, measureable and agreed on by all involved in providing the service.

4. Service standards are sets of agreements or understandings amongst service staff that help them to provide their best to their customers.

5. A service level that cannot be measured is not worth a standard, as it cannot be applied consistently.

6. Effective service consultants apply the agreed upon service standards to maintain a consistently high level of customer service.

7. Development and implementation of effective service standards is a process that requires everyone's participation: the front line, the support departments, the customers, the suppliers and the management.

8. You'll never have a product or price advantage again. They can be easily duplicated, but a strong customer service culture can't be copied.

Chapter 25

"This is not the material I selected from the samples you showed me!"

MAKE THE MOST OF COMPLAINTS

Customer complaints are the schoolbooks from which we learn.

Unknown

Case Study 25:

Simon went to a car showroom to buy a brand new car. The salesman there was more interested in talking with his colleagues than showing cars to Simon! Simon was very upset by the inattentiveness of the salesman and went to the manager's office to lodge a complaint.

The manager seemed busy with his cronies who all were smoking and drinking coffee. After a few seconds, the manager noticed Simon standing there in his office and inquired if there was anything he could do for Simon. Simon apologized for barging into his office and complained about the way the salesman treated him. The manager didn't seem to care much about Simon's complaint and asked him to come back the next morning so he could personally assist him! Simon left the showroom in a huff and bought a car from another dealer.

Later, Simon sent a letter of complaint to the owners of the car dealership, and to his surprise, they did not even acknowledge his complaint. Upon sending numerous requests for an acknowledgement, he got a two-lined response that confirmed receipt of his complaint and stated that they were taking all necessary action! Simon was very disappointed with the attitude of the car dealer and vowed that he would never go to that showroom again. Whenever Simon got a chance, he told all of his acquaintances how badly he was treated by this car dealer.

What do you think happened here?

Customers get doubly upset, first when they are mishandled, and second, which is worse, when their complaints go unacknowledged!

Mak

If you get everybody in the company involved in customer service, not only are they 'feeling the customer' but they're also getting a feeling for what's not working. That's the key - listening to make sure that you understand the customers and that you make them feel that you understand. When a customer calls up with a complaint, we obviously can't change the past. But we have to deal with the problem.

Penny Handscomb

WHY CUSTOMERS COMPLAIN

Customers complain whenever there is a marked difference between their expectations and the services they receive. Furthermore, most customers prefer not to complain if the matter is not so serious and they have an easier alternative; rather than buying from you, next time they will go to one of your competitors!

I won't complain. I just won't come back.

Brown & Williamson
Tobacco Advertisement

Here are some reasons why your customers may complain:

1. Your services could fall short of their expectations in any of the following areas:
    *   Disrespectful or rude behavior on the part of the service agent
    *   Lack of proper attention
    *   Customer not being understood
    *   Irresponsive service
    *   Lack of product knowledge or lack of service-related information

2. Your focus on policy, procedures, and company rules, rather than the customer's needs

3. Inconvenience caused to the customer due to:

   - Sloppy service
   - Frequent breakdowns and no alternative arrangements leaving the customers in a limbo
   - Lack of accurate and reliable information and updates
   - Access difficulties (e.g., location, company personnel, service, or products)

4. Loss or damage to the customer's person or property due to negligence or defective products

5. Lack of safety procedures and standards

6. Inferior quality (e.g., flimsy products, inadequate or unhygienic facilities)

7. Design faults

8. Sometimes, customers also complain when they are having a bad day and they take it out on you. For example, they may provoke you and try to pick a fight with you because they had a quarrel with their spouse or the police may have given them a ticket! In such situations, duck the complaint and avoid retaliating or taking it personally. If you want to understand a customer who is complaining, learn to see and feel things from his perspective.

"Go on! Blame me if our neighbor's wife elopes with a gorilla!"

Most customers complain when their expectations go unmet and they have no other option.

WHY ARE COMPLAINTS IMPORTANT FOR YOUR BUSINESS?

Complaints are like physical pain. Pain tells us what is wrong with our bodies and ensures that we take action to remove the cause of the pain. If we didn't have physical pain, we would not notice injuries to our bodies and take no action to cure or prevent them. Not tending to our injuries would obviously make the injuries fester until we succumb to them.

Similarly, complaints tell us what our customers don't like about us or our services, and this allows us to remove the kinks in our services. Customers continue to do business with us because they feel we attend to their complaints. The remedial action also helps us to improve our products or services and prevent other complaints from taking place.

Most customers don't complain when they get bad service. They find it easier to get what they want from a competitor than to go through the hassle and embarrassment of making a complaint. For that reason, complaining customers are special to us; they take the trouble to let us know that they are unhappy with our services. *They actually give us a second chance to improve on our services, which is beneficial for us as well as all other clients using our services.*

Therefore, it is important that we entertain and facilitate complaints and treat the complaining customers as special. Besides, if you are a little more patient and take the trouble to listen to them, they would gladly tell you how to fix the problem as well, and free of charge!

Remember, resolving customers' complaints to their satisfaction are the shortest route to developing customer loyalty.

That is because customers are apprehensive about whether or not we can resolve their complaints to their satisfaction, and when we do so, they feel elated, relieved, and surprised. They develop a bond with us and become our loyal customers.

Complaining customers tell us what is wrong with our services, and at times, they can tell us how to fix them. Resolving customer complaints to their satisfaction is the shortest route to customer loyalty.

THE UPSIDE & DOWNSIDE OF CUSTOMER COMPLAINTS

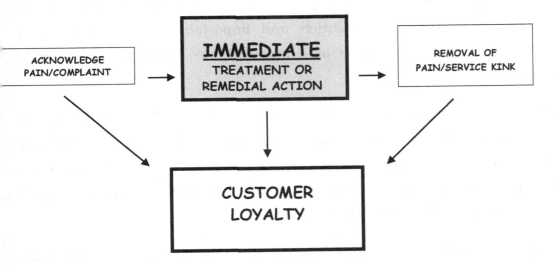

1. **Immediate Attention:** The advantage of promptly attending to the complaining customers and taking care of their problems is that they develop a level of faith and trust in us that keeps them loyal for a long time to come. In addition, not attending to a customer complaint immediately is same as ignoring the customer – a sure recipe for losing good customers who took the trouble to complain.

There is only one way to manage complaints and that is immediately. Delayed attention to complaints is like treating a patient after his demise!

Your most unhappy customers are your greatest source of learning.

Bill Gates

2. **Customers Would Rather Leave Than Complain:** Most customers don't bother to complain; they simply leave. According to one survey, 68% of customers leave a service provider if not treated properly, and most never return. Often, we don't realize until a large chunk of our clientele has slipped through our fingers and it is too late!

Customers find it easier to go to another service provider than to go through the embarrassment of complaining. On a subconscious level, most customers perceive the process of complaining as demeaning and stressful. This is because service providers usually don't give due attention and importance to customers who complain and don't look at complaints as a practical way of finding out what is wrong with their services.

The fact remains that complaining customers actually do us a favor by letting us know what is wrong with our services, and as mentioned above, they sometimes suggest very creative solutions that could save us millions of dollars in fixing the problem. Therefore, we should treat complaining customers with the utmost respect and thank them for taking the trouble to complain.

Remember, more often than not, complaining customers become loyal customers when they are attended to immediately and when their complaints are heard and resolved quickly.

Depending on the market and type of business you are in, a certain percentage of the customers will complain. It is absolutely normal and expected. As a matter of fact, a reasonable amount of customer complaint is healthy. It tells us where things are going wrong, giving us the opportunity to fix them and avoid future complaints of similar nature.

Most customers leave rather than go through the trouble and embarrassment of complaining.

3.   Acceptable levels of complaints: Every industry and market has an acceptable level of customer complaints that is indicative of how our customers feel about us. Complaints are healthy as long as they don't exceed the acceptable level mentioned above; in case you don't have one, you will have to set one based on your past level of complaints and those received by your competitors.

Ideally, we should strive to keep customer complaints as low as possible, although it would be foolhardy to expect no complaints. Complaints are an integral part of any business. Some things will go wrong, unexpected breakdowns will happen, and because of unforeseeable circumstances, service levels will fall at times.

Set a standard for an acceptable level of customer complaints for your business that will be indicative of how your customers perceive you.

4.   Customers with Unresolved Complaints Badmouth You: Customers that cannot complain are more likely to badmouth you, and you cannot afford to let any of your customers do this. Lodging a complaint helps the customer to vent their negative emotions towards an untoward incident and regain their disposition. Remember, the memory of a bad experience festers with time. Each time the customer remembers it, it is as if they are going through the bad experience again. Over time, other imagined negatives are added to the original bad experience, and the original memory of the bad experience goes from bad to worse.

In time, customers start believing in their imagined version of the bad experience, which is much worse than what actually happened.

The phenomenon is aptly described by Stephen R. Covey in his book "Seven Habits of Highly Effective People: *"Remember, it isn't the snake bite that does the serious damage; it's chasing the snake that drives the poison to the heart."*

Is it any wonder that each dissatisfied customer tells at least twenty other customers about their bad experience? They feel so frustrated that they have to vent their frustration by sharing their plight with others. Further, to get their audience's attention and sympathy, they add a lot of **'negative spicy perspective' (NSP)** to the incident.

When these twenty or more people relate the same story to others, they too add their own NSP! The end result can be ghastly and far from the truth. Therefore, don't be dismissive of complaining customers.

Mishandled complaints can destroy your reputation in the market.

MAKE IT EASY FOR YOUR CUSTOMERS TO COMPLAIN

1. **Set up a system to receive and respond to complaints:** Customers should be able to lodge their complaints at all service contact points through conveniently located complaint boxes, via dedicated telephone numbers and email addresses, and where possible, through face-to-face interviews with customer service complaint consultants.

2. **Encourage customers to lodge their dissatisfaction:** Encourage and invite customers to participate in customer service level surveys and incentivize the process through prizes, special offers, or any other suitable gifts so that customers participate in the surveys. Nothing is more frustrating to complaining customers

than service agents or customer service departments that don't respond to them. It should be our priority to attend to complaining customers promptly and efficiently.

A complaint well heard is a complaint half-resolved.

"I love spirited complainers. Most however leave quickly, & those that stay keep their peace forever."

PREPARE TO MANAGE COMPLAINTS

Manage complaints proactively. Preempt complaints during rush seasons by preparing for such periods. Do so by referring to patterns of complaints received during similar high seasons in the past. From previous trends and seasonal fluctuations, predict service shortfalls due to work pressure or other reasons, and organize your resources accordingly to manage customer rushes. Learn to communicate with disgruntled customers. Listen to them attentively, find out exactly what it is that is bothering them, and work on what it will take to appease them.

Personalize your approach with each complaining customer so that you can respond to him or her in the most effective manner. Don't take things personally when the customer shouts at you. Understand that he hardly knows you and is only venting his frustration regarding a service or product that did not meet his expectations. Avoid judging customers so that you can respond to them objectively and professionally.

Resolve to do everything possible for complaining customers and remain aware of their plight at all times. Keep your emotions in check and respond to the customer in the best possible manner.

SUMMARY

1. Customer complaints are the schoolbooks from which we learn.

2. Customers get doubly upset, first, when they are mishandled, and second, which is worse, when their complaints go unacknowledged!

3. Most customers complain when their expectations go unmet and they have no other option.

4. Complaining customers tell us what is wrong with our services and at times they can tell us how to fix them. Resolving customer complaints to their satisfaction is the shortest route to customer loyalty.

5. There is only one way to manage complaints and that is immediately. Delayed attention to complaints is like treating a patient after his demise!

6. Most customers leave rather than go through the trouble and embarrassment of complaining.

7. Set a standard for an acceptable level of customer complaints for your business that will be indicative of how your customers perceive you.

8. Mishandled complaints can destroy your reputation in the market.

9. A complaint well heard is a complaint half-resolved.

10. Resolve to do everything possible for complaining customers and remain aware of their plight at all times. Keep your emotions in check and respond to the customer in the best possible manner.

Organizations that encourage customers to voice their complaints give themselves a chance to resolve issues and convert complaining customers into advocates.

Matthew Hendry,
Charter UK

Chapter 26

HOW TO MANAGE AN IRATE CUSTOMER

There is only one boss. The customer. And he can fire everybody in the company from the chairman on down, simply by spending his money somewhere else.

Sam Walton

Case Study 26:

Peter was the sales manager of an international airline in Dubai. One morning, he received an irate customer in his office. One Mr. Sinclair from Holland, an elderly gentleman, was on his way back to Amsterdam after an around the world trip and was transiting Dubai. Mr. Sinclair had a short two-day stay in Dubai, after which he was to board his flight to Amsterdam. He was traveling first class and had a confirmed booking onwards.

On the day of his flight, he reported for the flight on time; however, the handling agent at the airport refused to allow him to board. There was a huge rush of passengers waiting with seemingly similar predicaments. The handling agent offered to rebook all such passengers on other available flights. It seemed that in the ensuing chaos, the handling agent at the airport forgot to brief Mr. Sinclair on why he couldn't accommodate him for the flight, and this made him angry. Mr. Sinclair's request to know why he was being offloaded was lost in the confusion and demands from other customers who were all talking at the same time.

What happened was that the aircraft on which Mr. Sinclair was to fly to Amsterdam had a technical problem, and on short notice, the airline replaced the original aircraft with a smaller aircraft. As a result, a large number of passengers who were holding confirmed bookings were offloaded! Mr. Sinclair waited near the check-in desk for a while, hoping that one of the handling agents would give him some attention; however, no one seemed to care!

He left the airport in a huff because of the way he was treated, and early next morning, he went to the airline's town office to lodge a complaint. It was at this point that he met Peter, the sales manager for the airline in Dubai.

Peter pacified Mr. Sinclair by offering tea and coffee and assured him of immediate action. His investigation revealed that Mr. Sinclair was a rich retiree and widower whose children had left the roost. He frequently travelled to far-off places to keep himself occupied. He loved writing about his travel episodes for local magazines, and his articles were given wide acclaim in Amsterdam. He did this to keep himself busy, rather than for the money.

Peter explained the situation to Mr. Sinclair, apologized on behalf of their handling agent, and offered to reimburse him for all of his hotel and incidental expenses incurred during his extra time in Dubai. He also made the necessary arrangements for him to take another flight out of Dubai the next morning. Further, to make up for the inconvenience caused, he offered a complimentary sightseeing tour of the city, a trip to the famous Gold Souk (souk means market in Arabic) and a dune dinner in the desert in the evening.

To Peter's surprise, Mr. Sinclair thanked Peter for his time and attention, but refused to take the airline's offer. He said he didn't need it, as he could afford all that on his own and could do with another day's rest anyway, before traveling onwards the next day. Mr. Sinclair transited via Dubai many times thereafter, and as a courtesy, he made it a point to either say hello to Peter over the telephone or visit him in his office.

What do you think happened here? Why did Mr. Sinclair not accept any recompense from the airline, and yet make it a point to lodge the complaint? You may have guessed it...

Mr. Sinclair was in no rush to reach Amsterdam, nor did he mind the additional day's stay in Dubai or the expenses. He was not particularly upset by the fact that he was denied boarding, either. He was upset at the way the handling agent treated him at the airport in spite of his being a regular and first-class passenger.

He wanted the airline to acknowledge him as one of their valued customers, and when Peter gave him that recognition, he was more than happy with nothing more than an arrangement to fly out the next day.

Find out exactly what the customer is complaining about and then address the issue accordingly.

When complaints are freely heard, deeply considered, and speedily reformed, then is the utmost bound of civil liberty attained that wise men look for.

John Milton

WHO IS AN IRATE CUSTOMER?

Irate customers are upset customers; they can be upset with us for a variety of reasons. Mostly, they are upset because they did not receive the services that they expected. In some rare situations, customers can be upset not because we failed to provide the agreed upon service, but because they are angry about something in their personal lives. They are grumpy at anyone they come across.

On other rare occasions, customers behave irately because they are under the influence of alcohol or drugs.

Whatever the reason for our customers' upset, it is important that we understand how our customers feel, especially when we can't keep our part of the bargain. *If we want to know how irate customers feel, the easiest way is to notice how we feel as customers when we are mistreated by a service provider.* It is important to understand that when customers are upset, they become emotional, and in that state of mind, their logical faculties are impaired. Customers in an emotional state are difficult to reason with, and if we want to communicate with them effectively, we first have to bring them out of their volatile emotional state into a calmer state. To do so requires a set of progressive steps that allows the customer to vent their anger and cool down, so that we can reason with them and communicate effectively.

Without going into unnecessary detail, it is enough to mention that whenever we human beings face any strong emotions because of perceived danger, anger, fear, etc., we automatically go into a state of fight or flight. As mentioned previously, the fight or flight response is our body's autonomic response to any danger or threat. It primes our body and mind to cope with the cause of danger by either fighting or fleeing from the source of danger. *In this state, we take on the adversarial position and perceive everything with hostility, suspicion, and scorn.*

When customers are upset, they are in the fight or flight state and see everything with hostility, suspicion, and scorn.

STEPS TO MANAGING AN IRATE CUSTOMER

Listed below is the suggested 'Fourteen-Step Method' that you may find useful when managing an irate customer:

1. Greet:

- ☐ Greet the customer and use their name. Using the customer's name brings about a feeling of connectedness with the customer that is lost when the customer is upset.

- ☐ Stop doing what you are doing and focus completely on the customer.

2. Listen without interruption:

- ☐ Give your undivided attention to the customer and take notes. Taking notes tells the customers that you care and allows you to capture the critical details of the complaint in one discussion.

Asking an irate customer to repeat the details only adds to their woe.

☐ Indicate to the customer that you're listening intently by nodding your head or saying words like "yes" or "hmm...."

☐ Don't interrupt the customer; rather, let him vent his anger. Even if you know what the complaint is about, listen without interrupting. Listening intently triggers the customer's parasympathetic response discussed earlier, and brings them out of their emotional state into a calmer and neutral state. Once the customer calms down, their logical brain function kicks in so that you can have a meaningful dialogue with him.

3. **Understand the customer by listening**: Listen to what he is saying, how he is saying it, and <u>what he is not saying</u>. Read his body language and notice the tone of his voice as he reveals what is bothering him. If the complaint is complicated, or if you don't understand the customer's main reason for complaining, restate your understanding to make sure you have fully understood the customer and that you have captured all the details.

4. **Don't react**: Don't react emotionally. Learn to respond calmly and stay composed.

5. **Acknowledging the complaint: It is an important step in calming the** customer because he feels someone understands him and cares. For example, you might say, "So what you're saying, Mr. Sheen, is that you didn't get a wakeup call this morning, and because of that, you were late for an important meeting?"

6. **Apologize and/or empathize:** When you see the customer calming down, apologize for any inconvenience caused. One word of caution, though: You should apologize only when you are sure that some service compromise has taken place. Otherwise, an apology could imply an inappropriate acceptance of liability on your company's behalf and that may not be the case.

For example, the wakeup calls were made repeatedly and recorded by the hotel's automated wakeup call system, but the guest had turned off the telephone's ringer the night before so as not to be disturbed by any incoming call rings while he worked. Before going to bed that night he completely forgot about it, and didn't reactivate the ringer.

If you're unsure of whose fault it is, empathize with the customer by letting them know that you understand the situation. For example, you might say "Mr. Sheen, we understand how inconvenient it is for you to be rushing to an important meeting, and we will investigate this matter thoroughly and get back to you."

7. **Ask questions if necessary:** Seek the customer's permission to ask questions with a valid cause and consequence. For example, "Can I ask you some questions so I'm sure I understand you fully? It will help me to help you better." Seeking permission gives the customer a sense of control and helps in reconnecting with him. Asking questions helps us to clarify the finer details of the customer's complaint and uncover his expectation so that we can provide satisfactory solutions to the problem.

8. **Assure:**

   ☐ *After the apologies are over, don't spend too much time justifying why things went wrong. Justifications keep the customer's attention and feelings on the negative aspects of the complaint and that can make him more irritated and aggressive.*

☐ Rather, quickly move on to <u>assuring</u> the customer that action will be taken to put things right immediately. Use statements like, "<u>We</u> need to resolve your problem *immediately*." Notice that using the word "we" puts you and the customer on the same side of the fence, rather than as adversaries.

☐ Offer to investigate the complaint later and emphasize your intention and the importance of first resolving the complaint quickly. For example, you might say, "Ms. Susan, we understand your predicament, and right now, we need to ensure that you get on the next flight to London which leaves in two hours' time; we will investigate what happened in the meantime and let you know on your return."

9. Offer alternatives:

☐ Once you understand the situation, offer appropriate alternatives. Like seeking permission to ask questions, offering alternatives also gives customers a sense of control that induces the parasympathetic response discussed above.

☐ Explain the pros and cons of each alternative so that the customer can make an educated choice.

☐ Recommend an alternative that you think is most befitting to the customer's needs and make sure he sees the benefits to him in the solution you recommended.

10. Agree on an alternative:

☐ Agree on an alternative with the customer.

☐ Whether the customer agrees to your recommendation or not is immaterial, as it is all about the customer's choice.

☐ Commend the customer's choice anyway, and make him feel more confident about his choice.

☐ Ask the customer if there is anything else you could help him with.

11. Tell the customer what action you're going to take:

☐ Explain to the customer what action you are going to take and explain what he can expect. Many service agents fail to explain to their customers how their problems will be resolved, and in the process, keep their customers guessing, which is not a comfortable position to be in.

12. Take action and keep the customer informed on progress if appropriate:

☐ Take action.

☐ Keep the customer informed of any changes to what was agreed upon.

☐ Where appropriate, keep customers informed on progress made on their order so they are assured that their work is being attended to

☐ In case of any change, inform the customer up front with specific reasons and possible alternatives/remedies from which the customer can choose. Customers should be advised of any changes as early as possible to give them ample time to take any other course of action that they may want to take.

13. Thank the customer:

☐ Thank the customer for taking the trouble of complaining and for his patience and understanding.

☐ Invite him back with assurance that next time you will do better.

14. Advise relevant departments:

☐ Document the complaint and action taken and send it to colleagues in relevant departments so they too are aware of the situation and can work together to avoid such complaints in the future.

☐ For recurring complaints, invite ideas from colleagues as well as customers and initiate action to preempt such complaints from happening.

Note: The above fourteen-step method is just a guideline, and there could be situations where it would be more practical to ignore certain steps or repeat some sequence of steps for a better grasp and resolution of the complaint. Use common sense and keep the needs and feelings of your customer paramount at all times.

Before you empathize or attempt to resolve their complaint, first let them vent their feelings.

SUMMARY

1.   There is only one boss. The customer. And he can fire everybody in the company from the chairman on down, simply by spending his money somewhere else.

2.   Find out exactly what the customer is complaining about and then address the issue accordingly.

3.   When customers are upset, they are in the fight or flight state and see everything with hostility, suspicion, and scorn.

4.   Before you empathize or attempt to resolve their complaint, first let them vent their feelings.

Chapter 27

SERVICE RECOVERY

What separates service leaders from the rest of the pack is how they handle those mistakes, how they meet the challenge of turning a disgruntled customer into one who sings their praises and becomes a customer for life.

John
Tschohl
International Management Consultant

Case Study 27:

Jim was a businessman and had to travel on business quite often. On one business trip, he had a frustrating experience at the airport. When he reported for the flight, the airline refused to accept him because he did not have a confirmed booking and the flight was full! The travel agent had booked Jim for the next day's flight by mistake!

Jim was extremely upset and disappointed. He called his agent and lodged a complaint in the strongest possible terms. The manager of the travel agency, one Ms. Jessie, listened to his complaint and invited him to her office so she could look into the complaint. While driving to the travel agency, Jim felt that most travel agencies were scam operations and wondered what excuses Ms. Jessie had cooked up for him to justify the fiasco. The receptionist gave Jim a broad smile and asked if she could be of any assistance to him. Jim wondered if the receptionist's welcoming attitude was guile or a genuine offer to assist him. Jim decided to ignore the receptionist and stormed into Ms. Jessie's office.

Jim expected Ms. Jessie to justify their mistake by making a lot of excuses, but instead, she surprised Jim by listening intently and showing empathy. She said that she had probed into the incident and confirmed that it was a mistake on their part. She inquired whether Jim would like to be booked on the next available flight, and at Jim's consent, proceeded to make the necessary arrangements herself.

Upon confirming the next available flight, she again apologized to Jim for the inconvenience, and to make up for the inconvenience caused to him, she offered to upgrade Jim to business class at no additional cost the next time he traveled.

Jim was surprised by the way Ms. Jessie handled the situation. He had expected an exchange of harsh words and avoidance tactics by the agent. Instead, they had taken complete responsibility for their mistake and even apologized for it. They not only took immediate action to rectify the situation, but also offered to make up for the inconvenience by upgrading Jim to business class at no additional cost on his next trip.

How do you think Jim felt after all that? If you were in Jim's shoes, would you have continued buying tickets from this travel agency?

Customers expect the service providers to acknowledge their mistakes and take immediate action to correct them.

Customers don't expect you to be perfect. They do expect you to fix things when they go wrong.

Donald Porter

WHAT IS SERVICE RECOVERY?

Perhaps the best way to explain service recovery is through an example that pertains to personal relationships. Imagine that you promise to take your wife to the movies. You agree to pick her up from home after work at 8 p.m. so you can comfortably reach the cinema by 9 p.m.

Now, imagine that as you are leaving the office at 6 p.m., your boss suddenly calls you for an emergency meeting concerning a project that requires immediate attention. Because of your close involvement with the project, you completely forget that you were supposed to take your wife to the movies. You don't call her to let her know that you won't be able to make it to the movies. The meeting ends by 10 p.m., and as you get into your car, to your horror you realize that you were supposed to take your wife to the movies. When you reach home, she is upset and not ready to listen to your side of the story!

After profuse apologies and explanations about the emergency meeting, your wife reverts to speaking terms, but remains displeased by the incident. What would you do to eliminate her disappointment? Would you take her to the movies the next evening, invite her to a candlelit dinner at her favorite restaurant, or buy her the gift of her choice to make up for the disappointment?

In the above example, you probably would make up with your wife by doing the following:

1. You would **apologize** for not taking her to the movies and also for forgetting to tell her or keep her waiting.

2. **Empathize** and explain briefly why you couldn't make it.

3. Offer to **take her to the movies** the next evening.

4. Make it up to her by **offering something extra** (e.g., inviting her to dinner).

5. **Thank her for her patience and reassure her** that such a slip will not happen again.

Similar to the above, whenever we fail to provide the service we promise to our customers, we need to take steps to recover our relationship with them. This recovery process involves the following:

a.   Apologize and empathize

b.   Briefly explain how and why things went wrong

c.   Take <u>immediate steps</u> to fulfill the service

d.   Offer something tangible to the customer (over and above the original service agreement) to make up for the inconvenience caused

e.   Thank the customer for lodging the complaint (as it helps us to improve our services) and assure the customer that things will be better the next time.

As explained earlier, please note that step "b" should be kept as brief as possible because explanations or justifications keep the customer's thoughts on service compromises – a negative area. Move to step "c" as quickly as possible, as this step offers the solution – a positive perception for the customer. This is where the service recovery process starts.

> *Service recovery involves undoing the damage and then compensating for the inconvenience caused.*

CUSTOMERS TALK WHEN THEIR EXPECTATIONS ARE NOT MET

Go back to a time when you, as a customer, had a bad experience. Think of the way you felt and the negative thoughts that went through your head. Maybe the customer service agent was rude, the product you bought didn't work, or they gave you the wrong product. Now, when you think about the incident, does it churn up negative feelings of some kind? Notice that although the incident may have happened some time ago, it still hasn't lost its power to annoy you to some extent.

Since the time of the above incident, how many people have you told about how badly you were treated? Further, whenever an opportunity presents itself, wouldn't you repeat the story to others?

We as human beings are always looking for attention, and what better way to get attention and sympathy than to exaggerate about how inconsiderately you were treated. Every time we talk about the incident, don't we keep adding a little spice to the incident to make our talk more interesting? **(Negative Spicy Perspective (NSP) - page 392).**

Furthermore, when you repeat your sad story a number of times, you actually start believing what you say (including the added spice and dramatization) over what actually happened. Additionally, let's not forget that your audience tells the story to others, and they too add some more spice of their own to make their talk more interesting! It's no wonder that wronged customers never forget and try to get back at you by telling everyone they meet. In contrast to the above, when you get what you expect (i.e., good service), you hardly think about it and your mind gets preoccupied with other things that are more interesting.

Recently, I read on the Internet that on average, customers tell two to three other customers about the good service they received, while dissatisfied customers tell up to twenty to twenty-five others about how bad the service was! Not to mention how many others the twenty-five would tell!

Some people think that successful businesses don't have or have few customer complaints. However, you can rest assured that nothing could be further from the truth. The truth is that the more business you have, the more complaints you can expect to receive. No matter how careful you are with your service, things will occasionally breakdown, systems will fail, and mistakes will be made.

However, the resilient businesses are those that recover quickly through their efficient service recovery programs. They have deliberately learned, developed, and applied service recovery processes that work. In such businesses, there seems to exist an unwritten, unquestioned, and agreed upon culture that puts the customer first in anything and everything they do.

Advertising will get a customer through the door to your business once, but it is service that will keep them coming back. Advertising is aimed at the masses; customer service is aimed at the individual. Service recovery creates word-of-mouth advertising that is 100 times cheaper and more powerful than traditional advertising.

John Tschohl

STEPS TO AN EFFECTIVE SERVICE RECOVERY

Customer service recovery is not about how much you give, but how much you care. Think of it like a lover's tiff; the estranged party is the customer and you want to try and win them back. When you make up with someone, don't you try to undo what you have done wrong and compensate for it by giving extra for the hurt or inconvenience caused? Therefore, compensation has to be something that the (particular) customer likes or appreciates. You wouldn't compensate your partner by taking her to a movie if she prefers going to an opera, would you?

> *Service recovery has to be suited to the personality of the customer. It is more about what would satisfy the customer, but can only be implemented after undoing the wrong done to him.*

FOUR STEPS TO SERVICE RECOVERY

1. Act quickly:

This means acting speedily (i.e., within seconds). John Tschohl, the world-renowned guru on service recovery, says, *"Don't say you'll get back to the customer tomorrow. Do whatever needs to be done—and do it now. The cost of handling a complaint escalates as it moves up the corporate ladder. And the longer it takes for a complaint to be resolved, the angrier the customer gets."*

2. Apologize and take responsibility:

"Too many employees want to blame someone else for mistakes," says Tschohl. *"The customer doesn't care who made the mistake; he wants the employee standing in front of him to take care of it. You must own the problem. Apologize on behalf of your organization and then take whatever steps are necessary to solve the problem."*

3. Be empowered:

"Empowerment is the backbone of service recovery," says Tschohl. *"Service recovery requires empowerment at all levels of the organization. Unfortunately, most employees are petrified at the thought of making an empowered decision. They're afraid the management would reprimand them, deduct their salaries with what they give away to customers, or lose their jobs for making mistakes while serving customers. As a result, the service agents worship at the altar of procedures and policies. For then they can hide behind procedures or policy and not risk being on the wrong side of the management. How often have you heard service agents saying, 'I'm sorry; our company policy doesn't allow for ...,' which only makes an angry customer angrier. If there is any policy regarding service recovery, it should be one that requires service agents to do whatever it takes to satisfy their customers."*

4. Compensate the customer:

"Service recovery doesn't end when you solve the customer's problem," says Tschohl. *"Give her something of value that excites her. Every company has products or services that have value in the eyes of the customer that don't cost the company a lot of money. Identify five or ten products or services your organization has that you could give away when your organization makes a mistake. Vail Resorts has a system in place that provides free drinks when the ski lift shuts down for a few minutes and free lift tickets when it's down for more than 15 minutes."* *"A restaurant,"* Tschohl adds, *"can waive the cost of a meal or offer a free dessert. A software company can provide a free upgrade. A computer company can give the customer a free one-year extended warrantee."*

The acronym "RECOVER" in Table – 1, below, further explains the steps by drawing an analogy between service recovery and personal relationship recovery. When things go wrong, you may find the analogy intriguing:

Sr. No:	Service Recovery in Business	Personal Relationship Recovery	Remarks
	Similarities between business and personal relationship recovery strategies when things go wrong		
1.	**R**espond rapidly	*Call your sweetheart (her/him) immediately*	The longer you wait the more difficult it becomes to make up
2.	**E**ndorse the complaint	*Apologize/empathize*	Accept that you treated her/him unfairly and take responsibility
3.	**C**ontain negative emotions by undoing the service compromise	*Undo your wrong doing as quickly as possible otherwise the negative emotions could fester and become worse – you could face sanctions on relational benefits and privileges!*	Pacify and duck allegations/accusations etc., – ensure situation doesn't get out of hand. _Keep the original promise,_ do what you were supposed to do, e.g., take her to the movies at the first possible opportunity - high priority
4.	**O**ffer compensation for the hurt or inconvenience. This is extra-over and above the replacement of the original promise	*Compensate by offering to take her out for dinner after the movie or something similar*	Repair the damaged relationship and bond
5.	The compensation should be of **V**alue to the customer	*The compensation should be something that your sweetheart likes or prefers*	The compensation should show the other person that you care
6.	**E**nchanting the customer with the compensation	*While at dinner, do everything possible to please and **reassure** your partner*	Reassure that it will not happen again
7.	**R**evalidate their patronage so they return to you.	Reassure them and tell them that you love them.	Do this with sincerity, care and finesse

(Table – 1)

BENEFITS OF SERVICE RECOVERY

Repeat business/customer loyalty: *"When you solve a customer's problem and give her something of value, you will have a customer who will be loyal for life,"* says Tschohl. *"In fact, studies show that she then will be more loyal to your company than if she hadn't experienced a problem with you. Superior service, supported by service recovery, will generate positive word-of-mouth advertising, increase your customer loyalty, bring in new customers—and send your sales and profits soaring."* Research indicates that repeat customers spend 67% more than new customers. If you want to have satisfied customers, you cannot worship at the altar of policies and procedures. *"When a customer has a problem, you must act quickly, take responsibility, be empowered, and compensate the customer,"* says Tschohl. *"Do that and you will have a customer who will be loyal for life."*

Cut marketing costs: As mentioned earlier, it is much cheaper to retain the patronage of existing customers than to acquire new customers. However, many companies focus on gaining new customers at the cost of retaining existing customers. Surveys have proven that it costs companies ten to fifteen times as much money to gain a new customer as it does to retain an existing one.

Word of mouth advertisement: When you effectively practice service recovery, you are creating a customer who will be so satisfied with your services that he will tell all his close acquaintances about it. Recommendations from a satisfied customer are very convincing. Such word of mouth publicity is very powerful and doesn't cost a dime. It is said that word of mouth advertising is ten times more powerful than other forms of advertisement and twenty times cheaper.

Improve your bottom line: In the long term, an effective service recovery program can prevent customer defections and contribute towards increasing your sales and profits.

Reduce employee turnover: Further, it will prevent employee defection. Service agents that are trained to provide excellent customer service and empowered to make decisions to assist their customers have a higher level of job satisfaction. Employees with high levels of job satisfaction rarely leave for another employer.

> *With effective service recovery, both your internal and external customers will think twice before leaving you.*
>
> *Mak*

In the long term, it will create a customer-focused culture in the company. The service staff will keep responding to their customers by being creative and applying innovations that aren't utilized in companies run by policies, rules, and procedures.

Keep competition at bay: Service recovery will put you and your organization ahead of the competition. The competition will find it more difficult to snatch your customers, as your customers will prefer to deal with you.

WHY BUSINESSES FAIL AT SERVICE RECOVERY

Most companies don't understand the implications of not having an effective service recovery program. Although some seem to nod their heads in agreement, they only give lip service to the importance of service recovery.

Many spend millions of dollars to get the customers in, but very little or nothing at all to ensure that the customers that they won keep coming back. They fail miserably at ensuring that customers already with them are not deterred from returning because of bad service or non-existent service recovery processes.

It is similar to trying to fill up a bucket with water that has gaping holes; no matter how much water you pour into the bucket, the water leaks out eventually. It's not difficult to see why most companies fail to keep their fair share of customers. Some of the common reasons are:

Lip service: Service recovery is only lip service with these companies. The higher echelons in these companies don't practice what they preach, even with their internal customers.

Lack of employee empowerment: Their front-line employees are not empowered to make decisions that are crucial to satisfying customers; everything is about rules, policies, and procedures, and is subject to management approval.

Training: Companies who fail to empower their front-line employees are usually the same companies that don't invest in training their employees! Why? Because their focus is on the development of products, procedures, bottom line, and they  ignore the people who are responsible for managing the products, applying the procedures, and adding to the bottom line of the company.

Personnel recruit employees who may be efficient, but not necessarily customer-savvy: This is so rampant that even a blind person can see it, and yet no one seems to take any action to correct this anomaly. Intelligence is not the only criterion that is indicative of service potential. In addition to being smart, the staff selected for customer service should be inherently and intrinsically customer-service oriented. They should enjoy serving others and it should come naturally to them.

Inappropriate recruitment not only harms the company and the customers, but also those employees, who then find their jobs uninteresting. The company strives to motivate, discipline, and train such staff, but seldom gets the desired results. Staff members that do not have the aptitude or interest in assisting customers hardly ever display the customer-oriented behavior, no matter their qualifications.

Whatever the reason, these companies are paying a heavy price for recruiting people that are smart, but not particularly motivated in serving others.

Mak

Lack of customer service culture: In the final analysis, these companies lack the service culture. They do things for their own convenience and are focused on their own needs. The customers' needs and preferences are, at best, buzzwords that are better left in the books and for small talk at parties and social gatherings.

Service recovery is action-based, rather than promise-based.

WHAT DO COMPANIES WITH SUCCESSFUL SERVICE RECOVERY PROGRAMS DO DIFFERENTLY?

*Successful companies realize that they are in a **service business** and not a computer, airline, healthcare, or restaurant business.*

They know the importance of repeat business and customer loyalty, and spend considerable resources to ensure that their employees know how to provide service in a way that generates profits as well as builds relationships with customers. Let's look at what the staffs of these companies do differently:

Focus on customer-centered culture: These companies have a customer service culture that permeates from the boardroom right down to the front-line. They make sure their policies, procedures, and systems are all customer-friendly. *The* *governing rule is that everything exists to make things convenient and pleasurable for the customers.*

Focus on building relationships rather than making sales:

The front-line and back office staffs in these companies focus on building relationships rather than making sales. That way, the customer not only keeps coming back for more, but also recommends them to other customers. When you add up the lifetime value of all such customers, the figures become enormous.

Recruit customer service-oriented employees: They hire people who inherently like helping others and have aptitude in customer service. Recruiting the right people in the first place saves them from the unnecessary hassles of managing indifferent staff, not to discount the damage such staff members can do in the time before they leave for another job that is more meaningful to them.

Train their staff: These companies invest heavily in training. They train their front-line employees and supervisors in the art of customer service delivery and encourage their staff to keep learning and developing their customer service skills. *These companies understand that training in the area of customer service is not a onetime intervention, but something that needs to be ingrained by repeated training.* Otherwise, after a while front-line staffs tend to cut corners because of work pressure or pure negligence. A constant and focused realignment to best practices must be intermittently provided through refresher training to reinforce the service culture and best practices. Onetime training intervention results in nothing more than awareness that is hardly ever applied!

A consistent high level of customer service requires repeated training exposure that keeps service staff motivated, realigned, and in touch with best practices.

Empower their employees—especially their front-line staff:

CONTRACT

"I'll NEVER say 'yes' to customers without first checking with my Supervisor!"

They empower their employees. They give them authority to deviate from the rules within justifiable limits to satisfy the customer. *They understand that empowerment is the backbone of service recovery.* Employees must have the authority to make reasonable decisions to resolve customers' problems and see them off fully satisfied.

Many company executives that I have come across reiterate that they strongly believe in empowering their employees. However, they lament that their front-line employees are nothing but a breed of nonentities that cannot be empowered, and as such, their service recovery suffers. I once asked one such executive what it made him if he were the leader of these so-called nonentities!

Now, with that kind of an attitude, what do you think the executives do to control the front-line employees? You guessed it; they impose a lot of unbreakable rules, procedures, and systems that leave the service providers with no power to assist their customers, particularly in a service recovery situation. Empowerment is a difficult concept for many managers to internalize. It takes away their control and they feel exposed. They would rather install policies, procedures, and sets of instructions that eliminate the need for the front-line employee to think and make decisions, especially when something unexpected happens or when something goes wrong. What these managers don't realize is that their tendency to micromanage prevents their front-line employees from providing the very service they yearn for - an excellent level of service that keeps the customers coming back for more.

Recognize and reward outstanding service: These companies recognize and reward the front-line employees that provide excellent and exemplary service. In fact, some companies keep pushing the limits to which customer service can be elevated and keep challenging their employees to do better and better through various reward and recognition schemes.

A lot of companies have the service agent of the year, which is okay, but the question remains as to how the award makes other service agents feel who also toiled to put the company where it is now. *Why does it have to be one award? Why not have many awards that recognize different good things done by staff anytime of the year, and why not make it an ongoing process?*

Progressive companies look after their employees, and the employees in turn look after the customers.

The positive attitudes of effective customer service staff in progressive companies can be attributed to the following:

- ☐ They have a sense of belonging.
- ☐ They feel their work is recognized and appreciated.
- ☐ They feel they are meaningfully contributing to the company's bottom line.
- ☐ They have the opportunity to express themselves, to be creative, and innovate.
- ☐ They are treated fairly.
- ☐ They find themselves reasonably secure in their jobs.
- ☐ They have the opportunity to learn.
- ☐ They have the possibility for career growth.

Service recovery has to be as deeply satisfying to the service provider as it is to the customer.

MAKE THE SERVICE RECOVERY PROCESS MORE EFFECTIVE

It is worthwhile to ask ourselves how we can make our company's service recovery process more successful. You, as the front-line staff, can contribute immensely in the formulation of effective processes and procedures that facilitate the service recovery process. You are the eyes and ears of the company, and the feedback and suggestions you provide to the management will help them to support you better so that the customer service you provide is par excellence.

Let us have a look at what you, as a front-line staff, can do to empower yourself even though your employer may not have an effective customer service recovery process in place:

i. **Take personal responsibility in managing customer complaints:** You can take personal responsibility for all the customer complaints you handle and do so with dedication. Use personal influence and connections (networking) to ensure that the complaining customer is fully satisfied and encouraged to continue doing business with you. Watch out for some superiors who may not be particularly appreciative of your devotion to service recovery. However, don't let their lukewarm attitude discourage you. It is not uncommon to hear of situations where instead of being appreciated for taking extra care of the customers, the staff member was asked to stick to company procedures and not try to be overly smart! However, helpful staff can't keep themselves from bending procedures (within limits) every now and then to help their customers. Assisting the customers seems to be in their blood, and their self-worth seems to come from having fully satisfied customers that profusely thank them for their interest, involvement, and initiative.

ii.   **Job knowledge:** Acquire full and complete technical knowledge of the job that you do so that you attain the level of being referred to as an expert. Make sure that you have the relevant product or service information. For example, if you're working as a front-line staff member in a rental car company, you had better be an expert on the local car rental rules and regulations, your company's rates and policies, and the legal implications of accidents, late vehicle returns, etc.

How can you get all that information? Start by asking the seniors in the company, analyze previous records, and take interest in areas in which you don't have adequate knowledge or skills.

iii.   **Learn to relate the benefits of your services to your customers:** You should learn to show your customers how your product or services will benefit them, rather than highlight and sell the features of the product. Focusing on the features ignores your customer and their needs. Rather, find out what the customer wants and then link the benefits in your product to those wants; be customer focused.

Respond, rather than react, to your customers. Most mediocre service agents react to their customers (i.e., answer customers' questions or provide information). Expert customer service agents, on the other hand, go beyond answering questions by trying to discern the real concerns of the customer and respond accordingly. For example, if the customer inquires about the availability of a certain product over the telephone, the mediocre service agent will probably say "yes" or "no." However, expert service agents will not only answer the query, but they will also find out more information on what the customer needs and offer a range of similar products from which the customer can choose.

iv. **Behave like a specialist:** Think of yourself as a specialist in your area of work and provide consultancy service. Guide the customers so they can benefit from your expertise and depend on your recommendations.

v. **Discreetly bend the rules to assist your major customers:** I know of a cargo agency in town that has a large notice on its window telling its customers that photocopying facilities are not available. However, one of the service agents there helps his major customers by photocopying one or two pages for them discreetly. When I asked him why he was going against the department's policy of not providing photocopies to clients, he explained, "Our major customers use our services regularly and expect the service from us. Besides, I can't be sending these customers back just for photocopies – most of them have found a parking space after going around for 15 to 20 minutes! If we keep sending our customers back for such a petty thing, we will soon be without customers!"

Upon further inquiry, I found that the staff had taken the matter up with their manager on many occasion and with little success. The manager was a cost-cutting enthusiast. He was promoted to the position of a senior manager by showing higher profits that he thought could be sustained through cutting costs to the bone.

One word of caution, though: You should be very careful when you bend the rules. Company rules and procedures are usually there to protect your interests, to protect the company's interests, and to avoid unnecessary litigation and legal claims. There are unscrupulous people out there who wouldn't think twice about getting you in trouble for their personal gain.

For example, perhaps your company policy doesn't allow staff to provide rides to customers in company vehicles. However, you don't think much of it, and with good intentions, you provide a lift to one of your customers. Now, God forbid you meet with an accident and the customer in the car is injured. How can you guarantee that he will not sue you or your company for his injuries?

Here is a simple but powerful rule – always give people more than what they expect to get.

Nelson Boswell

One of the deep secrets of life is that all that is really worth doing is what we do for others.

Lewis Carol

SUMMARY

1. What separates service leaders from the rest of the pack is how they handle those mistakes, how they meet the challenge of turning a disgruntled customer into one who sings their praises and becomes a customer for life.

2. Customers expect the service providers to acknowledge their mistakes and take immediate action to correct them.

3. Service recovery involves undoing the damage and then compensating for the inconvenience caused.

4. Advertising will get a customer through the door to your business once, but it is service that will keep them coming back. Advertising is aimed at the masses; customer service is aimed at the individual. Service recovery creates word-of-mouth advertising that is 100 times cheaper and more powerful than traditional advertising.

5. Service recovery has to be suited to the personality of the customer. It is more about what would satisfy the customer, but can only be implemented after undoing the wrong done to him.

6. With effective service recovery, both your internal and external customers will think twice before leaving you.

7. Service recovery is action-based, rather than promise-based.

8. A consistent high level of customer service requires repeated training exposure that keeps service staff motivated, realigned, and in touch with best practices.

9. Service recovery has to be as deeply satisfying to the service provider as it is to the customer.

10. One of the deep secrets of life is that all that is really worth doing is what we do for others.

Chapter 28

Honk, honk...

TEAMWORK

Did you know that in our world, the word "geese" means "team" – a team that works, plays and survives together?

Mak

THE GEESE - OUR STORY:

LET ME INTRODUCE YOU TO OUR TEAM (FORMATION)

It may surprise you to know that we achieve the unachievable only because of teamwork. We migrate hundreds of miles at a stretch without a break and it is tough–we succeed in doing so because we fly together, in a formation that looks like a "V." Below are some interesting facts about how we work together and benefit from it, something that you can adopt in your workplace as service specialists and consultants.

FACT 1:

When we flap our wings to fly, it creates "uplift" for our colleagues flying behind us. You may have seen a lot of us flying in a "V" formation, and we do that because flying in that formation enables the whole flock to fly more than 70% more distance than we could fly if we flew alone.

Lesson for you:

A service team that has a common purpose and shares the work achieves what they want quickly and easily, and enjoys their work because they support and back each other up.

> Teamwork is the ability to work together toward a common vision. It is the fuel that allows common people to attain uncommon results.

Andrew Carnegie

FACT 2:

When we fall out of the formation, we suddenly feel the drag and resistance of flying alone! We quickly move back into formation to take advantage of the lifting power of our colleagues in front of us; why work hard unnecessarily and waste the flying power of the formation?

Lesson for you:

When service specialists work together and stay aligned to the common purpose, they complement each other's efforts; they accept and extend help to each other.

Successful people are always looking for opportunities to help others. Unsuccessful people are always asking, "What's in it for me?

Brian Tracy

FACT 3:

When our lead goose in the formation gets tired, he or she goes back to the end of the formation and another goose takes the lead; we keep doing this so we can rest from leading the formation and yet fly hundreds of miles non-stop.

Lesson for you:

When service specialists take turns at doing the tough and unpleasant chores, everyone's stress levels stay down. It allows everyone to rest and recuperate before returning to stressful and challenging tasks.

What is without periods of rest will not endure.

Ovid

FACT 4:

While flying, those of us in the back of the formation constantly honk to encourage those braving the winds in the front of the formation to keep up a steady speed; our feedback gives those in the front strength and support and the whole formation benefits by reaching the destination more quickly.

Lesson for you:

Service specialists need to constantly encourage, provide support to each other, and give positive feedback to their colleagues working at the front, especially those working in direct contact with customers. Support and encouragement makes those at the front feel good, and they in turn make their customers feel good.

You need to be aware of what others are doing, applaud their efforts, acknowledge their successes, and encourage them in their pursuits. When we all help one another, everybody wins.

Jim Stovall

FACT 5:

When one of us is sick, wounded, or shot, two geese from the team drop out of the formation and follow the disabled goose to take care of him and protect him. The three geese stay together until the disabled colleague has fully recovered. Then, they join other formations to catch up with their original formation.

Lesson for you:

In any service area, considerable pressures of all kinds build up during peak hours. During such stressful periods, people tend to make mistakes. It is at such times that service specialists need help from their colleagues.

Build for your team a feeling of oneness, of dependence on one another, and of strength to be derived by unity.

Vince Lombardi

********* ***Based on work by Milton Olson*** *********

WHAT IS TEAMWORK?

In simple words, teamwork can be defined as a group of people working together towards a common purpose or goal. In effective teams, people communicate with each other and focus on how they can complement each other's efforts. They understand that unity is strength, and make use of each other's expertise; "the right job for the right person" applies.

One example of good teamwork is a decent marriage in which the wife and the husband focus on the common good of the family rather than on themselves.

Another good example is found in a football team where the players play together by passing the ball to the right position so the team can score goals. Even a corporation in which the various departments work together towards common goals provide a clear illustration of teamwork.

A team is a small number of people with complementary skills who are committed to a common purpose, performance goals, and approach for which they are mutually accountable.

Katzenbach and Smith

Customer service is something that can't be provided by a service agent or a department on their own. Excellent service is always the result of the combined effort of service agents working in the front as well as the back offices of various departments. The customer comes in touch with various contact points where the service agents provide a component of the service. It is their combined effort that makes the customer's experience memorable. The practice of teamwork also applies within a department where a group of people doing similar jobs assists each other and synergize their efforts to provide the best possible service to their customers.

We cannot be separated in interest or divided in purpose. We stand together until the end.

Woodrow T. Wilson

What we need to do is learn to work in the system, by which I mean that everybody, every team, every platform, every division, every component is there not for individual competitive profit or recognition, but for contribution to the system as a whole on a win-win basis.

W. Edward Deming

CHARACTERISTICS OF A HIGH PERFORMANCE CUSTOMER SERVICE TEAM

COMMON GOALS & VISION

1. All the members of the team fully understand their company and departmental goals, especially goals relating to customer service.

2. They align their individual goals to the above-mentioned broader goals. They develop a common vision and encourage each other towards its achievement.

"Guys, my fiancé is watching, so let me make it clear once again - no one plays better than me!"

3. Anything and everything that they do is driven by the need to give the best possible service to their customers.

They may see things differently, but have common interests: to be of service to their customers, their employers, and themselves.

Mak

EFFECTIVE COMMUNICATION

1. All members of the team communicate with each other to keep each other informed on customer service issues and expect the same from other members of the team.

2. The team members brief each other on what they are doing, why, and what is expected; they collaborate to find the best possible way of doing things.

3. The team members tend to be patient with each other and focus on understanding the other's point of view or position rather than imposing their own. In case of disagreements, they don't stop working together, they "agree to disagree" and find a common path with the customers' and the company's interests in mind.

4. They understand and respect the standard operating procedures of the company, and when exceptions have to be made, they do so keeping all relevant colleagues informed so that they all act in unison.

The best communication is when you feel what others feel and others feel what you feel.

Mak

BELIEF IN HONESTY & INTEGRITY

1. Members of the team accept the responsibility entrusted to them and do their utmost to live up to those expectations.

2. When someone makes a mistake, other team members are supportive and understand that making mistakes is a part of learning; the member who made the mistake takes responsibility for the mistake and ensures that such a mistake is not repeated.

3. They are not shy to ask each other for help, and the other team members are more than eager to assist.

Humble yourself and you shall be honored. Honor yourself and you shall be humbled.

RESPECT FOR EXPERTISE

1. They recognize the expertise of their colleagues and make use of such expertise by letting others take over tasks they are good at. As much as possible, they delegate tasks to the most suitable person on the team.

2. They constantly coach each other on their expertise, talent, and experience so that the whole team's performance is enhanced and the team becomes more flexible to respond to all kinds of service situations and difficulties, especially when the experts are not on duty.

3. All members of the team believe in multitasking and strive to enhance their skills and competencies by learning from one another.

Never become so much of an expert that you stop gaining expertise. View life as a continuous learning experience.

Denis Waitley

MUTUAL SUPPORT

1. The team members take pride in being part of the team; there is a sense of belonging that is dear to all on the team.

2. Under pressure, they don't ask who is supposed to do what; rather, they ask themselves how they can help their colleagues. The byproduct of such

an attitude of camaraderie is a win-win for all. The service providers themselves, the customers, and the company all benefit.

3. Team members agree on how they will share the workload, set schedules, resolve conflicts, and make decisions, and stick by such agreements.

4. The team members hold each other accountable so that there is an automatic and perpetual check from within the service team rather than from the outside. Team members are not offended by questions asked by colleagues in this context, and are always willing to explore better ways of doing things. Team members take up differences between them on a one-to-one basis and never snitch on each other; politics is shunned and looked down upon by all team members. In fact, team members stand by each other and are protective of their colleagues when things go wrong.

5. They are highly appreciative of the help they receive from their colleagues and reciprocate without being asked for any assistance; for them, the team comes before self-interest.

It is probably not love that makes the world go around, but rather those mutually supportive alliances through which partners recognize their dependence on each other for the achievement of shared and private goals.

Fred Allen

SHARING THE GLORY

1. Team members rejoice in their successes together and congratulate each other's contributions to the success.

2. Often, such teams review and discuss their performance issues together. They often meet informally to brainstorm on problem solving or to discuss

how to simplify difficult procedures or any other area in which services can be improved.

3. In most cases, team members meet socially outside the office or work environment and share other activities like hobbies, games, and other common interests.

BENEFITS OF TEAMWORK

The benefits of working together are enormous. Listed below are some of the benefits that a service team experiences when they work together:

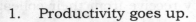

1. Productivity goes up.
2. The quality of service improves.
3. The workload is shared, so no one is made to carry the extra load, and stress levels come down.
4. Work processes improve because team members talk to each other.
5. It becomes relatively easier to solve customer problems quickly.
6. Team members learn from each other.
7. There is cooperation and coordination between the team members.
8. Everyone is involved, and as such, there is greater job satisfaction and fun.

ARE YOU A TEAM PLAYER?

Gauge your own tendencies towards teamwork. To get an accurate picture, be honest with your responses to the following questions.

Sr. No:	Questions	1 Not true	2	3	4	5 True	Remarks
1	Your own success is more important than the team's success.						
2	Your own goals are well aligned with the departmental goals.						
3	You prefer working alone to working in a project with others.						
4	When working with others, you keep others informed as to what you're doing, and appreciate others doing the same for you.						
5	You can cooperate with others even when the group turns down your ideas or suggestions.						
6	Sometimes, when you do go against the group consensus, you don't believe in keeping the group members informed or feel the need to explain to them why you're doing so.						

7	When you accept an assignment, you keep the group members informed on your progress and frequently consult them for their input.					
8	You don't find it easy to own up to your mistakes and abhor guidance from colleagues.					
9	If the group decides not to assign a task that you had in mind for yourself, you become detached from the team and do only as much as is absolutely necessary thereafter.					
10	You are eager to expand your repertoire of skills so you can assist others when needed.					
11	You don't mind staying back after office hours to assist a colleague who couldn't finish his/her work.					
12	You take the initiative of discussing with your colleagues the tasks at hand, who is going to do what, the work schedule, etc.					
13	When your ideas or suggestions conflict with those of a colleague, you tend to take it personally.					
14	You never hesitate to check with a colleague if and when they don't deliver on an assignment.					

15	You're not so open to ideas from junior or younger colleagues.					
16	You're appreciative of good work that other group members accomplish.					
17	You're grateful to your colleagues for any assistance and keep on the lookout for any opportunity to assist them.					
18	You feel attending meetings to keep group members abreast of your work and progress is a waste of time; it can be done via email, saving everyone's time.					
19	You don't like to celebrate completion of projects with team members if you haven't contributed much to the project.					
20	You don't believe in meeting colleagues outside work because it feels artificial and hypocritical.					

(Self-Assessment – 5)

Scoring:

a. Add up your scores for questions
    2, 4, 5, 7, 10, 11, 12, 14, 16, and 17

b. Similarly, add up your scores for questions
    1, 3, 6, 8, 9, 13, 15, 18, 19, and 20

To calculate your score subtract (a – b = ___)

- A positive score indicates that you're more a team player than a lone ranger.

- A negative score indicates that you prefer working alone. The higher the negative score, the higher your tendency to work alone.

- A neutral or near neutral score indicates that you don't have a dominant tendency to work in a team or alone.

A consistent high level of customer service is the result of service agents in various departments working together and towards a common goal, to exceed customers' expectations.

Mak

SUMMARY

1. Did you know that in our world, the word "geese" means "team" – a team that works, plays and survives together?

2. Teamwork is the ability to work together toward a common vision. It is the fuel that allows common people to attain uncommon results.

3. Successful people are always looking for opportunities to help others. Unsuccessful people are always asking, "What's in it for me?

4. What is without periods of rest will not endure.

5. You need to be aware of what others are doing, applaud their efforts, acknowledge their successes, and encourage them in their pursuits. When we all help one another, everybody wins.

6. Build for your team a feeling of oneness, of dependence on one another, and of strength to be derived by unity.

7. A team is a small number of people with complementary skills who are committed to a common purpose, performance goals, and approach for which they are mutually accountable.

8. We cannot be separated in interest or divided in purpose. We stand together until the end.

9. They may see things differently, but have common interests: to be of service to their customers, their employers, and themselves.

10. *The best communication is when you feel what others feel and others feel what you feel.*

11. *Humble yourself and you shall be honored. Honor yourself and you shall be humbled.*

12. *Never become so much of an expert that you stop gaining expertise. View life as a continuous learning experience.*

13. *It is probably not love that makes the world go around, but rather those mutually supportive alliances through which partners recognize their dependence on each other for the achievement of shared and private goals.*

14. *When you learn to rejoice together, you learn to mourn together; you become a family.*

15. *Coming together is a beginning. Keeping together is progress. Working together is success.*

16. *A consistent high level of customer service is the result of service agents in various departments working together and towards a common goal, to exceed customers' expectations.*

NOTES:

"I have been in the business of selling life insurance for more than 24 years and anyone selling life insurance knows how difficult it can be - Mak's book is nothing less than a treatise on persuasion; the persuasion techniques discussed in the book are powerful & when applied diligently can only lead to lifelong business relationships that are mutually beneficial to both the customer and the service/sales agent."

___ Joseph Bassil,
Unit Manager,
American Life Insurance Company

"The book could have been captioned as 'Anything & Everything You Wanted to Know about Customer Service"

___ Jabeena Zakir,
Reservation Sales Supervisor,
DNATA

"Mak makes subtle yet constant emphasis on customer service throughout the book. He has created a simple yet effective 'encyclopedia' on customer service and I am recommending this to all my colleagues in The Emirates Group - particularly the front-line staff."

___ Zoher Campwala,
Learning & Development Specialist,
Emirates Aviation College

"If you don't know what your customers want or how they feel, than there is no way in the world you can satisfy them. This book shows you exactly how to find out what your customers want and then give it to them in the manner that they appreciate – fantastic examples that are live and practical!"

___ Hasan Hasanuzzoha,
Professor,
Centennial College

"If there was any one area of business that was essential for winning customers and keeping them than that would undoubtedly be 'customer service' and this book by Mak addresses the subject succinctly with relevant case studies and examples. Not to mention the emphasis on continuously developing and empowering oneself and monitoring service standards."

___ **Nasser H. Batha,**
Amadeus,
Regional Markets Director,
Middle East & Northern Africa

"I recommend this book to anyone who is working in any area of customer service; front office, back office or outside sales; anyone new to customer service or already dealing with customers directly or indirectly can benefit immensely from this book."

___ **Mohammed Al Amiri,**
Chairman,
Amiri Consultancy Group

"What I like about the book is that it is easy and fun to read and full of case studies, examples & practical ideas on customer service that anyone can relate to. A must read for frontline staff dealing with customers over the telephone or face to face."

___ **Shaz Aslam Peshimam,**
Manager Dubai & Northern Emirates,
Emirates Airlines

"I'm a soft skills trainer and consult on 'Customer Service' with major corporates in Bangladesh. I find this book a boon for many customer service staff in most industries that don't get a chance to attend training on customer service – the book literally shows you how to manage customers to their satisfaction so they keep coming back to you for more."

___ **S.M. Manzurul Islam Chowdhury,**
Chief Consultant,
Continuing Education Centre

INDEX